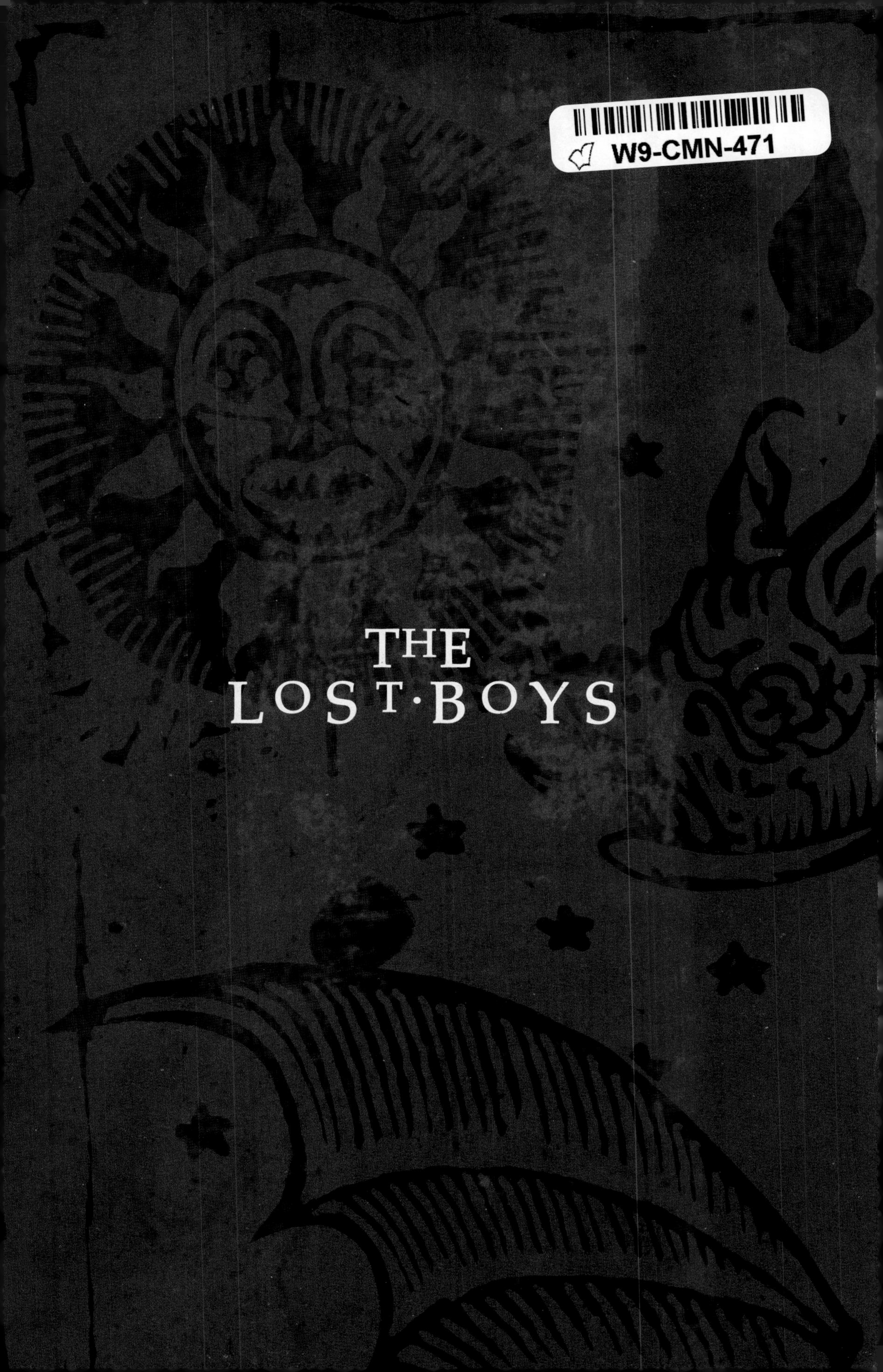

THE LOST·BOYS

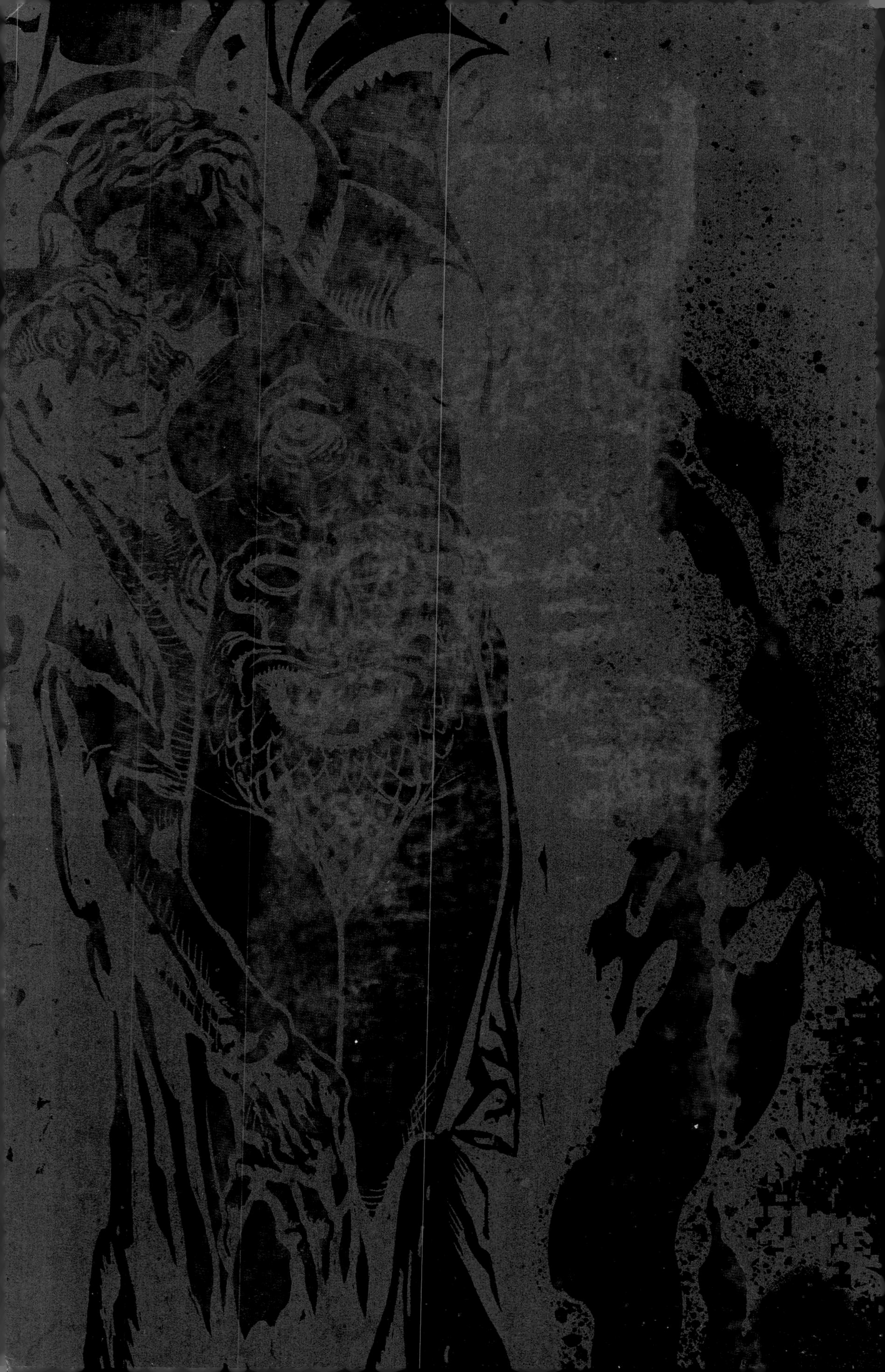

THE LOST·BOYS

Tim Seeley Writer
Scott Godlewski Artist
Trish Mulvihill   Michael Wiggam Colorists
Clem Robins Letterer
Tony Harris Cover Art and Original Series Covers

Jamie S. Rich Group Editor – Vertigo Comics and Editor – Original Series
Maggie Howell Assistant Editor – Original Series
Jeb Woodard Group Editor – Collected Editions
Scott Nybakken Editor – Collected Edition
Steve Cook Design Director – Books
Louis Prandi Publication Design

Diane Nelson President
Dan DiDio Publisher
Jim Lee Publisher
Geoff Johns President & Chief Creative Officer
Amit Desai Executive VP – Business & Marketing Strategy,
Direct to Consumer & Global Franchise Management
Sam Ades Senior VP – Direct to Consumer
Bobbie Chase VP – Talent Development

Mark Chiarello Senior VP – Art, Design & Collected Editions
John Cunningham Senior VP – Sales & Trade Marketing
Anne DePies Senior VP – Business Strategy, Finance & Administration
Don Falletti VP – Manufacturing Operations
Lawrence Ganem VP – Editorial Administration & Talent Relations
Alison Gill Senior VP – Manufacturing & Operations
Hank Kanalz Senior VP – Editorial Strategy & Administration
Jay Kogan VP – Legal Affairs
Thomas Loftus VP – Business Affairs
Jack Mahan VP – Business Affairs
Nick J. Napolitano VP – Manufacturing Administration
Eddie Scannell VP – Consumer Marketing
Courtney Simmons Senior VP – Publicity & Communications
Jim (Ski) Sokolowski VP – Comic Book Specialty Sales & Trade Marketing
Nancy Spears VP – Mass, Book, Digital Sales & Trade Marketing

THE
LOST BOYS

Published by DC Comics. Compilation and all new material Copyright © 2017 Warner Bros.
Entertainment Inc. All Rights Reserved.

Originally published in single magazine form as THE LOST BOYS 1-6. Copyright © 2016, 2017 Warner
Bros. Entertainment Inc. All Rights Reserved. All characters, their distinctive likenesses and related
elements featured in this publication are trademarks of Warner Bros. Entertainment Inc. VERTIGO is a
trademark of DC Comics. The stories, characters and incidents featured in this publication are entirely
fictional. DC Comics does not read or accept unsolicited submissions of ideas, stories or artwork.

DCCO39681

DC Comics
2900 West Alameda Avenue
Burbank, CA 91505
Printed in Canada. First Printing.
ISBN: 978-1-4012-7145-9

Library of Congress Cataloging-in-Publication Data is available.

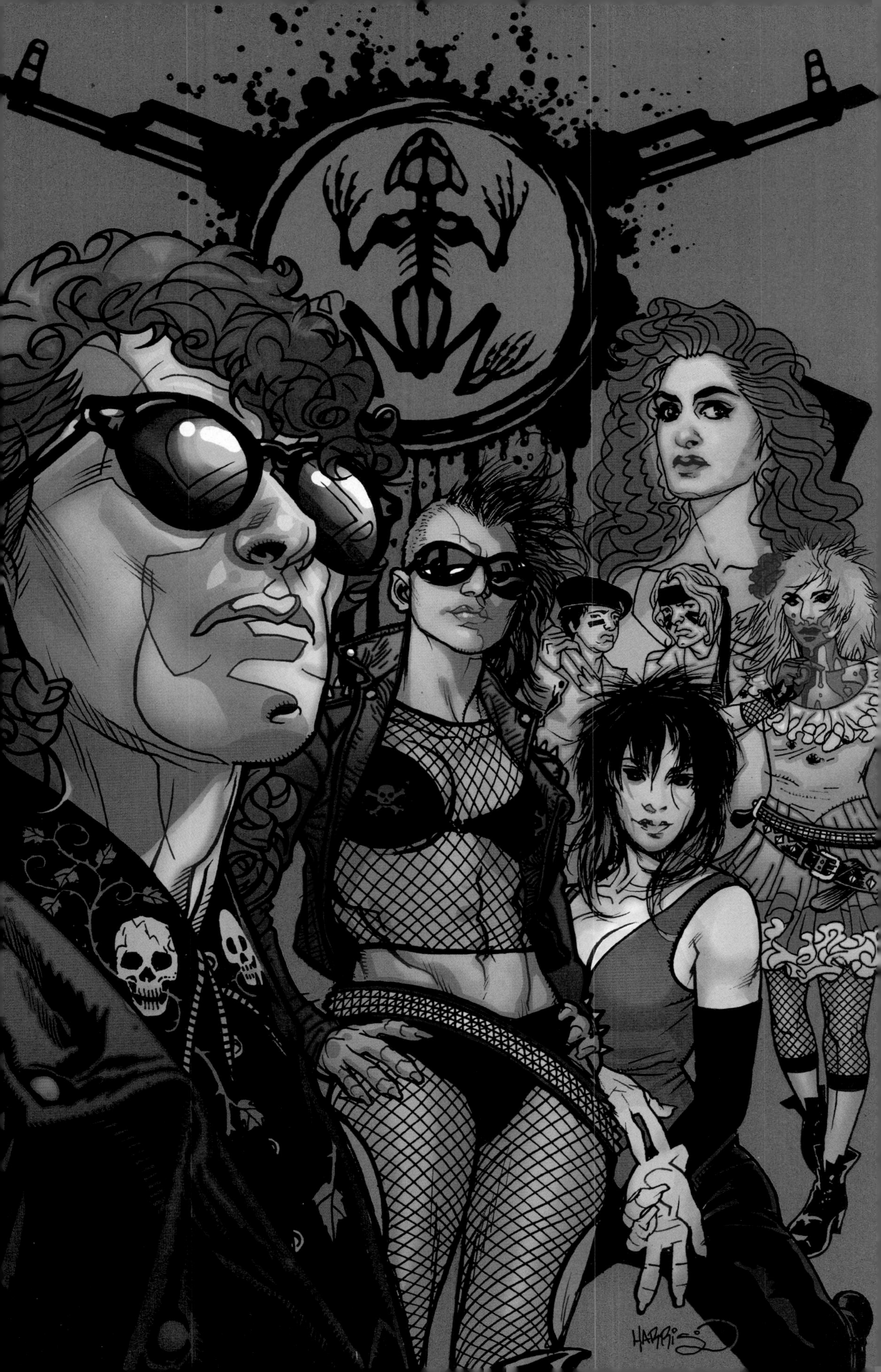

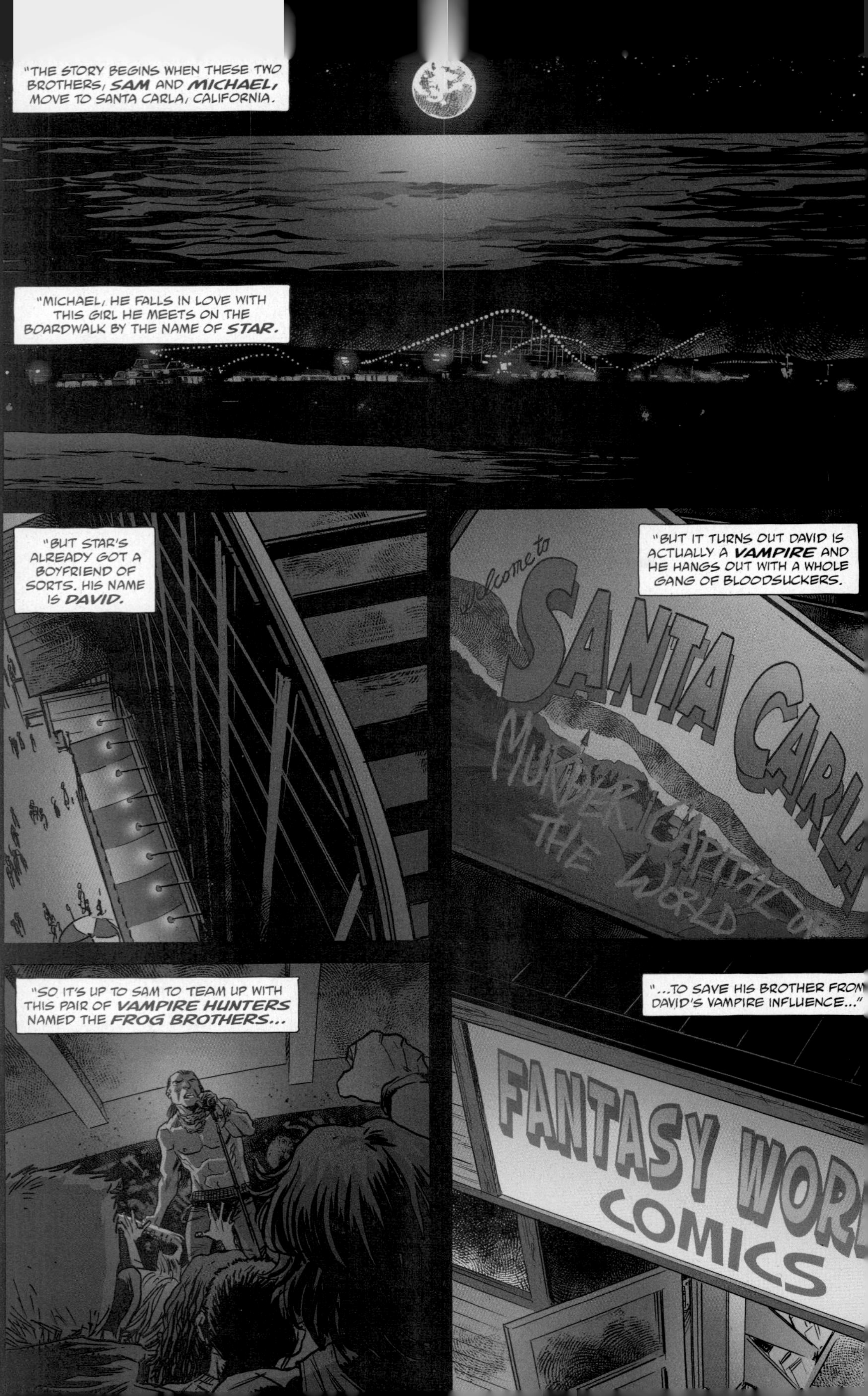
"THE STORY BEGINS WHEN THESE TWO BROTHERS, SAM AND MICHAEL, MOVE TO SANTA CARLA, CALIFORNIA.
"MICHAEL, HE FALLS IN LOVE WITH THIS GIRL HE MEETS ON THE BOARDWALK BY THE NAME OF STAR.
"BUT STAR'S ALREADY GOT A BOYFRIEND OF SORTS. HIS NAME IS DAVID.
"BUT IT TURNS OUT DAVID IS ACTUALLY A VAMPIRE AND HE HANGS OUT WITH A WHOLE GANG OF BLOODSUCKERS.
Welcome to
SANTA CARLA
MURDER CAPITAL OF THE WORLD
"SO IT'S UP TO SAM TO TEAM UP WITH THIS PAIR OF VAMPIRE HUNTERS NAMED THE FROG BROTHERS...
"...TO SAVE HIS BROTHER FROM DAVID'S VAMPIRE INFLUENCE..."
FANTASY WORL
COMICS

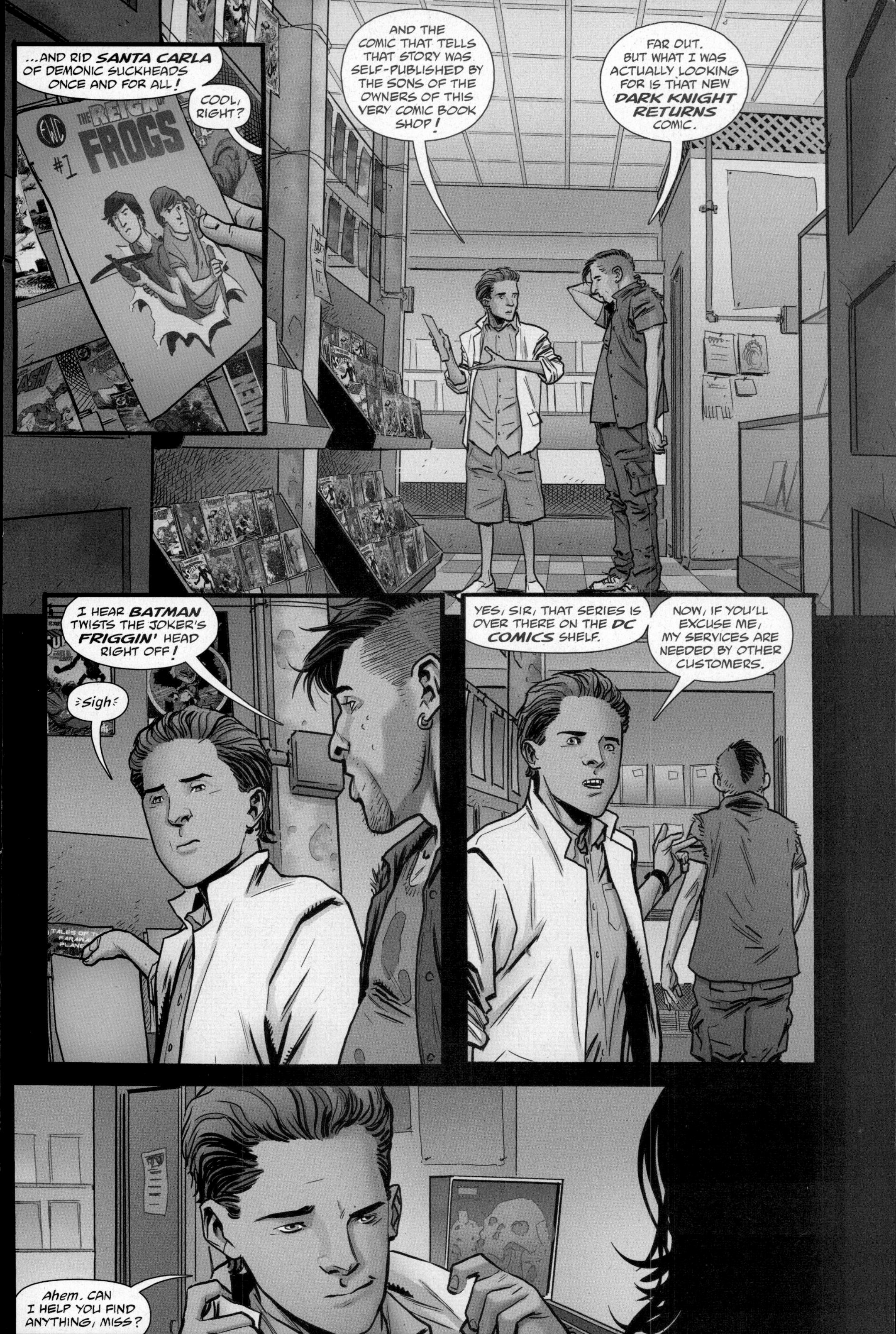
...AND RID SANTA CARLA OF DEMONIC SUCKHEADS ONCE AND FOR ALL!
COOL, RIGHT?
THE REIGN OF FROGS #1
AND THE COMIC THAT TELLS THAT STORY WAS SELF-PUBLISHED BY THE SONS OF THE OWNERS OF THIS VERY COMIC BOOK SHOP!
FAR OUT. BUT WHAT I WAS ACTUALLY LOOKING FOR IS THAT NEW DARK KNIGHT RETURNS COMIC.
I HEAR BATMAN TWISTS THE JOKER'S FRIGGIN' HEAD RIGHT OFF!
Sigh
YES, SIR, THAT SERIES IS OVER THERE ON THE DC COMICS SHELF.
NOW, IF YOU'LL EXCUSE ME, MY SERVICES ARE NEEDED BY OTHER CUSTOMERS.
Ahem. CAN I HELP YOU FIND ANYTHING, MISS?

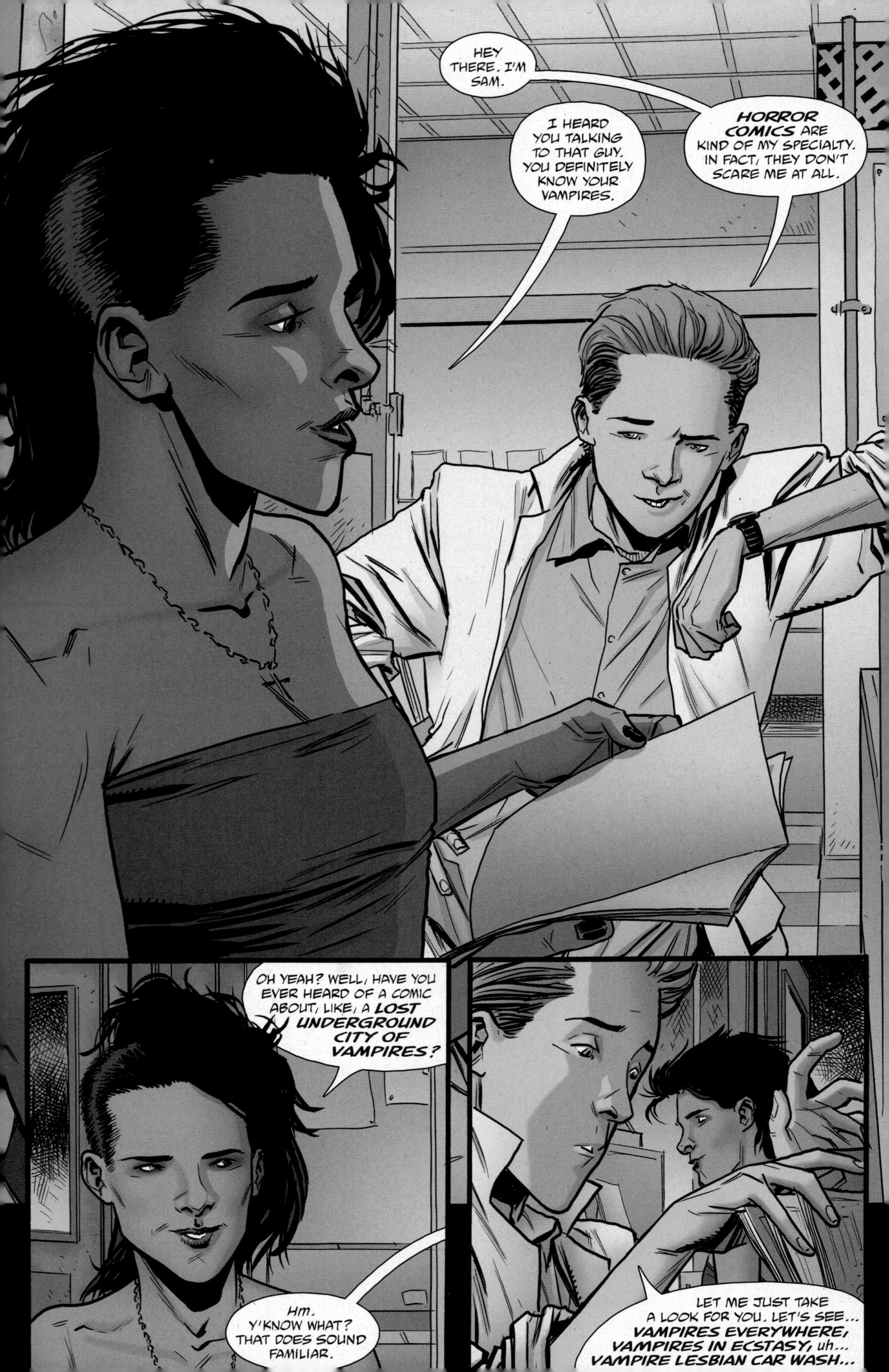
HEY THERE. I'M SAM.
I HEARD YOU TALKING TO THAT GUY. YOU DEFINITELY KNOW YOUR VAMPIRES.
HORROR COMICS ARE KIND OF MY SPECIALTY. IN FACT, THEY DON'T SCARE ME AT ALL.
OH YEAH? WELL, HAVE YOU EVER HEARD OF A COMIC ABOUT, LIKE, A LOST UNDERGROUND CITY OF VAMPIRES?
Hm. Y'KNOW WHAT? THAT DOES SOUND FAMILIAR.
LET ME JUST TAKE A LOOK FOR YOU. LET'S SEE... VAMPIRES EVERYWHERE, VAMPIRES IN ECSTASY, uh... VAMPIRE LESBIAN CAR WASH...

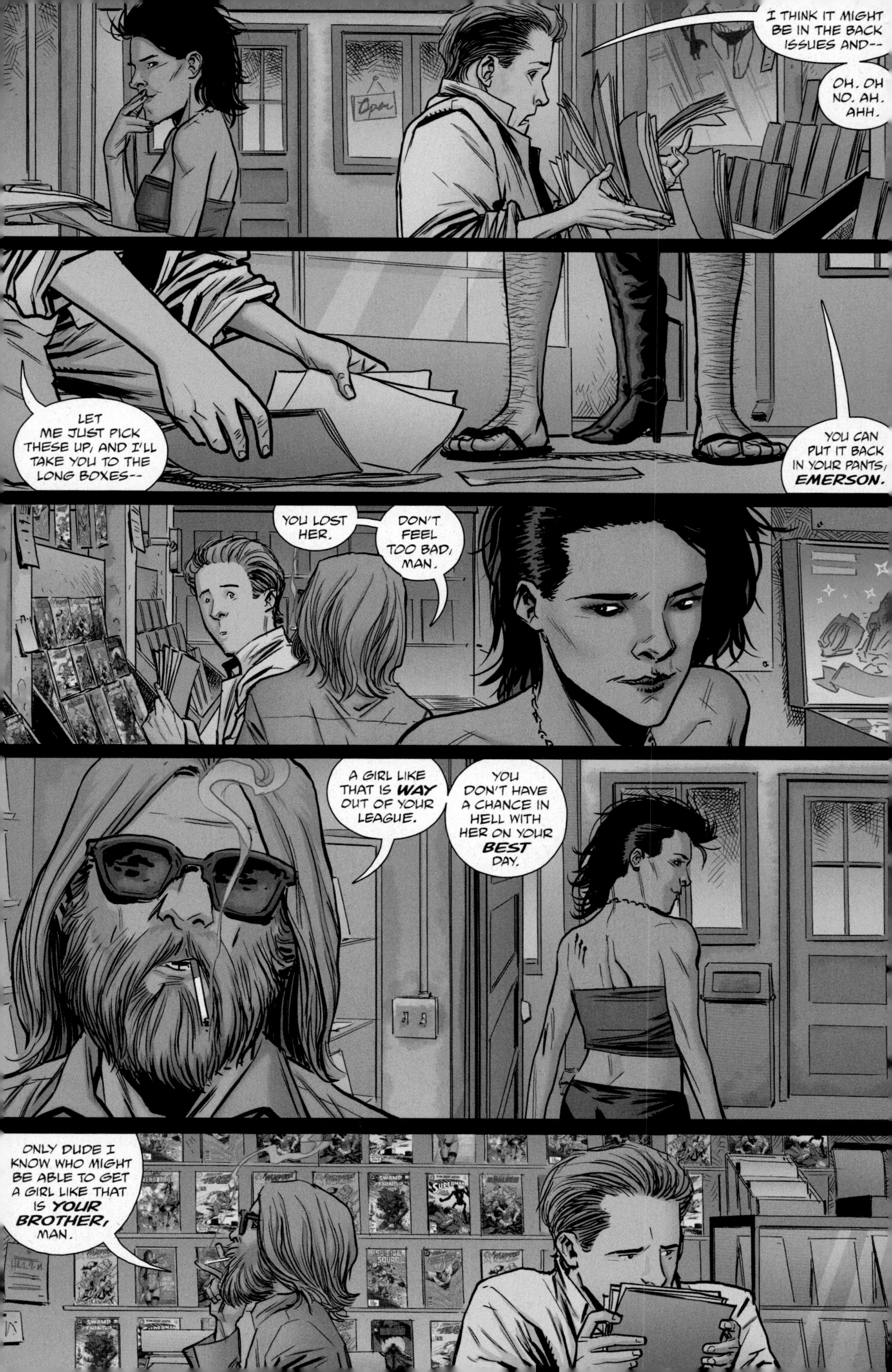

I THINK IT MIGHT BE IN THE BACK ISSUES AND--
OH. OH NO. AH. AHH.
Open
LET ME JUST PICK THESE UP, AND I'LL TAKE YOU TO THE LONG BOXES--
YOU CAN PUT IT BACK IN YOUR PANTS, EMERSON.
YOU LOST HER.
DON'T FEEL TOO BAD, MAN.
A GIRL LIKE THAT IS WAY OUT OF YOUR LEAGUE.
YOU DON'T HAVE A CHANCE IN HELL WITH HER ON YOUR BEST DAY.
ONLY DUDE I KNOW WHO MIGHT BE ABLE TO GET A GIRL LIKE THAT IS YOUR BROTHER, MAN.
SWAMP THING
SUPERMAN
SUICIDE SQUAD

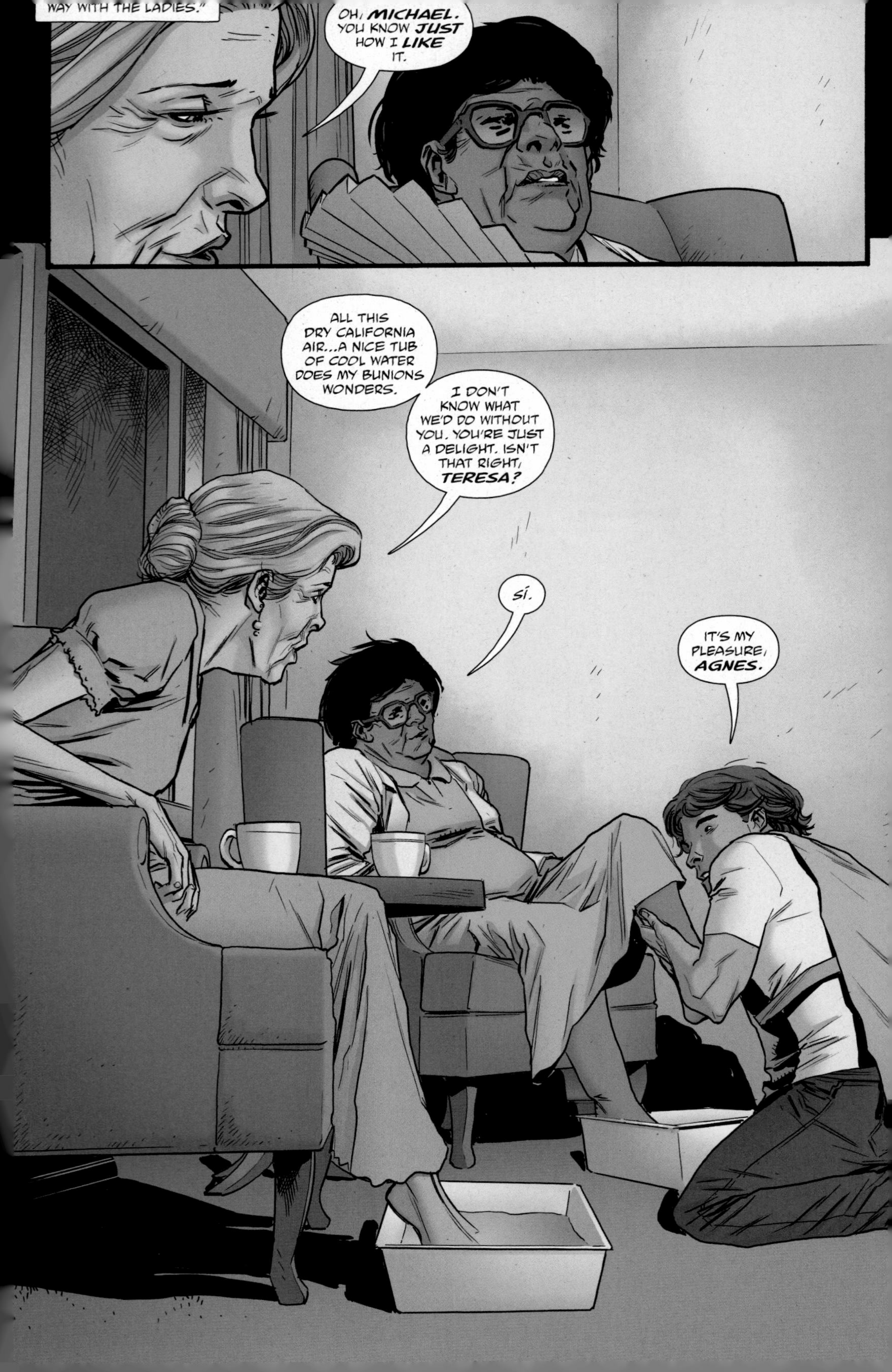
WAY WITH THE LADIES."
OH, MICHAEL. YOU KNOW JUST HOW I LIKE IT.
ALL THIS DRY CALIFORNIA AIR...A NICE TUB OF COOL WATER DOES MY BUNIONS WONDERS.
I DON'T KNOW WHAT WE'D DO WITHOUT YOU. YOU'RE JUST A DELIGHT. ISN'T THAT RIGHT, TERESA?
SÍ.
IT'S MY PLEASURE, AGNES.

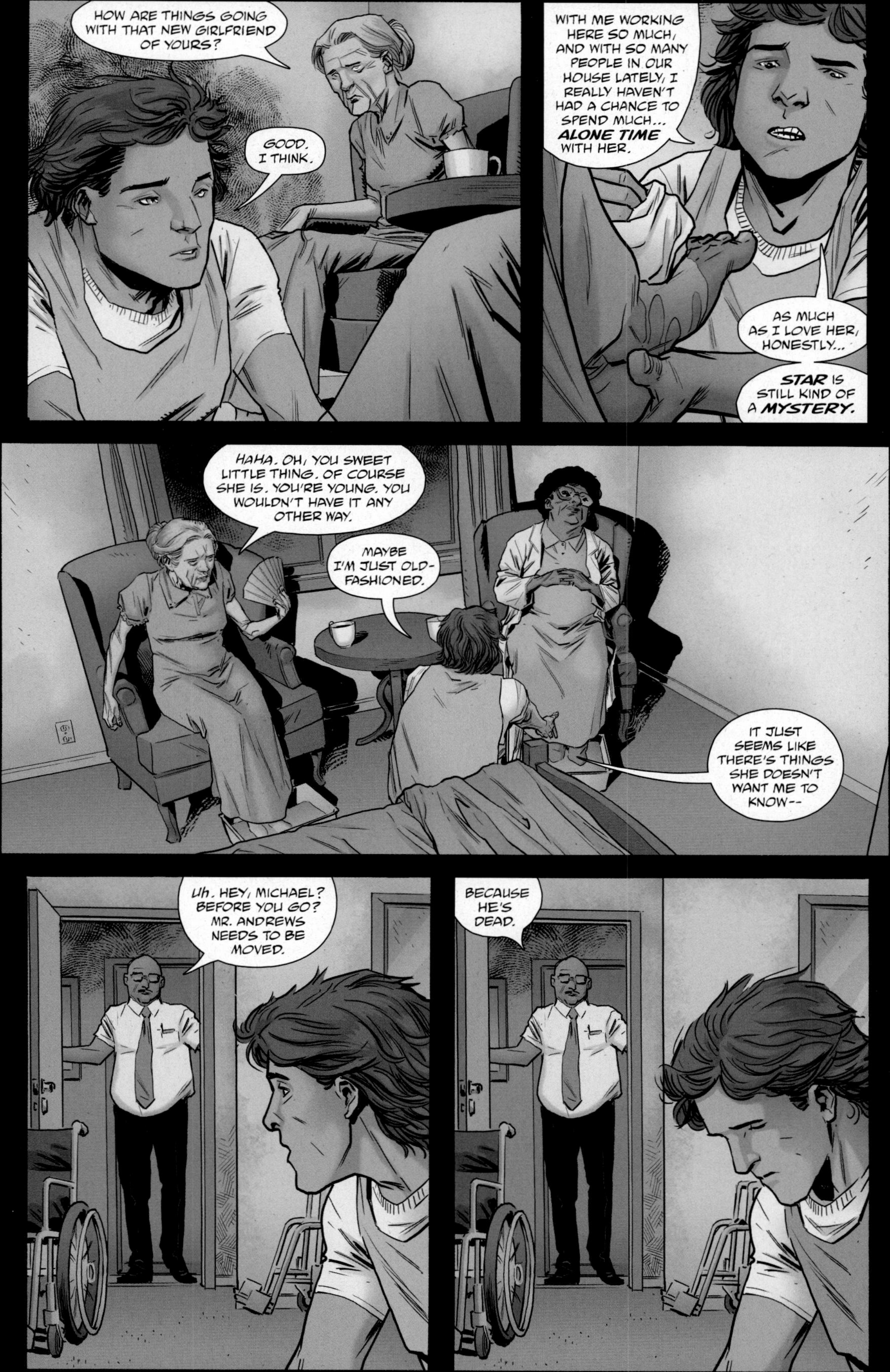
HOW ARE THINGS GOING WITH THAT NEW GIRLFRIEND OF YOURS?
GOOD. I THINK.
WITH ME WORKING HERE SO MUCH, AND WITH SO MANY PEOPLE IN OUR HOUSE LATELY, I REALLY HAVEN'T HAD A CHANCE TO SPEND MUCH... **ALONE TIME** WITH HER.
AS MUCH AS I LOVE HER, HONESTLY...
STAR IS STILL KIND OF A **MYSTERY.**
HAHA. OH, YOU SWEET LITTLE THING. OF COURSE SHE IS. YOU'RE YOUNG. YOU WOULDN'T HAVE IT ANY OTHER WAY.
MAYBE I'M JUST OLD-FASHIONED.
IT JUST SEEMS LIKE THERE'S THINGS SHE DOESN'T WANT ME TO KNOW--
UH. HEY, MICHAEL? BEFORE YOU GO? MR. ANDREWS NEEDS TO BE MOVED.
BECAUSE HE'S DEAD.

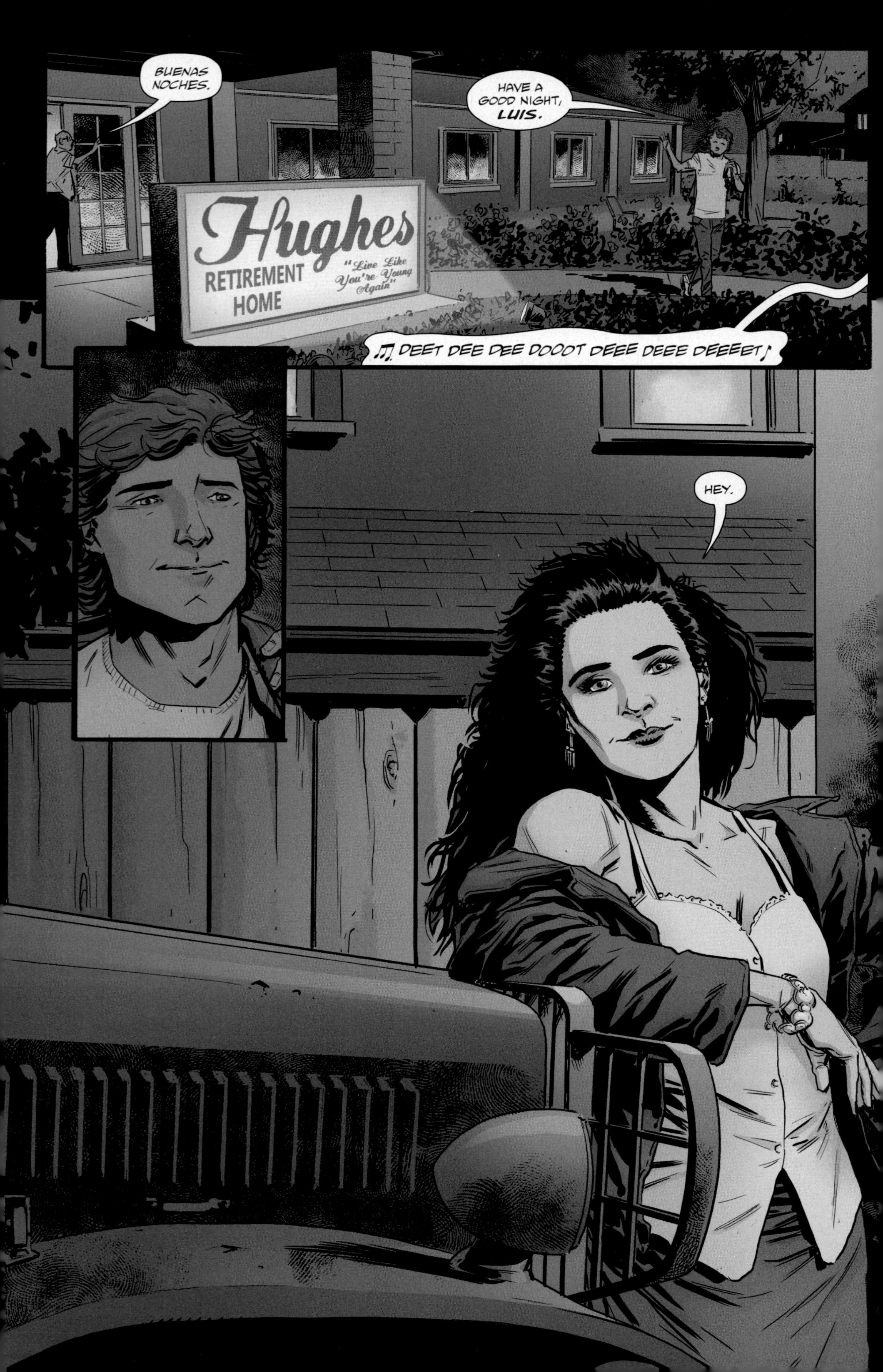
BUENAS NOCHES.
HAVE A GOOD NIGHT, LUIS.
Hughes
RETIREMENT HOME
"Live Like You're Young Again"
DEET DEE DEE DOOOT DEEE DEEE DEEEET
HEY.

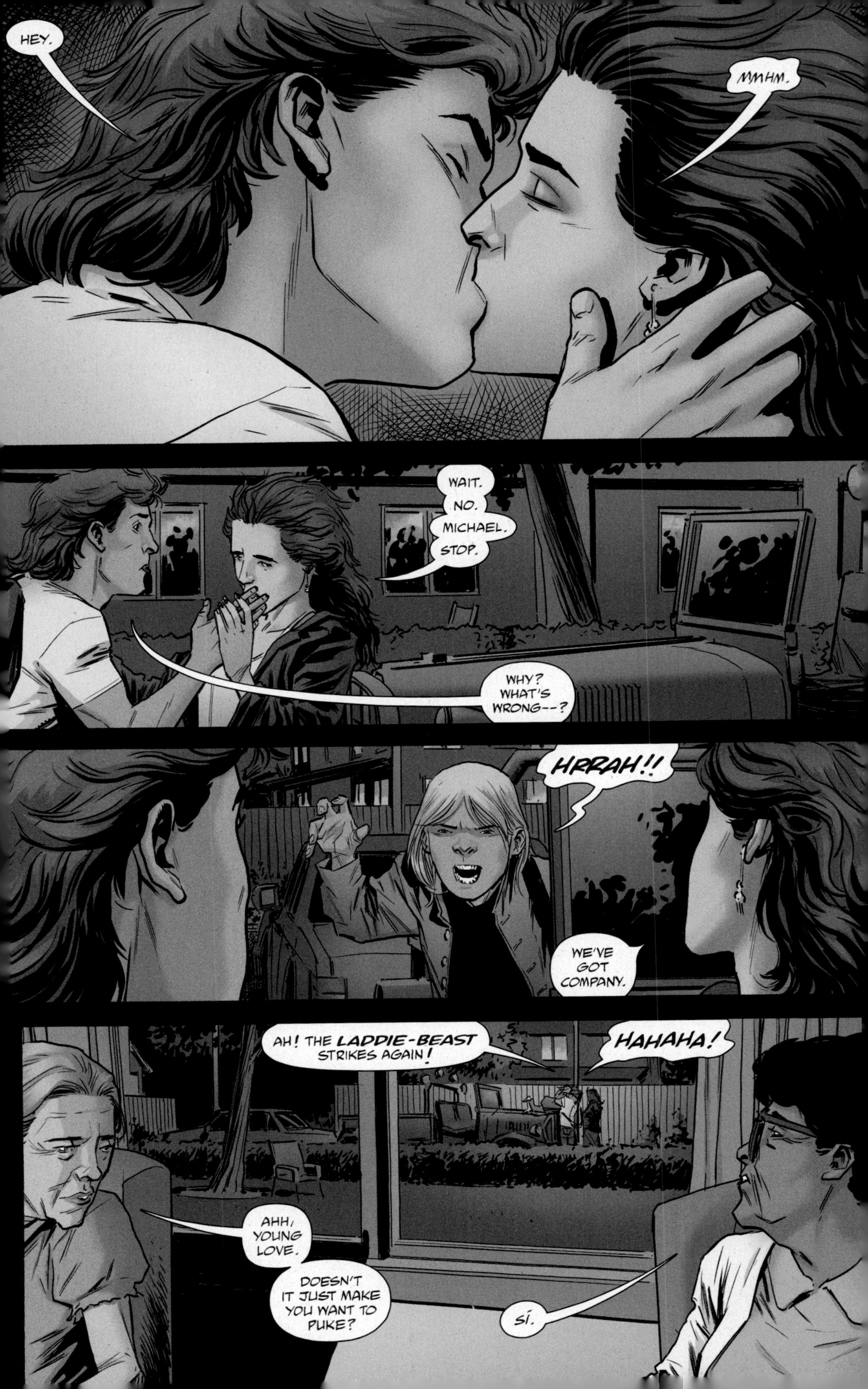
HEY.
MMHM.
WAIT.
NO.
MICHAEL.
STOP.
WHY? WHAT'S WRONG--?
HRRAH!!
WE'VE GOT COMPANY.
AH! THE LADDIE-BEAST STRIKES AGAIN!
HAHAHA!
AHH, YOUNG LOVE.
DOESN'T IT JUST MAKE YOU WANT TO PUKE?
SÍ.

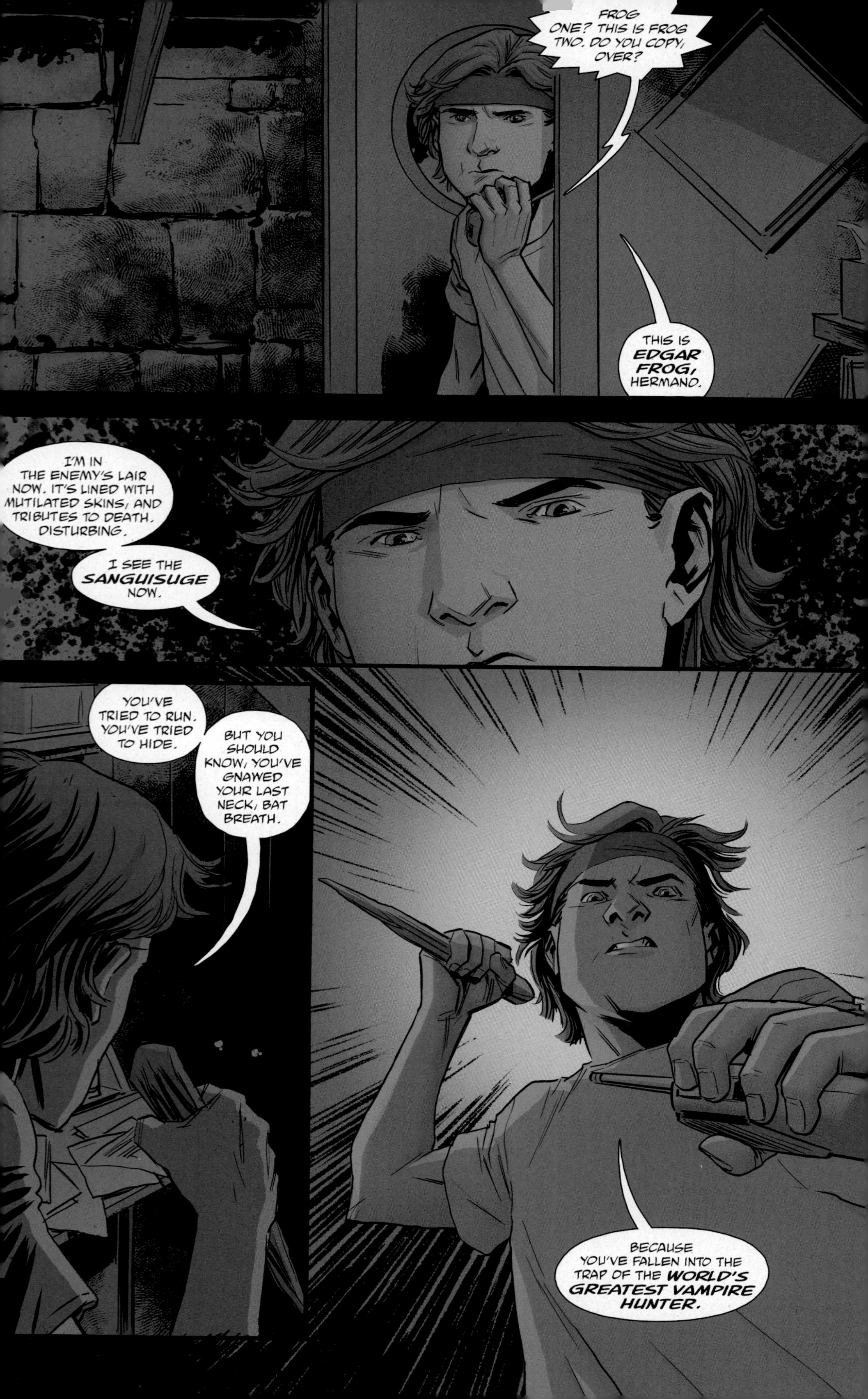
FROG ONE? THIS IS FROG TWO. DO YOU COPY, OVER?
THIS IS EDGAR FROG, HERMANO.
I'M IN THE ENEMY'S LAIR NOW. IT'S LINED WITH MUTILATED SKINS, AND TRIBUTES TO DEATH. DISTURBING.
I SEE THE SANGUISUGE NOW.
YOU'VE TRIED TO RUN. YOU'VE TRIED TO HIDE.
BUT YOU SHOULD KNOW, YOU'VE GNAWED YOUR LAST NECK, BAT BREATH.
BECAUSE YOU'VE FALLEN INTO THE TRAP OF THE WORLD'S GREATEST VAMPIRE HUNTER.

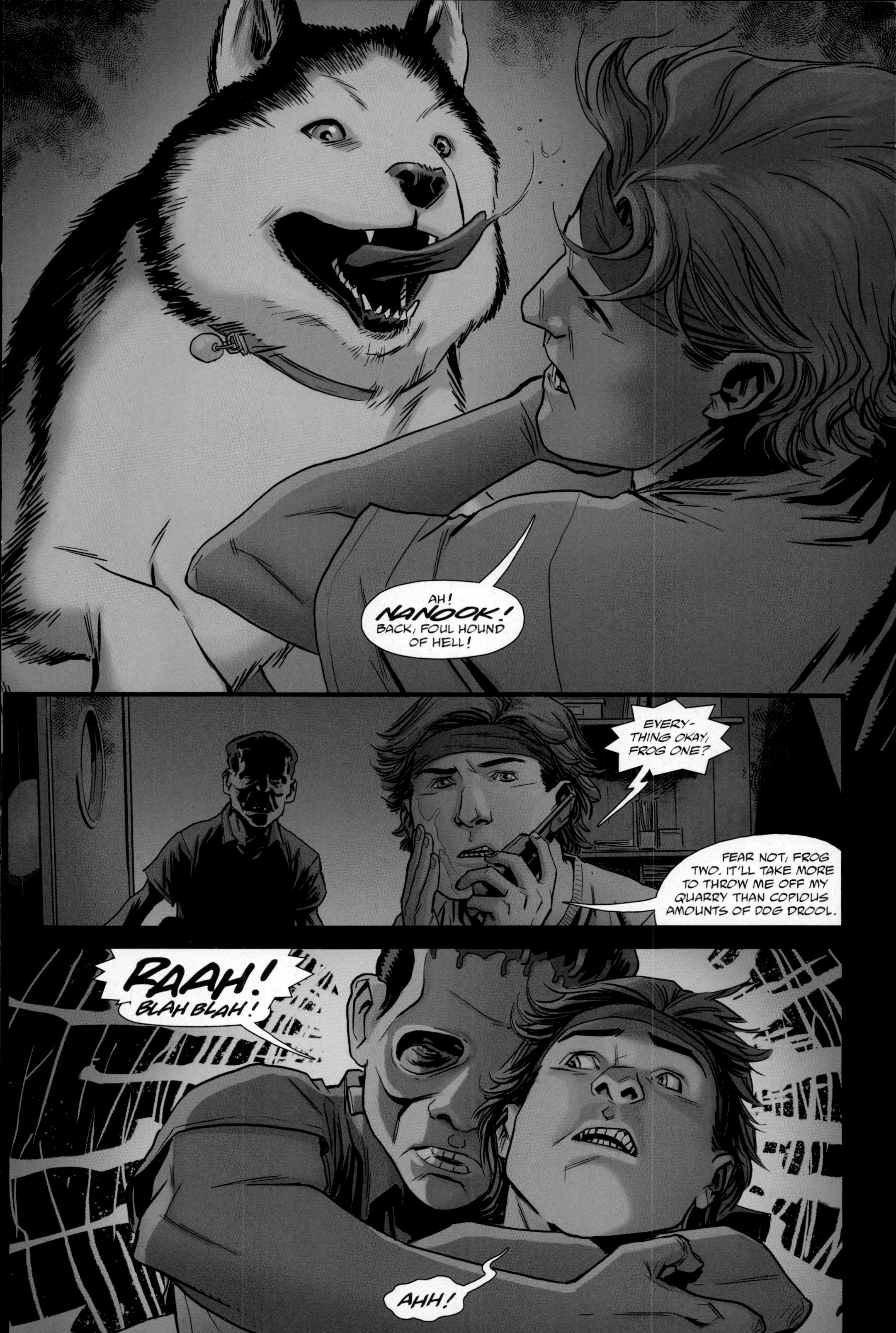
AH! NANOOK! BACK, FOUL HOUND OF HELL!
EVERY-THING OKAY, FROG ONE?
FEAR NOT, FROG TWO. IT'LL TAKE MORE TO THROW ME OFF MY QUARRY THAN COPIOUS AMOUNTS OF DOG DROOL.
RAAH! BLAH BLAH!
AHH!

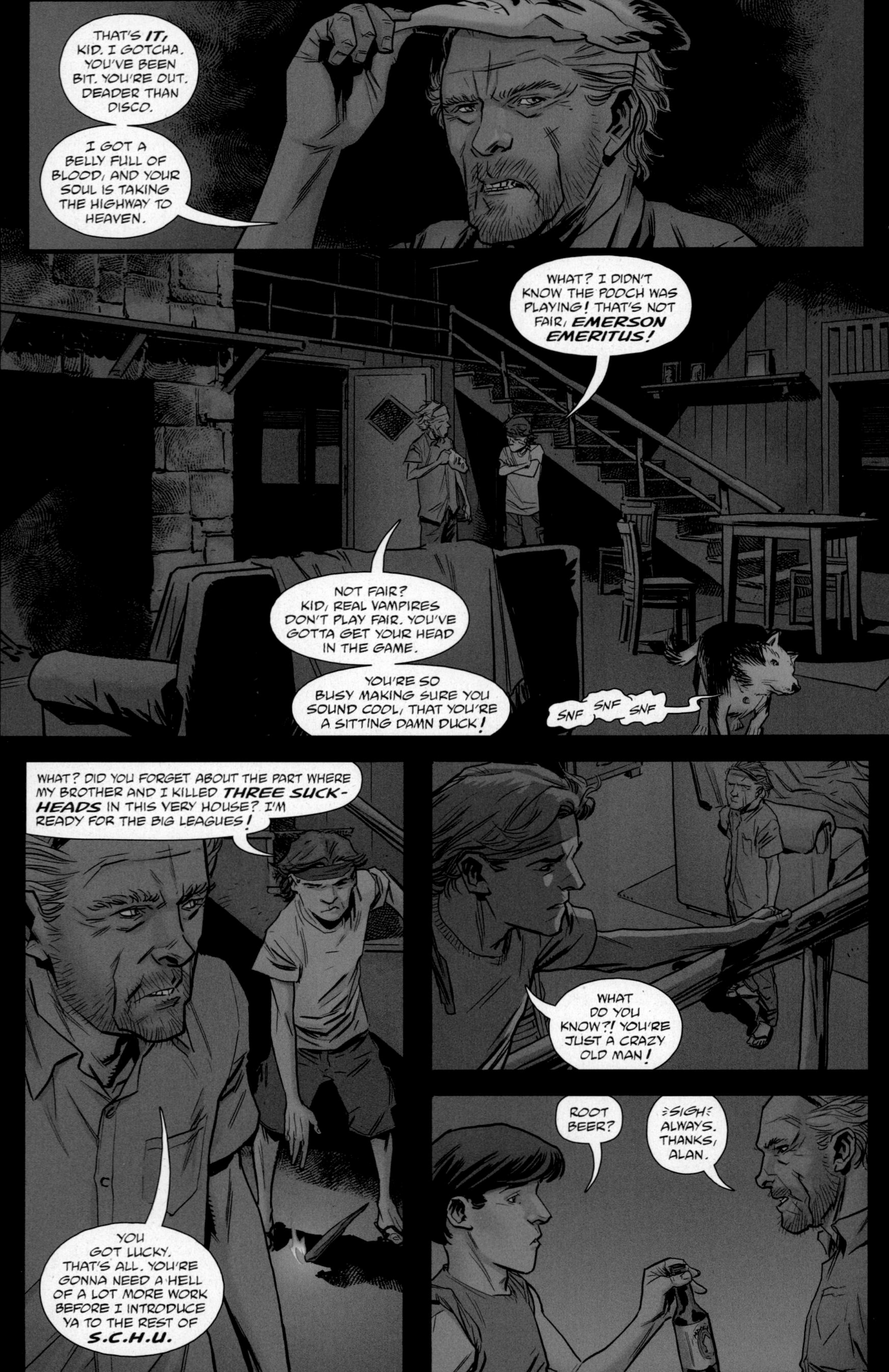
THAT'S IT, KID. I GOTCHA. YOU'VE BEEN BIT. YOU'RE OUT. DEADER THAN DISCO.
I GOT A BELLY FULL OF BLOOD, AND YOUR SOUL IS TAKING THE HIGHWAY TO HEAVEN.
WHAT? I DIDN'T KNOW THE POOCH WAS PLAYING! THAT'S NOT FAIR, EMERSON EMERITUS!
NOT FAIR? KID, REAL VAMPIRES DON'T PLAY FAIR. YOU'VE GOTTA GET YOUR HEAD IN THE GAME.
YOU'RE SO BUSY MAKING SURE YOU SOUND COOL, THAT YOU'RE A SITTING DAMN DUCK!
SNF SNF SNF
WHAT? DID YOU FORGET ABOUT THE PART WHERE MY BROTHER AND I KILLED THREE SUCK-HEADS IN THIS VERY HOUSE? I'M READY FOR THE BIG LEAGUES!
YOU GOT LUCKY. THAT'S ALL. YOU'RE GONNA NEED A HELL OF A LOT MORE WORK BEFORE I INTRODUCE YA TO THE REST OF S.C.H.U.
WHAT DO YOU KNOW?! YOU'RE JUST A CRAZY OLD MAN!
ROOT BEER?
SIGH ALWAYS. THANKS, ALAN.

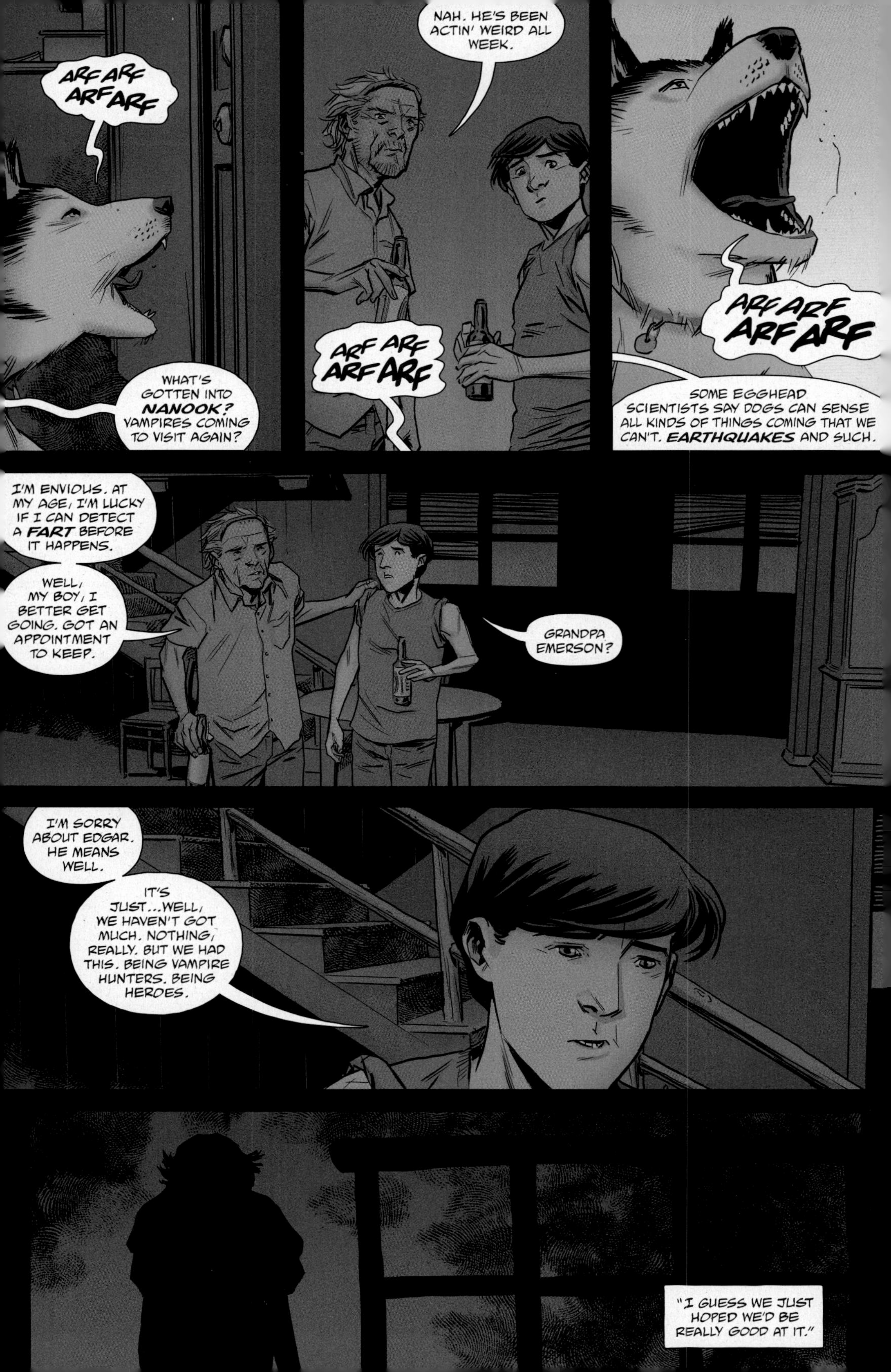
ARF ARF ARF ARF
WHAT'S GOTTEN INTO NANOOK? VAMPIRES COMING TO VISIT AGAIN?
NAH. HE'S BEEN ACTIN' WEIRD ALL WEEK.
ARF ARF ARF ARF
ARF ARF ARF ARF
SOME EGGHEAD SCIENTISTS SAY DOGS CAN SENSE ALL KINDS OF THINGS COMING THAT WE CAN'T. EARTHQUAKES AND SUCH.
I'M ENVIOUS. AT MY AGE, I'M LUCKY IF I CAN DETECT A FART BEFORE IT HAPPENS.
WELL, MY BOY, I BETTER GET GOING. GOT AN APPOINTMENT TO KEEP.
GRANDPA EMERSON?
I'M SORRY ABOUT EDGAR. HE MEANS WELL.
IT'S JUST...WELL, WE HAVEN'T GOT MUCH. NOTHING, REALLY. BUT WE HAD THIS. BEING VAMPIRE HUNTERS. BEING HEROES.
"I GUESS WE JUST HOPED WE'D BE REALLY GOOD AT IT."

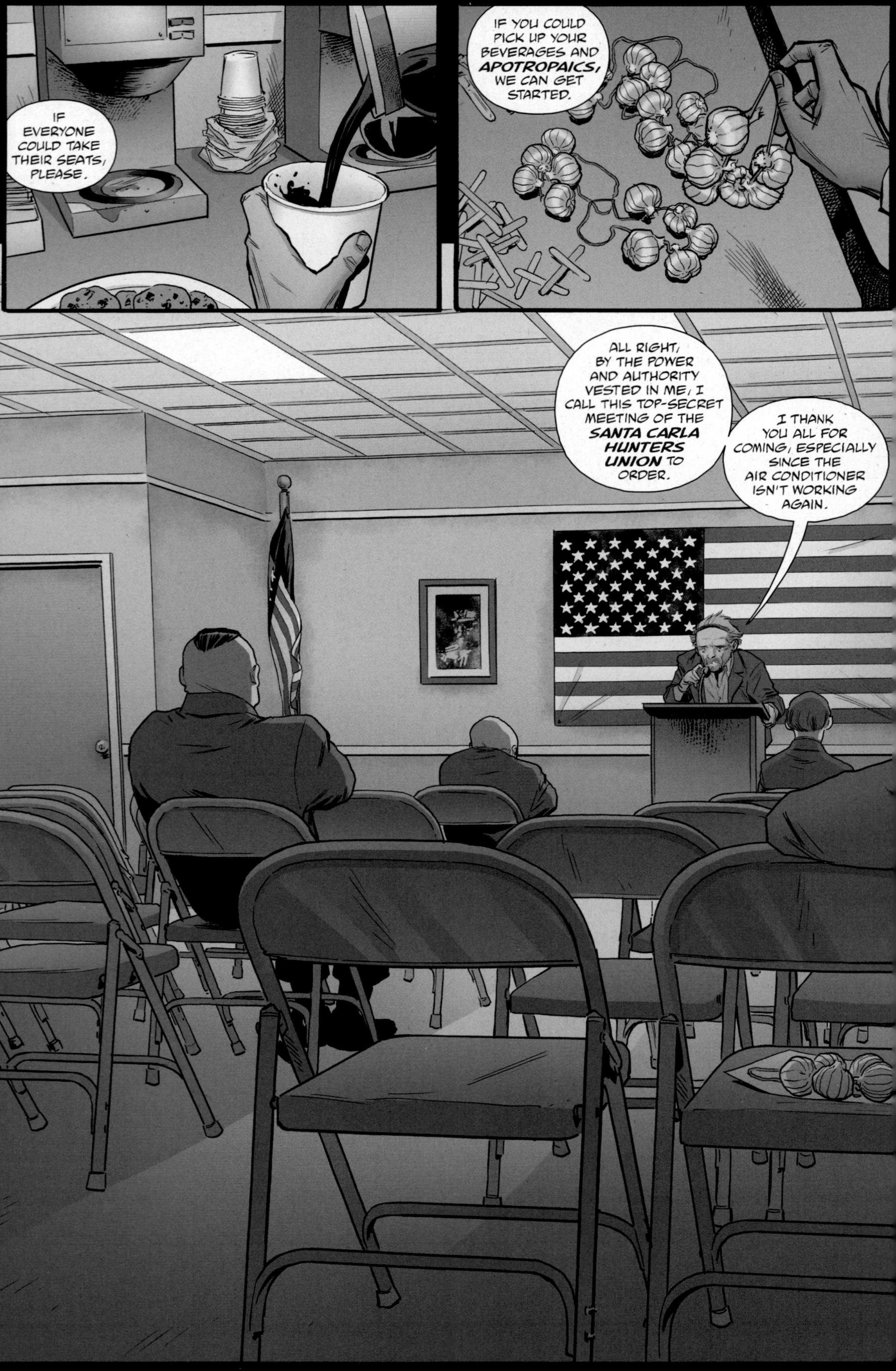
IF EVERYONE COULD TAKE THEIR SEATS, PLEASE.
IF YOU COULD PICK UP YOUR BEVERAGES AND APOTROPAICS, WE CAN GET STARTED.
ALL RIGHT, BY THE POWER AND AUTHORITY VESTED IN ME, I CALL THIS TOP-SECRET MEETING OF THE SANTA CARLA HUNTERS UNION TO ORDER.
I THANK YOU ALL FOR COMING, ESPECIALLY SINCE THE AIR CONDITIONER ISN'T WORKING AGAIN.

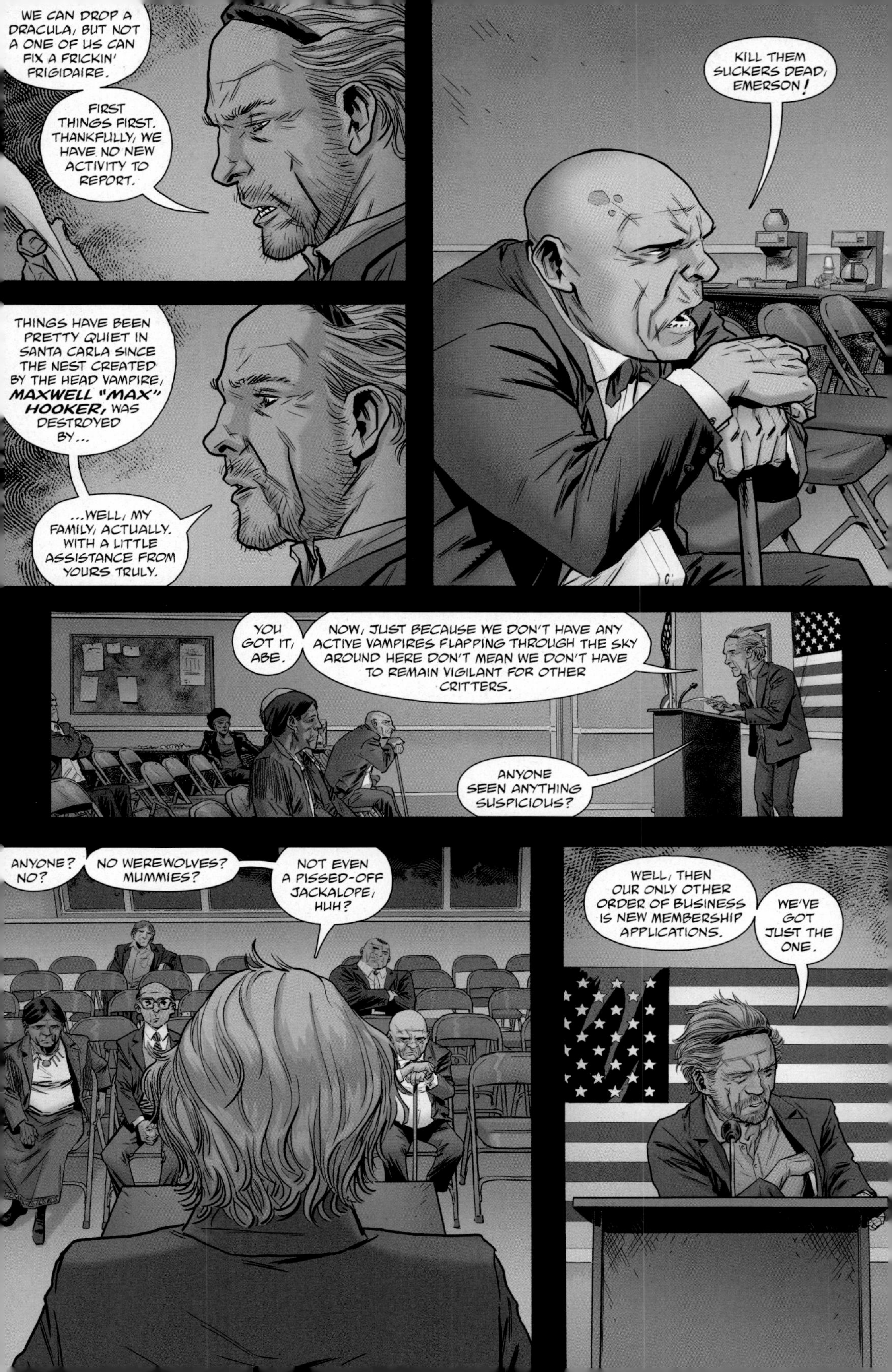
WE CAN DROP A DRACULA, BUT NOT A ONE OF US CAN FIX A FRICKIN' FRIGIDAIRE.
FIRST THINGS FIRST. THANKFULLY, WE HAVE NO NEW ACTIVITY TO REPORT.
THINGS HAVE BEEN PRETTY QUIET IN SANTA CARLA SINCE THE NEST CREATED BY THE HEAD VAMPIRE, **MAXWELL "MAX" HOOKER,** WAS DESTROYED BY...
...WELL, MY FAMILY, ACTUALLY. WITH A LITTLE ASSISTANCE FROM YOURS TRULY.
KILL THEM SUCKERS DEAD, EMERSON!
YOU GOT IT, ABE.
NOW, JUST BECAUSE WE DON'T HAVE ANY ACTIVE VAMPIRES FLAPPING THROUGH THE SKY AROUND HERE DON'T MEAN WE DON'T HAVE TO REMAIN VIGILANT FOR OTHER CRITTERS.
ANYONE SEEN ANYTHING SUSPICIOUS?
ANYONE? NO?
NO WEREWOLVES? MUMMIES?
NOT EVEN A PISSED-OFF JACKALOPE, HUH?
WELL, THEN OUR ONLY OTHER ORDER OF BUSINESS IS NEW MEMBERSHIP APPLICATIONS.
WE'VE GOT JUST THE ONE.

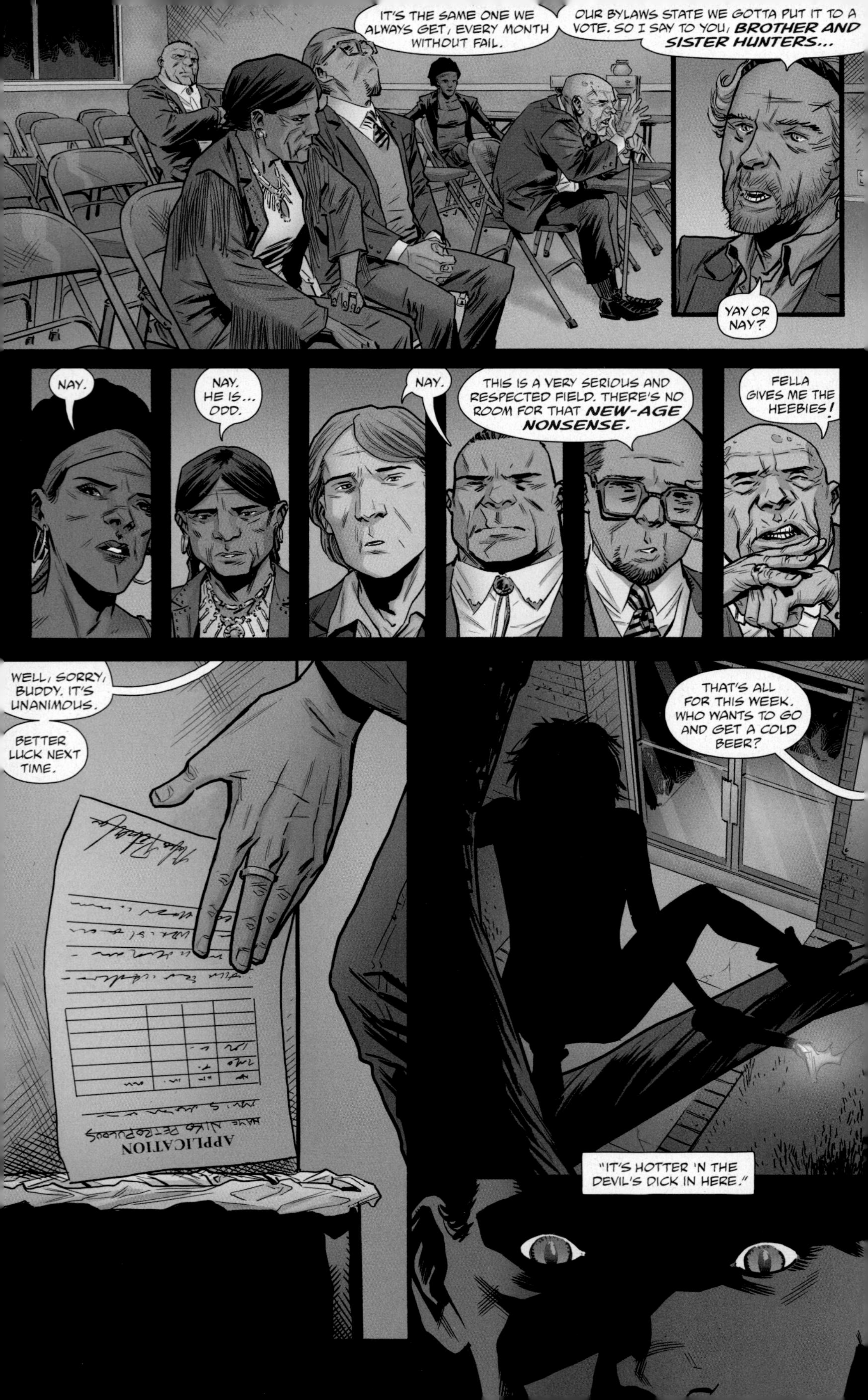
IT'S THE SAME ONE WE ALWAYS GET, EVERY MONTH WITHOUT FAIL.
OUR BYLAWS STATE WE GOTTA PUT IT TO A VOTE. SO I SAY TO YOU, BROTHER AND SISTER HUNTERS...
YAY OR NAY?
NAY.
NAY. HE IS... ODD.
NAY.
THIS IS A VERY SERIOUS AND RESPECTED FIELD. THERE'S NO ROOM FOR THAT NEW-AGE NONSENSE.
FELLA GIVES ME THE HEEBIES!
WELL, SORRY, BUDDY. IT'S UNANIMOUS.
BETTER LUCK NEXT TIME.
APPLICATION
THAT'S ALL FOR THIS WEEK. WHO WANTS TO GO AND GET A COLD BEER?
"IT'S HOTTER 'N THE DEVIL'S DICK IN HERE."

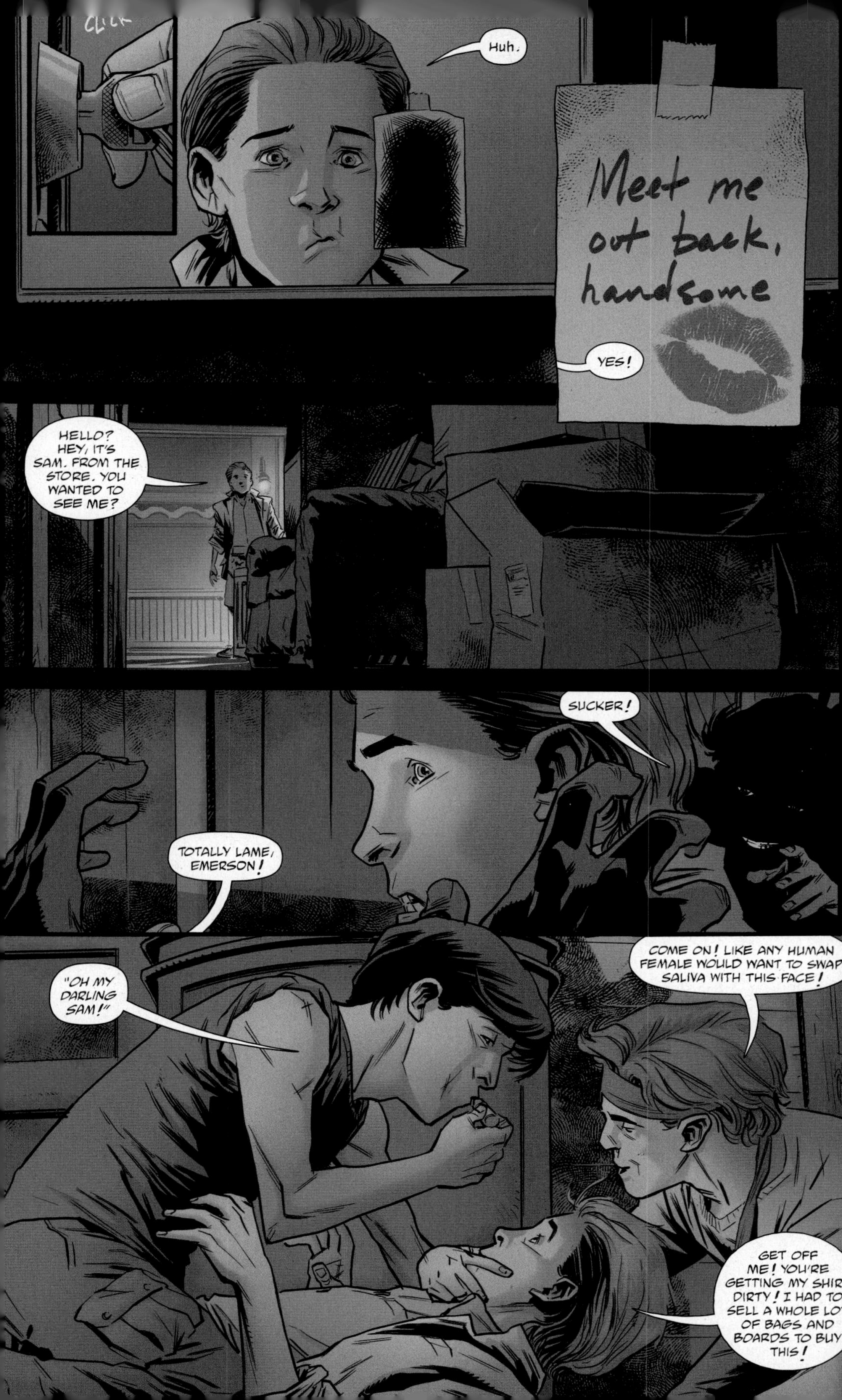
CLICK
Huh.
Meet me out back, handsome
YES!
HELLO? HEY, IT'S SAM. FROM THE STORE. YOU WANTED TO SEE ME?
SUCKER!
TOTALLY LAME, EMERSON!
"OH MY DARLING SAM!"
COME ON! LIKE ANY HUMAN FEMALE WOULD WANT TO SWAP SALIVA WITH THIS FACE!
GET OFF ME! YOU'RE GETTING MY SHIRT DIRTY! I HAD TO SELL A WHOLE LOT OF BAGS AND BOARDS TO BUY THIS!

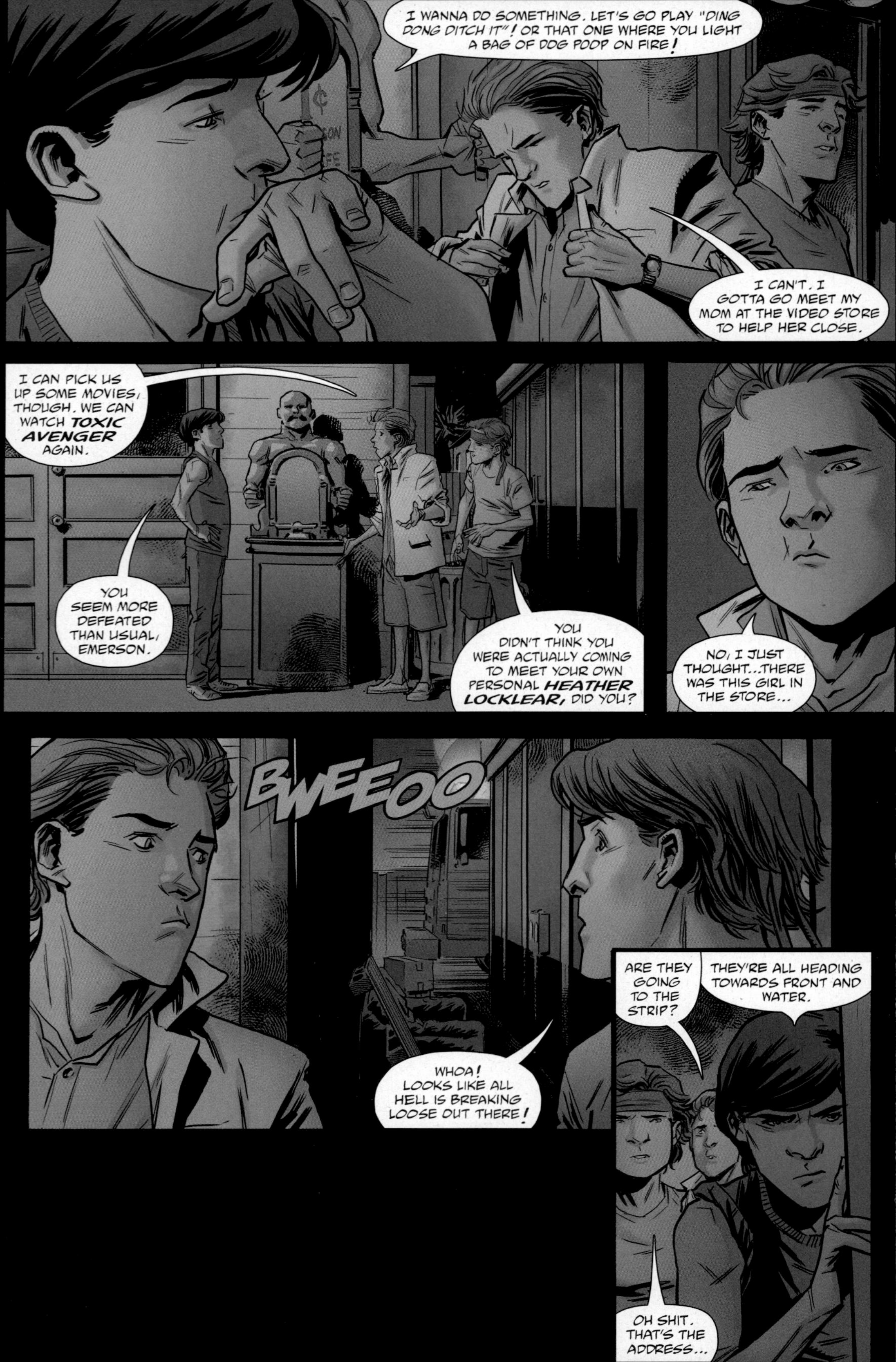
I WANNA DO SOMETHING. LET'S GO PLAY "DING DONG DITCH IT"! OR THAT ONE WHERE YOU LIGHT A BAG OF DOG POOP ON FIRE!
I CAN'T. I GOTTA GO MEET MY MOM AT THE VIDEO STORE TO HELP HER CLOSE.
I CAN PICK US UP SOME MOVIES, THOUGH. WE CAN WATCH TOXIC AVENGER AGAIN.
YOU SEEM MORE DEFEATED THAN USUAL, EMERSON.
YOU DIDN'T THINK YOU WERE ACTUALLY COMING TO MEET YOUR OWN PERSONAL HEATHER LOCKLEAR, DID YOU?
NO, I JUST THOUGHT...THERE WAS THIS GIRL IN THE STORE...
BWEEOO
WHOA! LOOKS LIKE ALL HELL IS BREAKING LOOSE OUT THERE!
ARE THEY GOING TO THE STRIP?
THEY'RE ALL HEADING TOWARDS FRONT AND WATER.
OH SHIT. THAT'S THE ADDRESS...

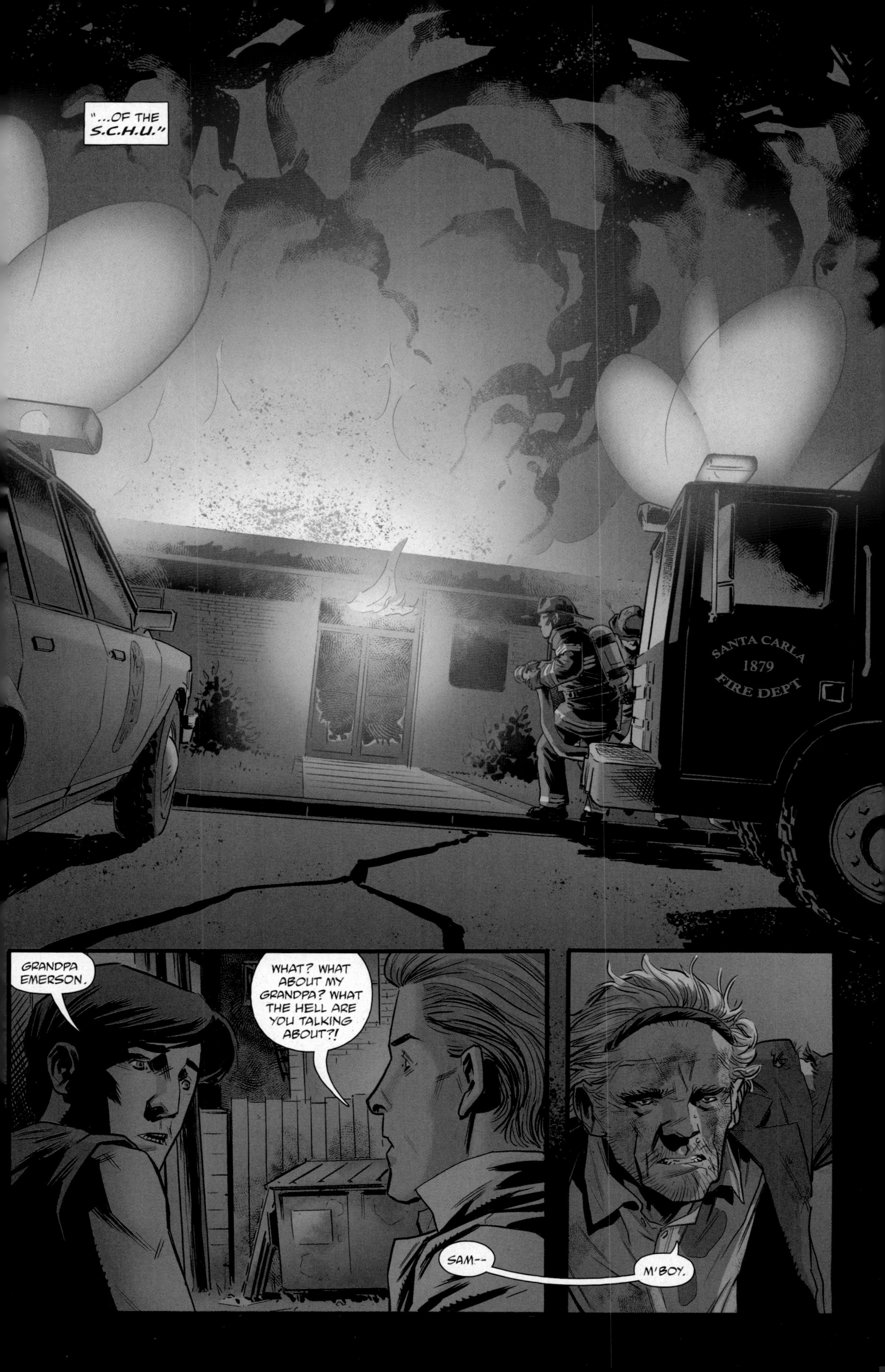
"...OF THE S.C.H.U."
SANTA CARLA 1879 FIRE DEPT
GRANDPA EMERSON.
WHAT? WHAT ABOUT MY GRANDPA? WHAT THE HELL ARE YOU TALKING ABOUT?!
SAM--
M'BOY.

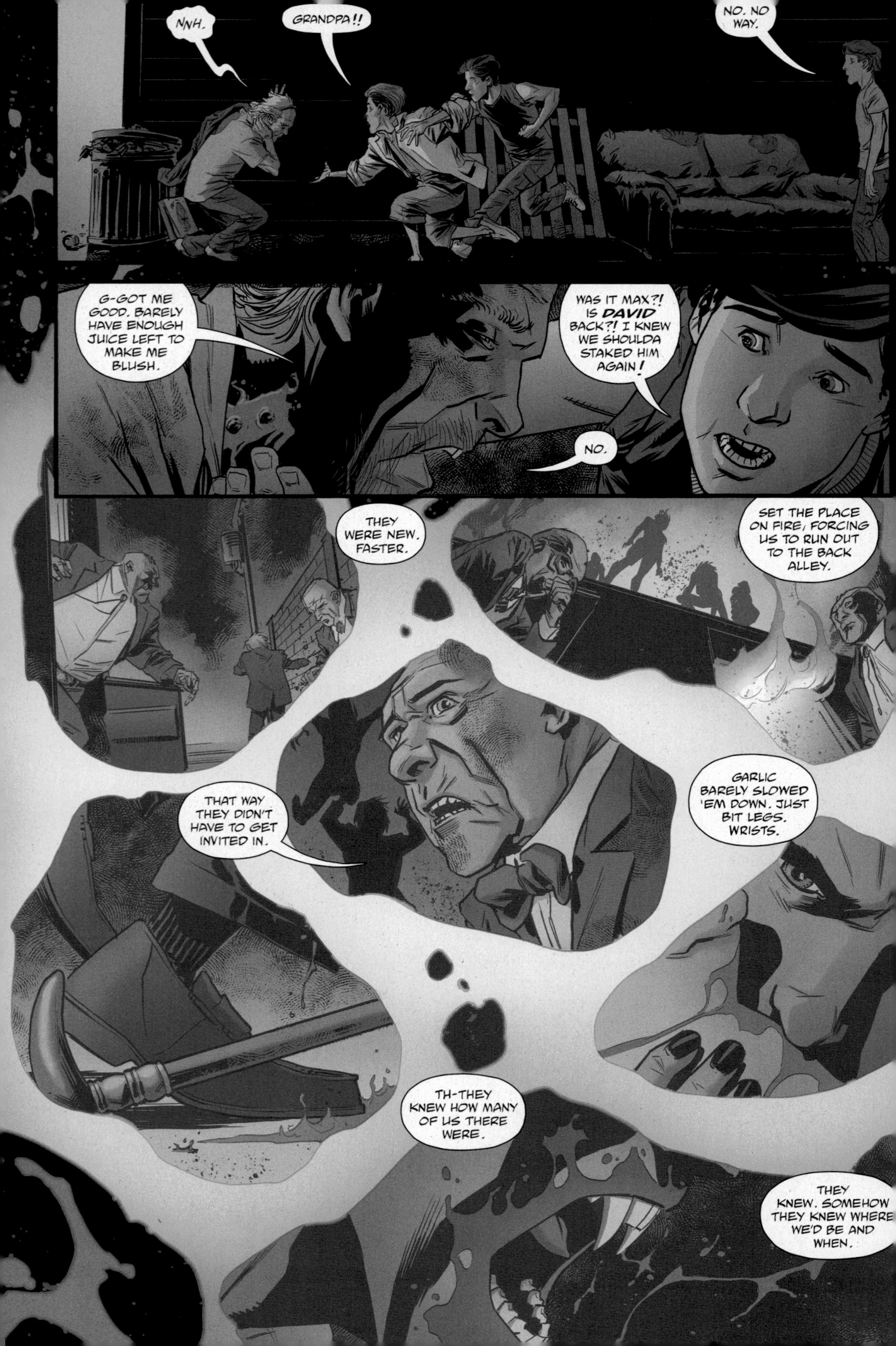
NNH.
GRANDPA!!
NO. NO WAY.
G-GOT ME GOOD. BARELY HAVE ENOUGH JUICE LEFT TO MAKE ME BLUSH.
WAS IT MAX?! IS DAVID BACK?! I KNEW WE SHOULDA STAKED HIM AGAIN!
NO.
THEY WERE NEW. FASTER.
SET THE PLACE ON FIRE, FORCING US TO RUN OUT TO THE BACK ALLEY.
THAT WAY THEY DIDN'T HAVE TO GET INVITED IN.
GARLIC BARELY SLOWED 'EM DOWN. JUST BIT LEGS. WRISTS.
TH-THEY KNEW HOW MANY OF US THERE WERE.
THEY KNEW. SOMEHOW THEY KNEW WHERE WE'D BE AND WHEN.

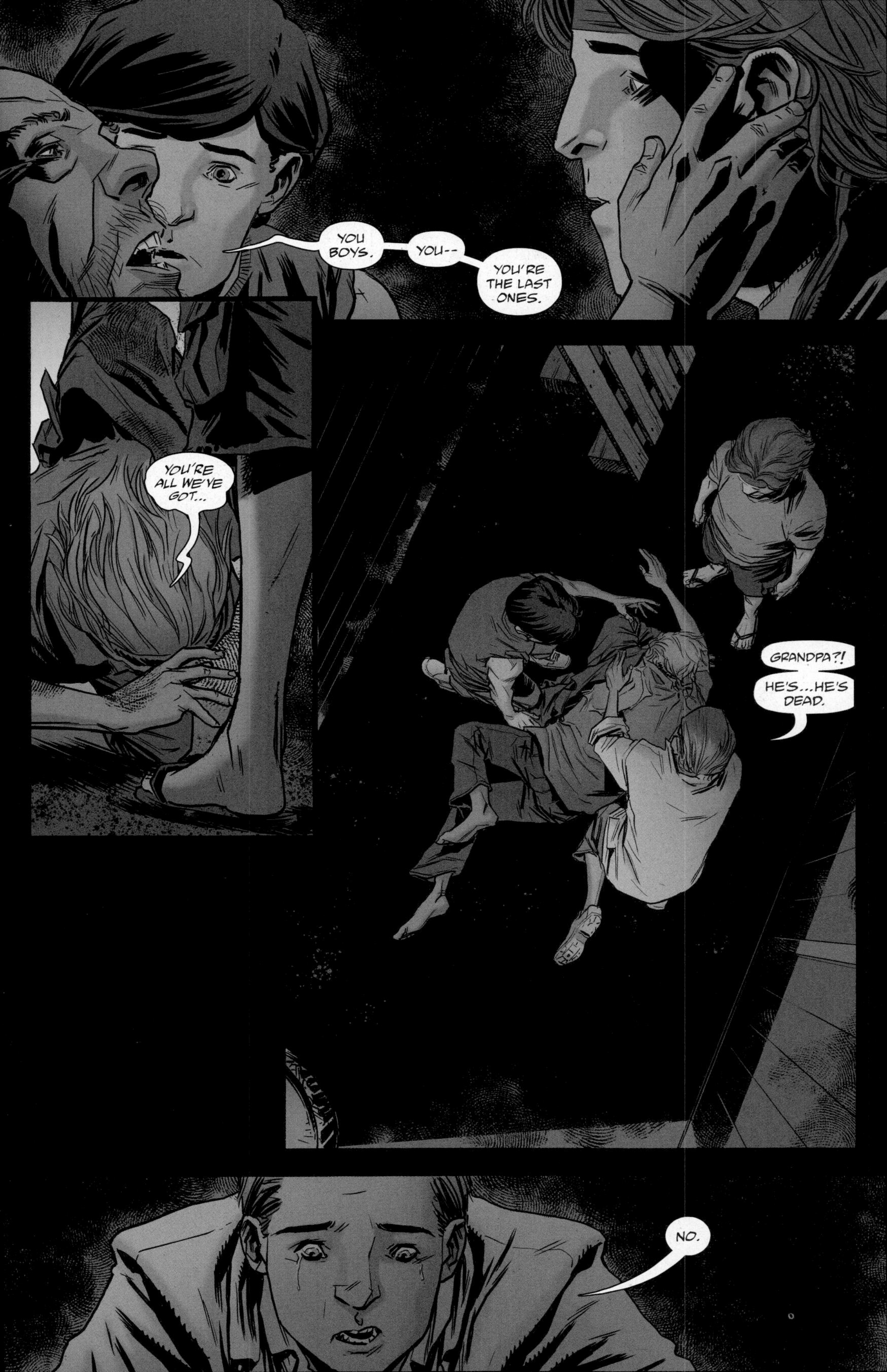
YOU BOYS.
YOU--
YOU'RE THE LAST ONES.
YOU'RE ALL WE'VE GOT...
GRANDPA?!
HE'S...HE'S DEAD.
NO.

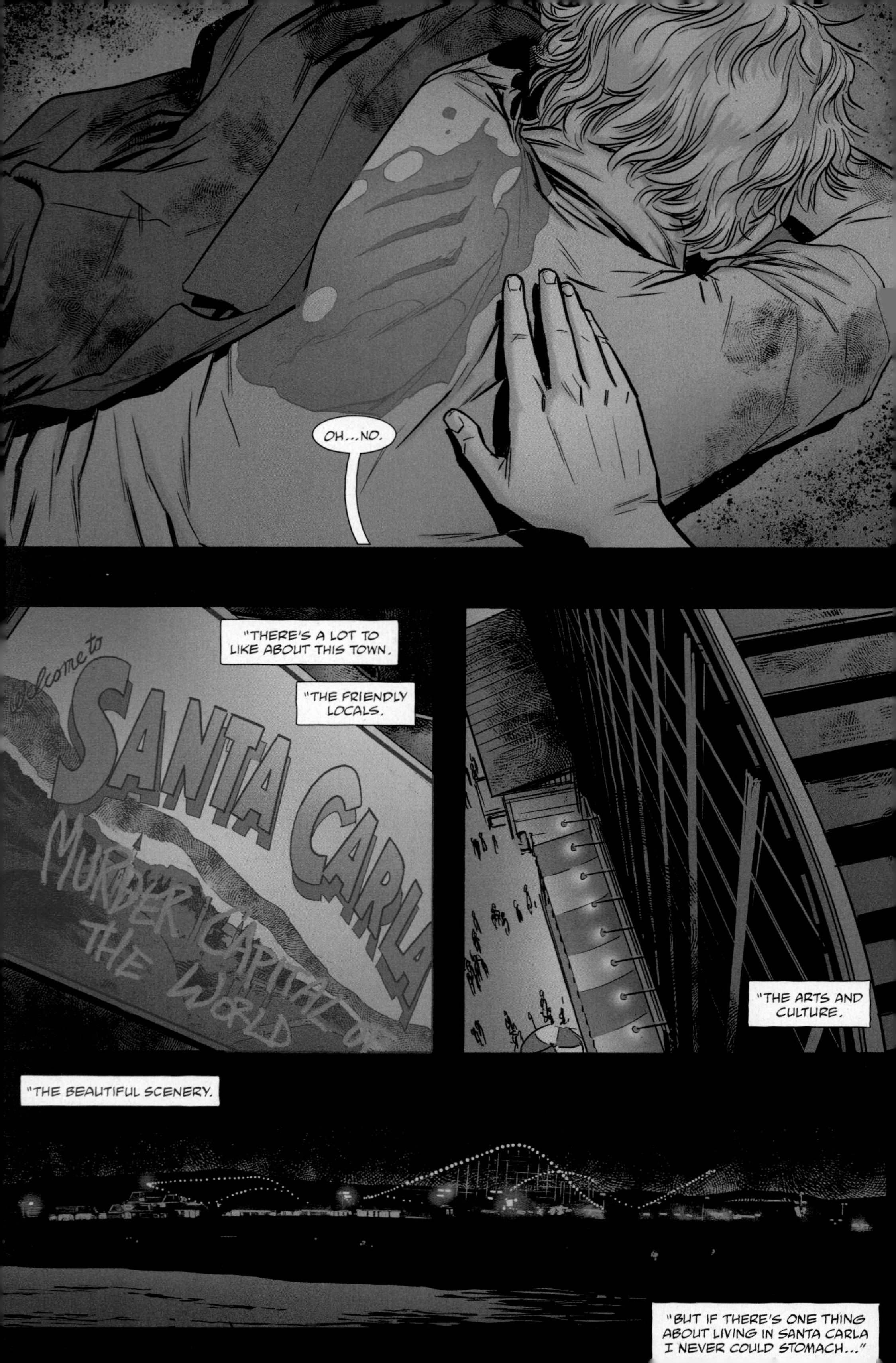
OH...NO.
"THERE'S A LOT TO LIKE ABOUT THIS TOWN.
"THE FRIENDLY LOCALS.
Welcome to
SANTA CARLA
MURDER CAPITAL
THE WORLD
"THE ARTS AND CULTURE.
"THE BEAUTIFUL SCENERY.
"BUT IF THERE'S ONE THING ABOUT LIVING IN SANTA CARLA I NEVER COULD STOMACH..."

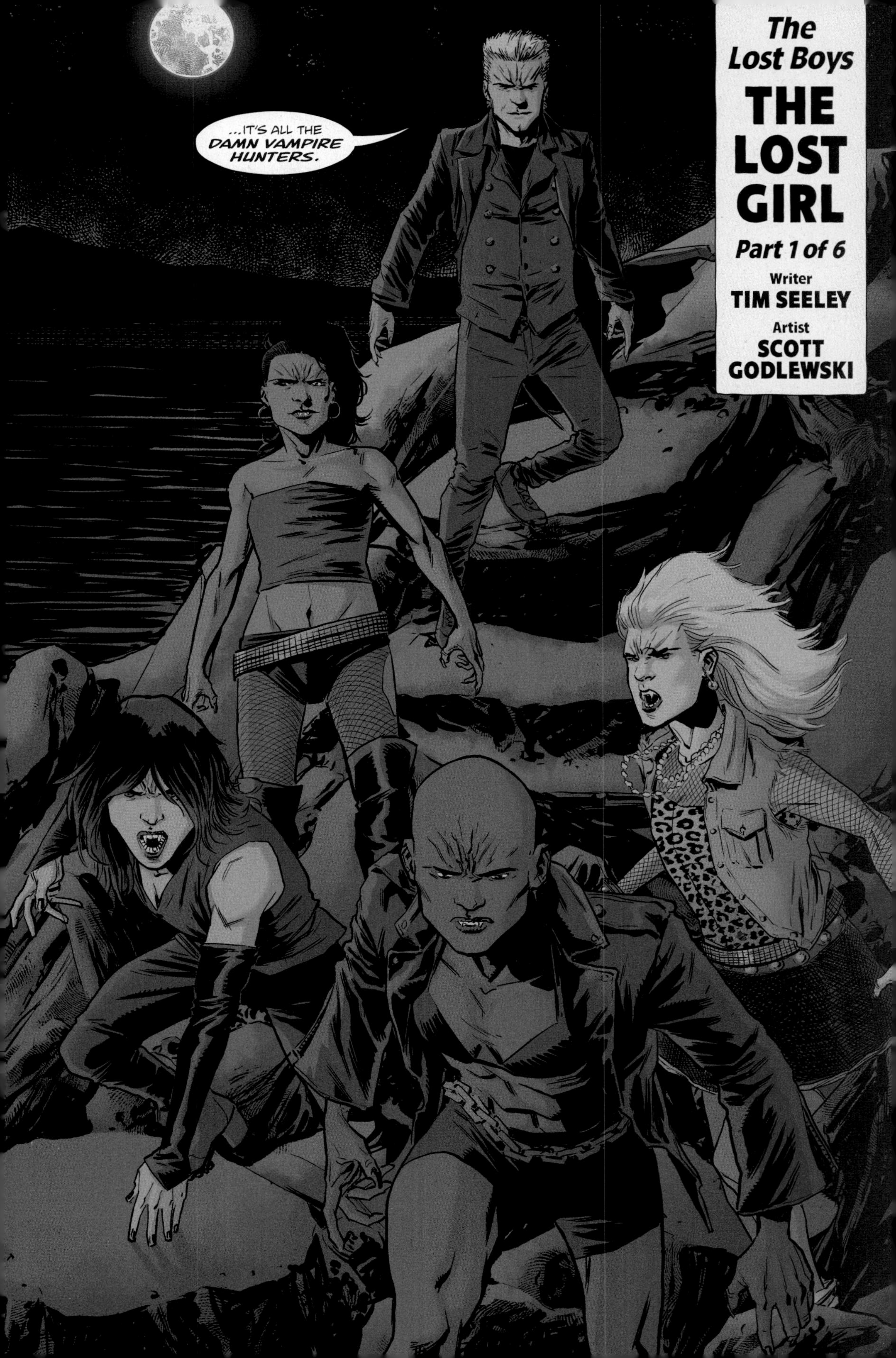
...IT'S ALL THE DAMN VAMPIRE HUNTERS.
The Lost Boys
THE LOST GIRL
Part 1 of 6
Writer TIM SEELEY
Artist SCOTT GODLEWSKI

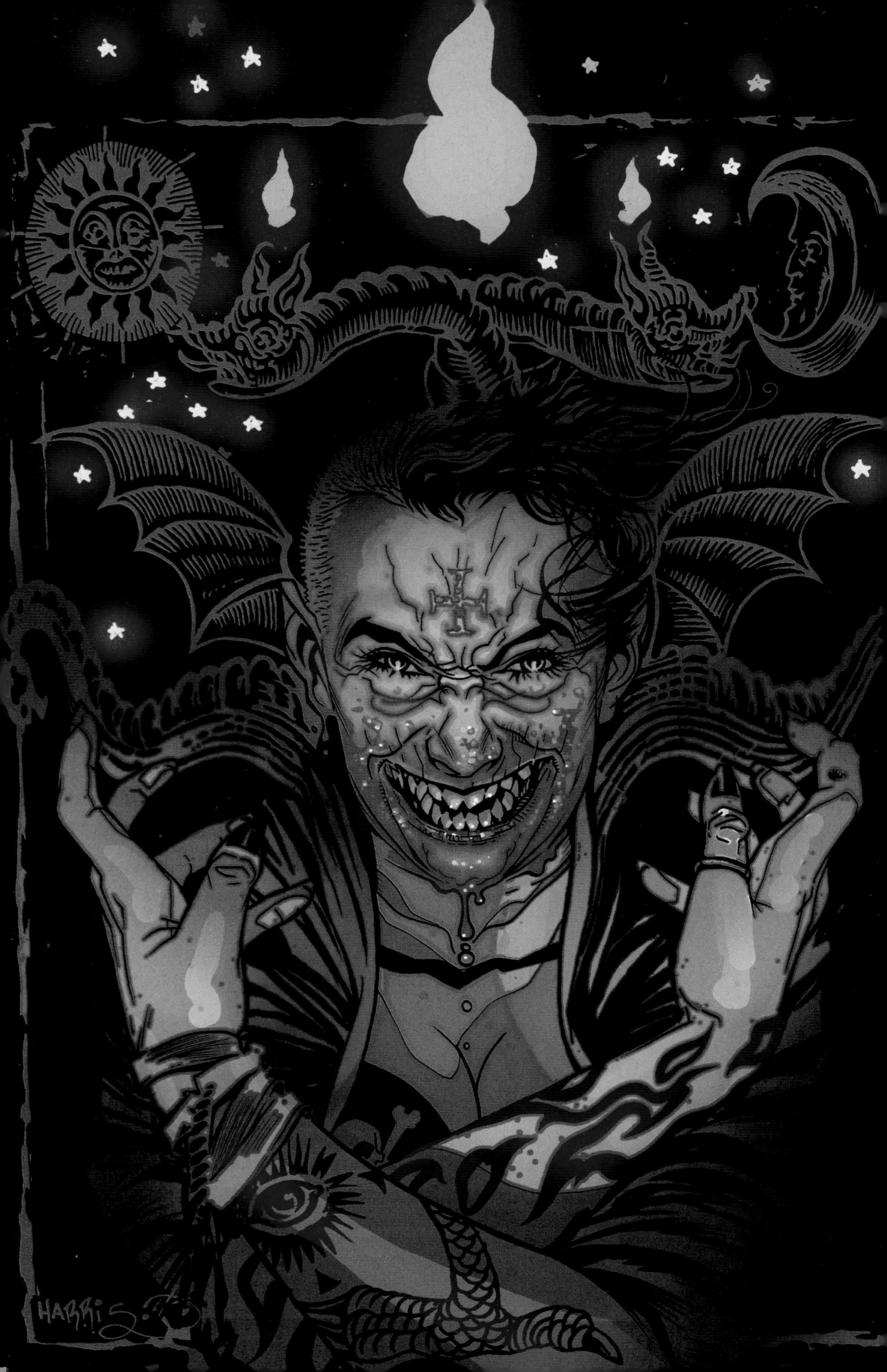
HARRIS

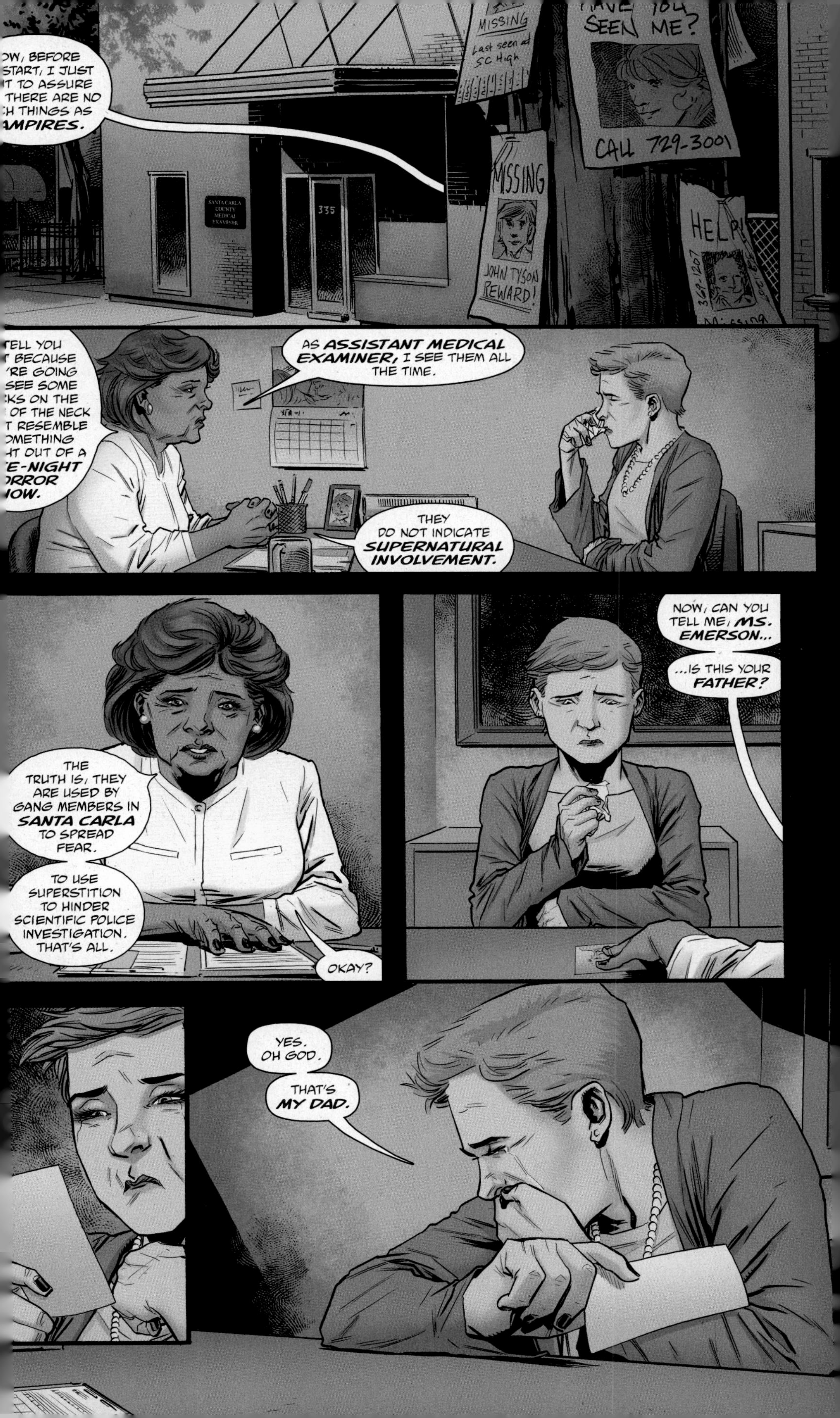
OW, BEFORE START, I JUST T TO ASSURE THERE ARE NO CH THINGS AS AMPIRES.
SANTA CARLA COUNTY MEDICAL EXAMINER
335
MISSING Last seen at SC High
HAVE YOU SEEN ME?
CALL 729-3001
MISSING
JOHN TYSON REWARD!
HELP
TELL YOU T BECAUSE 'RE GOING SEE SOME KS ON THE OF THE NECK T RESEMBLE OMETHING HT OUT OF A TE-NIGHT ORROR HOW.
AS ASSISTANT MEDICAL EXAMINER, I SEE THEM ALL THE TIME.
THEY DO NOT INDICATE SUPERNATURAL INVOLVEMENT.
THE TRUTH IS, THEY ARE USED BY GANG MEMBERS IN SANTA CARLA TO SPREAD FEAR.
TO USE SUPERSTITION TO HINDER SCIENTIFIC POLICE INVESTIGATION. THAT'S ALL.
OKAY?
NOW, CAN YOU TELL ME, MS. EMERSON...
...IS THIS YOUR FATHER?
YES. OH GOD.
THAT'S MY DAD.

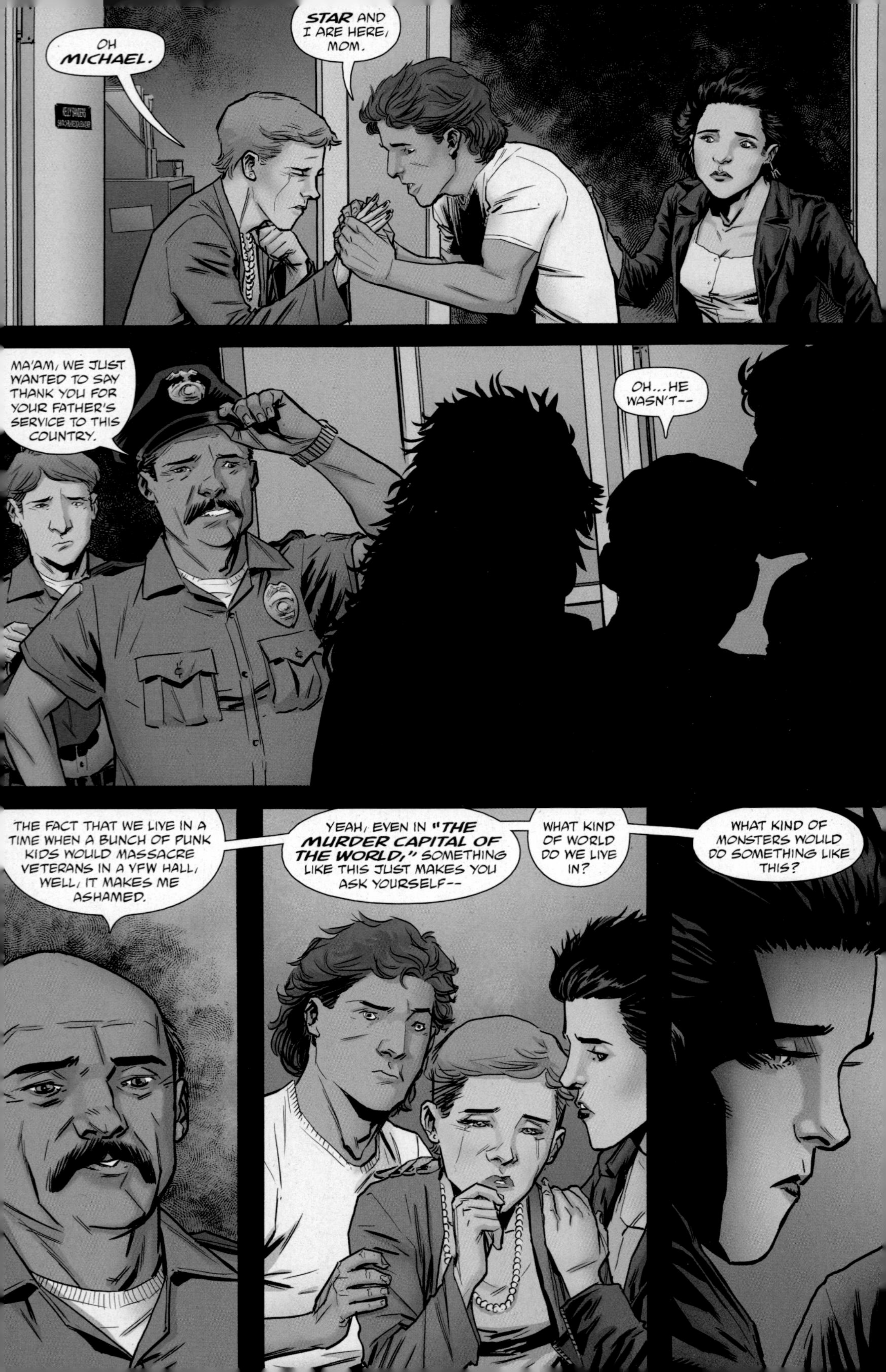
OH MICHAEL.
STAR AND I ARE HERE, MOM.
MA'AM, WE JUST WANTED TO SAY THANK YOU FOR YOUR FATHER'S SERVICE TO THIS COUNTRY.
OH...HE WASN'T--
THE FACT THAT WE LIVE IN A TIME WHEN A BUNCH OF PUNK KIDS WOULD MASSACRE VETERANS IN A VFW HALL, WELL, IT MAKES ME ASHAMED.
YEAH, EVEN IN "THE MURDER CAPITAL OF THE WORLD," SOMETHING LIKE THIS JUST MAKES YOU ASK YOURSELF--
WHAT KIND OF WORLD DO WE LIVE IN?
WHAT KIND OF MONSTERS WOULD DO SOMETHING LIKE THIS?

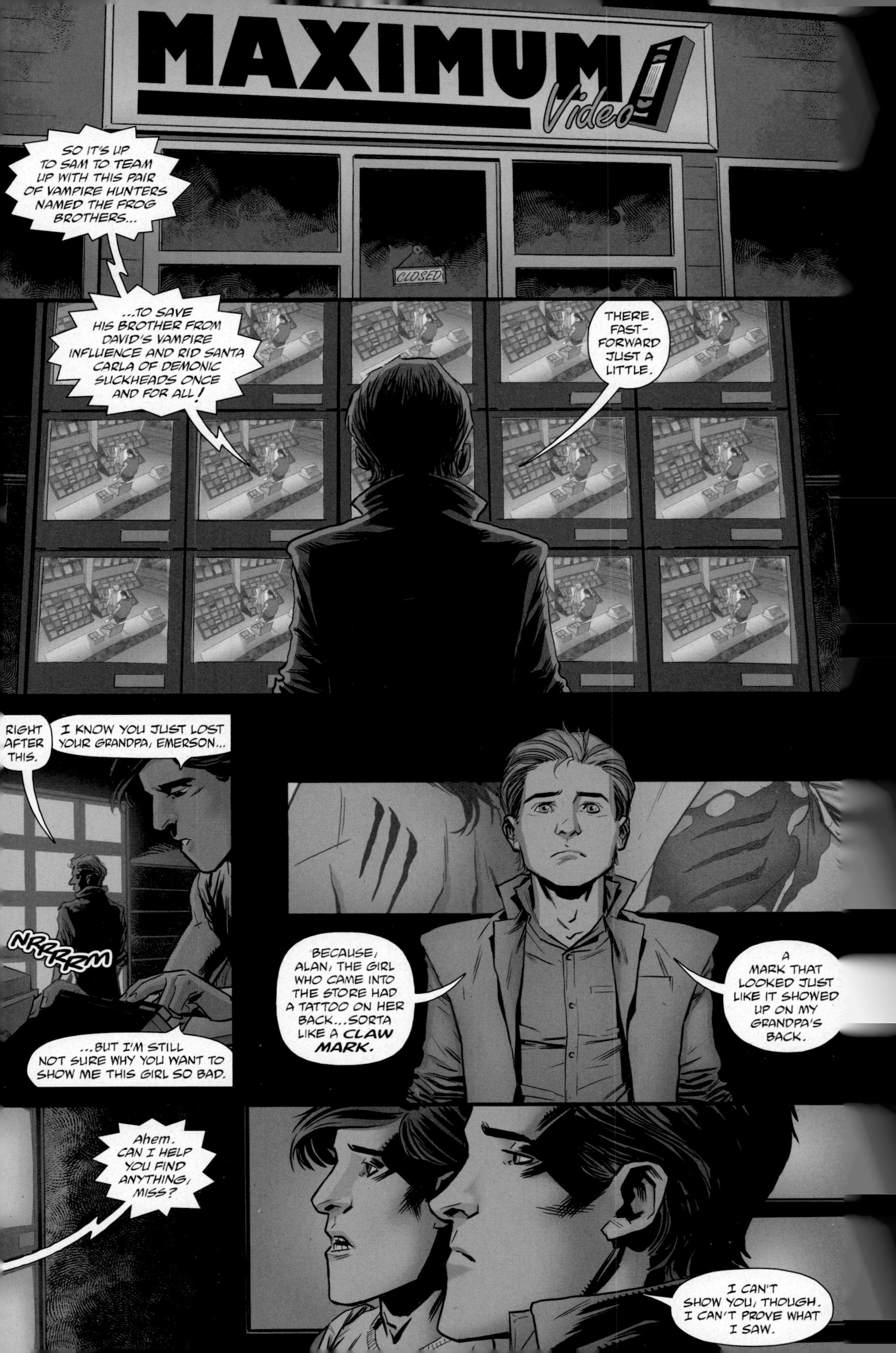
MAXIMUM Video
SO IT'S UP TO SAM TO TEAM UP WITH THIS PAIR OF VAMPIRE HUNTERS NAMED THE FROG BROTHERS...
CLOSED
...TO SAVE HIS BROTHER FROM DAVID'S VAMPIRE INFLUENCE AND RID SANTA CARLA OF DEMONIC SUCKHEADS ONCE AND FOR ALL!
THERE. FAST-FORWARD JUST A LITTLE.
RIGHT AFTER THIS.
I KNOW YOU JUST LOST YOUR GRANDPA, EMERSON...
NRRRRM
...BUT I'M STILL NOT SURE WHY YOU WANT TO SHOW ME THIS GIRL SO BAD.
BECAUSE, ALAN, THE GIRL WHO CAME INTO THE STORE HAD A TATTOO ON HER BACK...SORTA LIKE A CLAW MARK.
A MARK THAT LOOKED JUST LIKE IT SHOWED UP ON MY GRANDPA'S BACK.
Ahem. CAN I HELP YOU FIND ANYTHING, MISS?
I CAN'T SHOW YOU, THOUGH. I CAN'T PROVE WHAT I SAW.

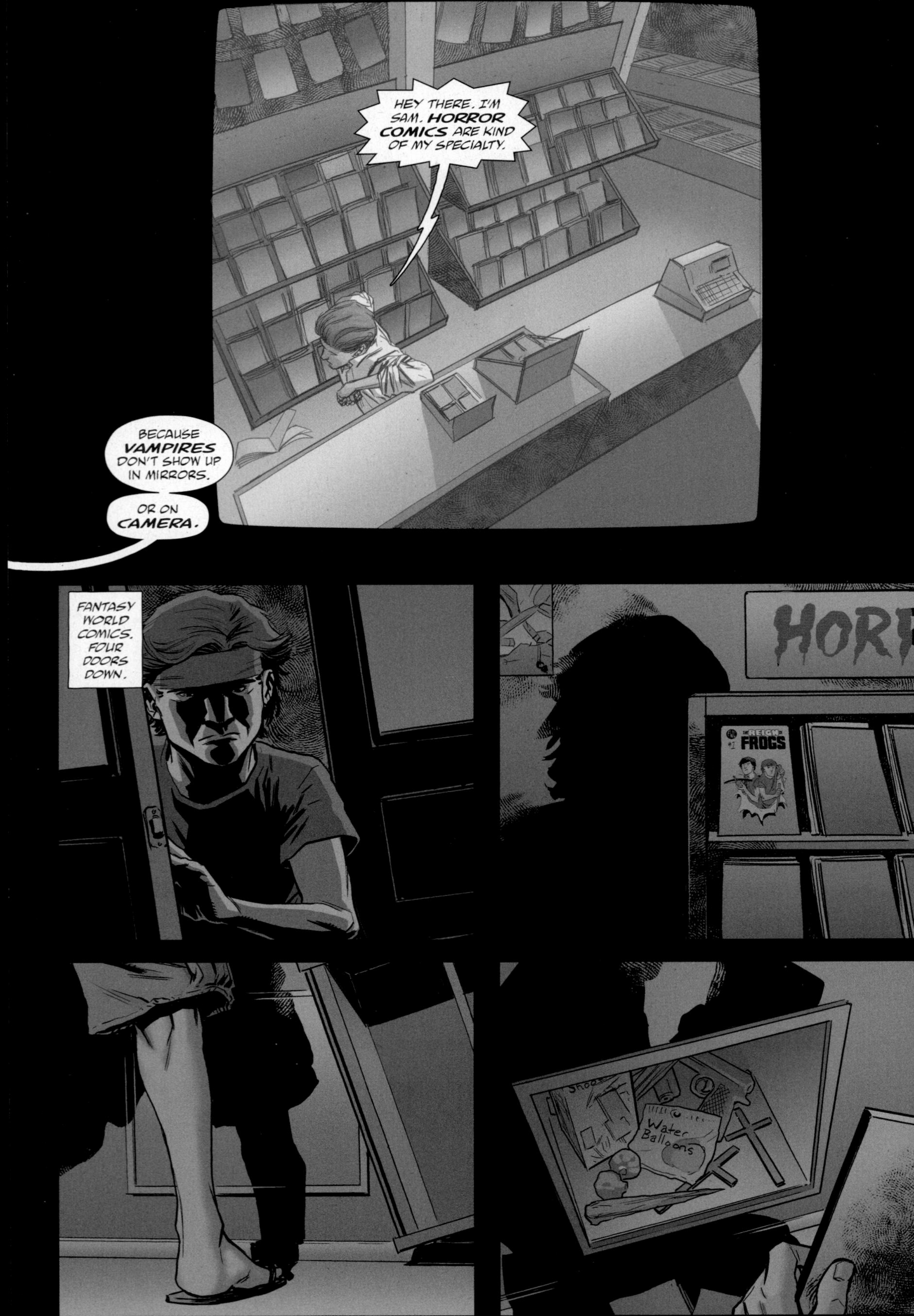
HEY THERE. I'M SAM. **HORROR COMICS** ARE KIND OF MY SPECIALTY.
BECAUSE **VAMPIRES** DON'T SHOW UP IN MIRRORS.
OR ON **CAMERA.**
FANTASY WORLD COMICS. FOUR DOORS DOWN.
HORR
THE REIGN OF FROGS #1
Water Balloons

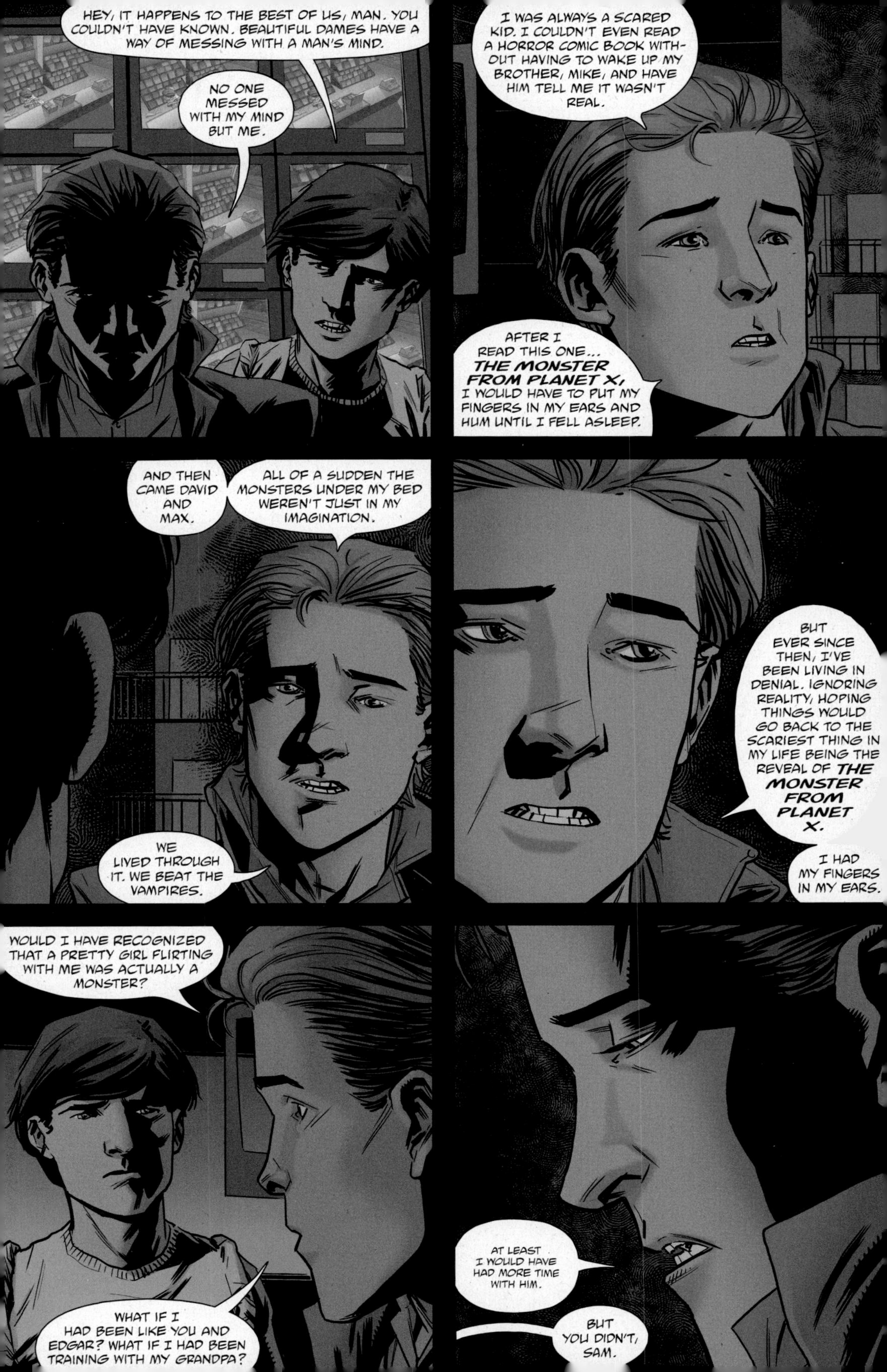
HEY, IT HAPPENS TO THE BEST OF US, MAN. YOU COULDN'T HAVE KNOWN. BEAUTIFUL DAMES HAVE A WAY OF MESSING WITH A MAN'S MIND.
NO ONE MESSED WITH MY MIND BUT ME.
I WAS ALWAYS A SCARED KID. I COULDN'T EVEN READ A HORROR COMIC BOOK WITH-OUT HAVING TO WAKE UP MY BROTHER, MIKE, AND HAVE HIM TELL ME IT WASN'T REAL.
AFTER I READ THIS ONE... THE MONSTER FROM PLANET X, I WOULD HAVE TO PUT MY FINGERS IN MY EARS AND HUM UNTIL I FELL ASLEEP.
AND THEN CAME DAVID AND MAX.
ALL OF A SUDDEN THE MONSTERS UNDER MY BED WEREN'T JUST IN MY IMAGINATION.
WE LIVED THROUGH IT. WE BEAT THE VAMPIRES.
BUT EVER SINCE THEN, I'VE BEEN LIVING IN DENIAL. IGNORING REALITY, HOPING THINGS WOULD GO BACK TO THE SCARIEST THING IN MY LIFE BEING THE REVEAL OF THE MONSTER FROM PLANET X.
I HAD MY FINGERS IN MY EARS.
WOULD I HAVE RECOGNIZED THAT A PRETTY GIRL FLIRTING WITH ME WAS ACTUALLY A MONSTER?
WHAT IF I HAD BEEN LIKE YOU AND EDGAR? WHAT IF I HAD BEEN TRAINING WITH MY GRANDPA?
AT LEAST I WOULD HAVE HAD MORE TIME WITH HIM.
BUT YOU DIDN'T, SAM.

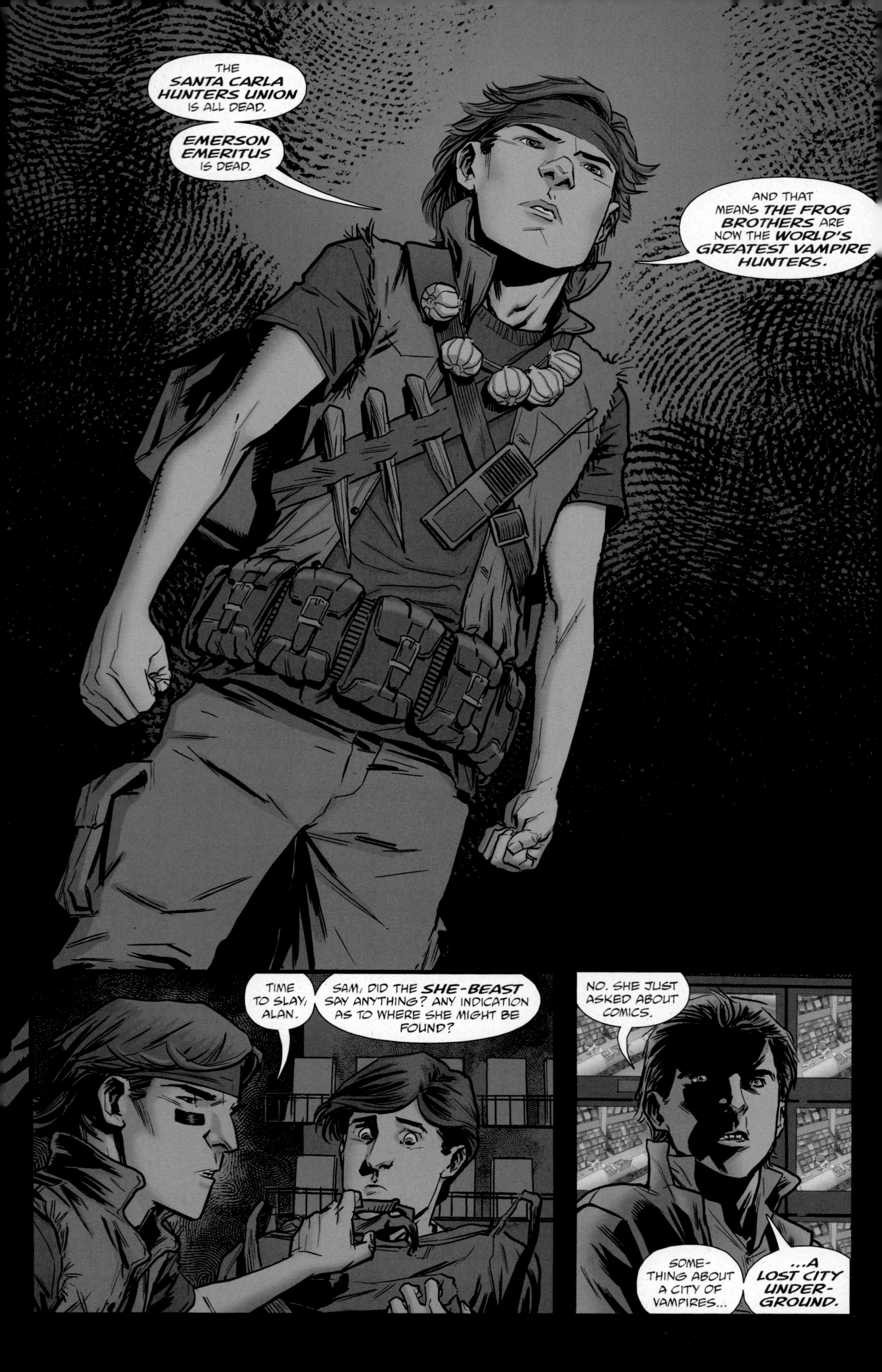
THE SANTA CARLA HUNTERS UNION IS ALL DEAD.
EMERSON EMERITUS IS DEAD.
AND THAT MEANS THE FROG BROTHERS ARE NOW THE WORLD'S GREATEST VAMPIRE HUNTERS.
TIME TO SLAY, ALAN.
SAM, DID THE SHE-BEAST SAY ANYTHING? ANY INDICATION AS TO WHERE SHE MIGHT BE FOUND?
NO. SHE JUST ASKED ABOUT COMICS.
SOME-THING ABOUT A CITY OF VAMPIRES...
...A LOST CITY UNDER-GROUND.

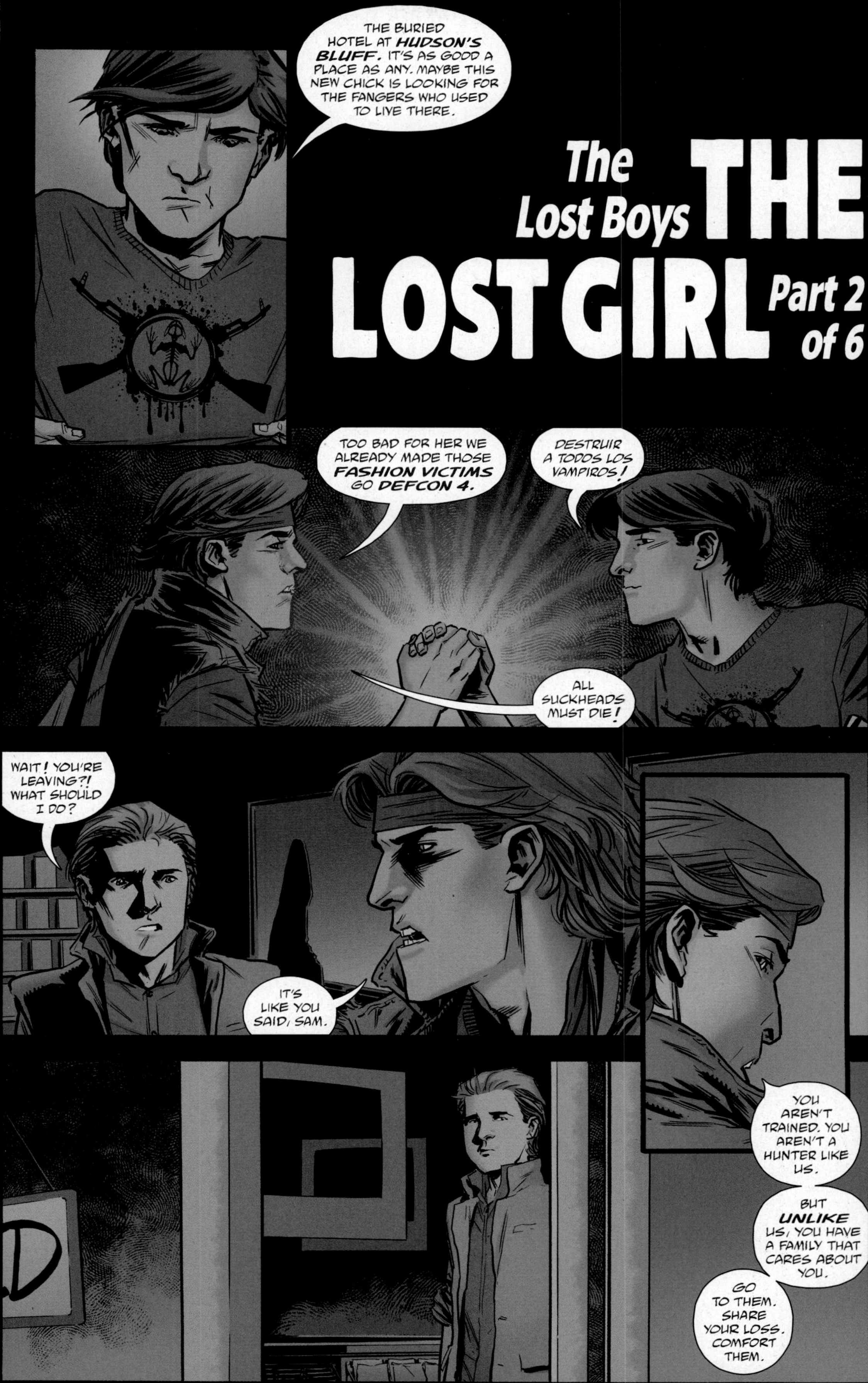
THE BURIED HOTEL AT HUDSON'S BLUFF. IT'S AS GOOD A PLACE AS ANY. MAYBE THIS NEW CHICK IS LOOKING FOR THE FANGERS WHO USED TO LIVE THERE.
The Lost Boys THE LOST GIRL Part 2 of 6
TOO BAD FOR HER WE ALREADY MADE THOSE FASHION VICTIMS GO DEFCON 4.
DESTRUIR A TODOS LOS VAMPIROS!
ALL SUCKHEADS MUST DIE!
WAIT! YOU'RE LEAVING?! WHAT SHOULD I DO?
IT'S LIKE YOU SAID, SAM.
YOU AREN'T TRAINED. YOU AREN'T A HUNTER LIKE US.
BUT UNLIKE US, YOU HAVE A FAMILY THAT CARES ABOUT YOU.
GO TO THEM. SHARE YOUR LOSS. COMFORT THEM.

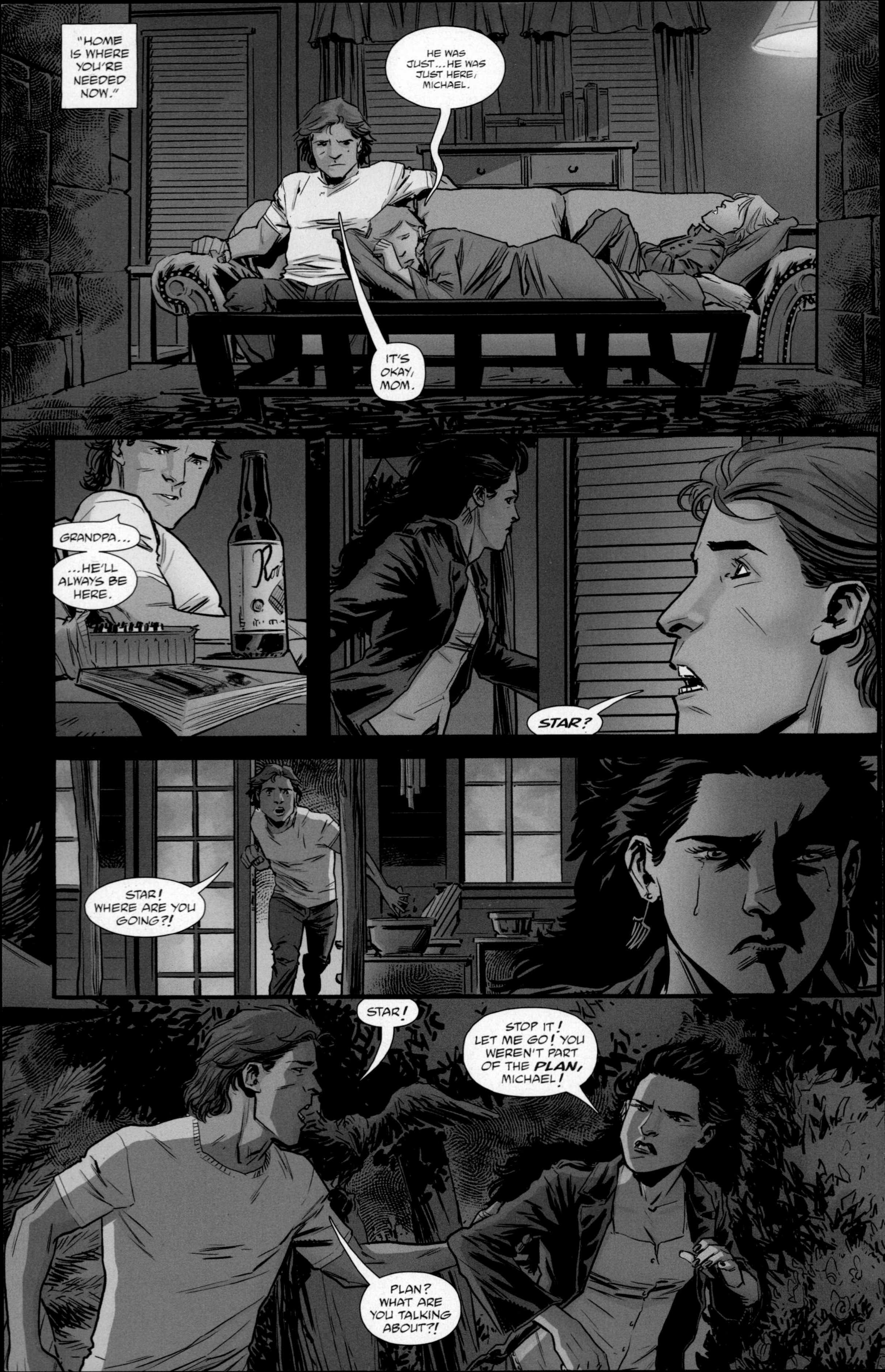
"HOME IS WHERE YOU'RE NEEDED NOW."
HE WAS JUST... HE WAS JUST HERE, MICHAEL.
IT'S OKAY, MOM.
GRANDPA...
...HE'LL ALWAYS BE HERE.
STAR?
STAR! WHERE ARE YOU GOING?!
STAR!
STOP IT! LET ME GO! YOU WEREN'T PART OF THE PLAN, MICHAEL!
PLAN? WHAT ARE YOU TALKING ABOUT?!

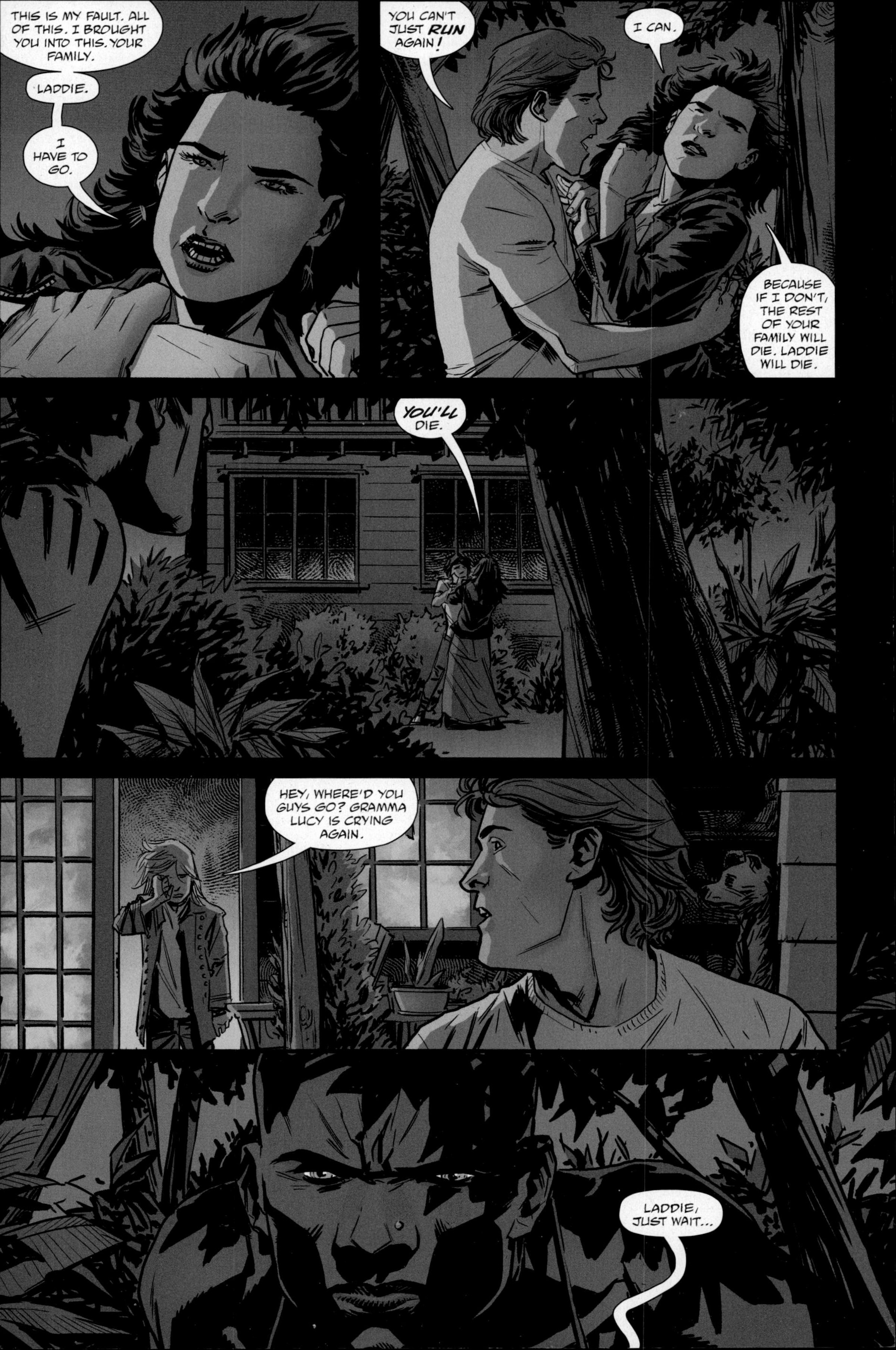
THIS IS MY FAULT. ALL OF THIS. I BROUGHT YOU INTO THIS. YOUR FAMILY.
LADDIE.
I HAVE TO GO.
YOU CAN'T JUST RUN AGAIN!
I CAN.
BECAUSE IF I DON'T, THE REST OF YOUR FAMILY WILL DIE. LADDIE WILL DIE.
YOU'LL DIE.
HEY, WHERE'D YOU GUYS GO? GRAMMA LUCY IS CRYING AGAIN.
LADDIE, JUST WAIT...

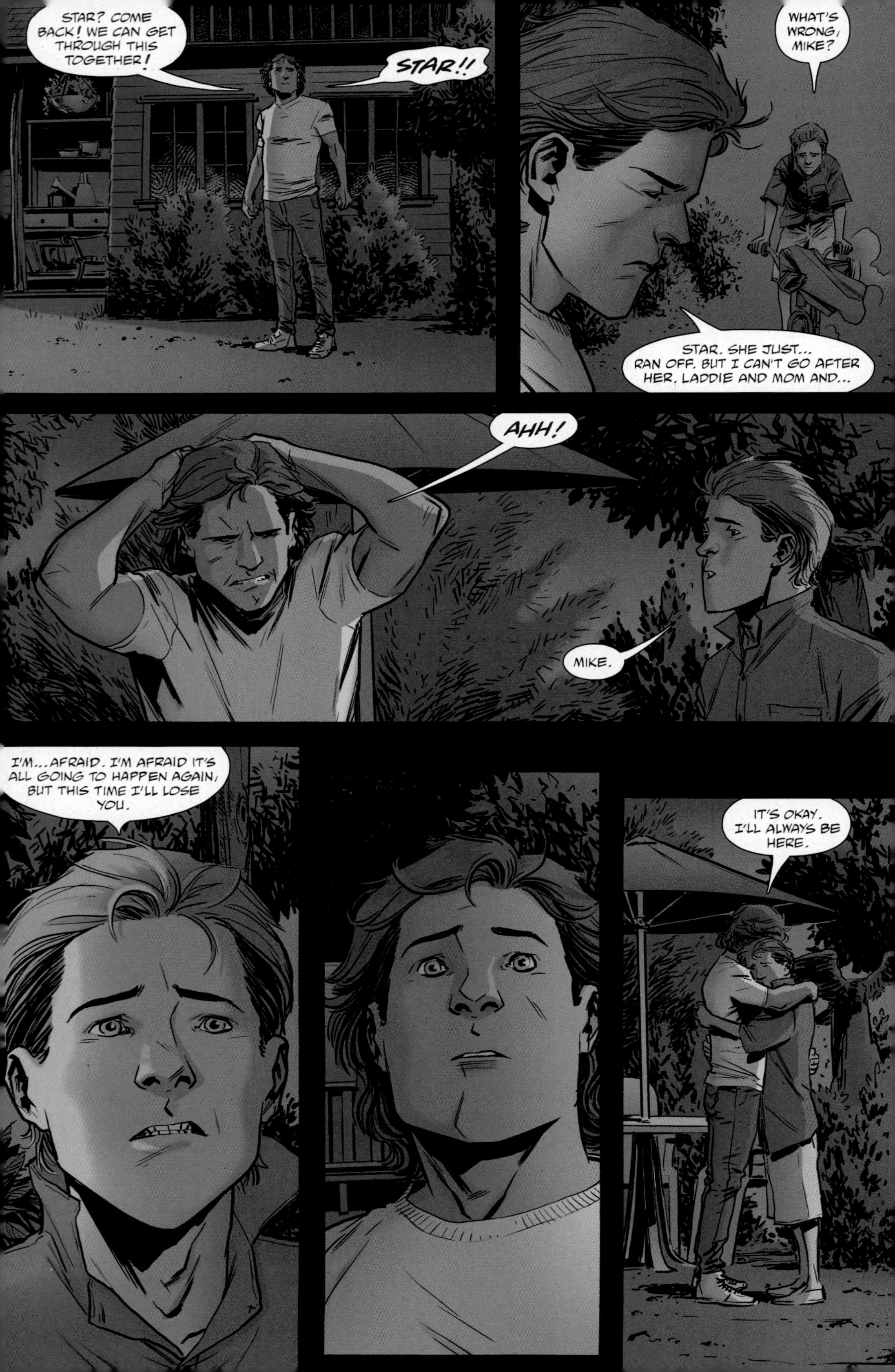
STAR? COME BACK! WE CAN GET THROUGH THIS TOGETHER!
STAR!!
WHAT'S WRONG, MIKE?
STAR. SHE JUST... RAN OFF. BUT I CAN'T GO AFTER HER. LADDIE AND MOM AND...
AHH!
MIKE.
I'M... AFRAID. I'M AFRAID IT'S ALL GOING TO HAPPEN AGAIN, BUT THIS TIME I'LL LOSE YOU.
IT'S OKAY. I'LL ALWAYS BE HERE.

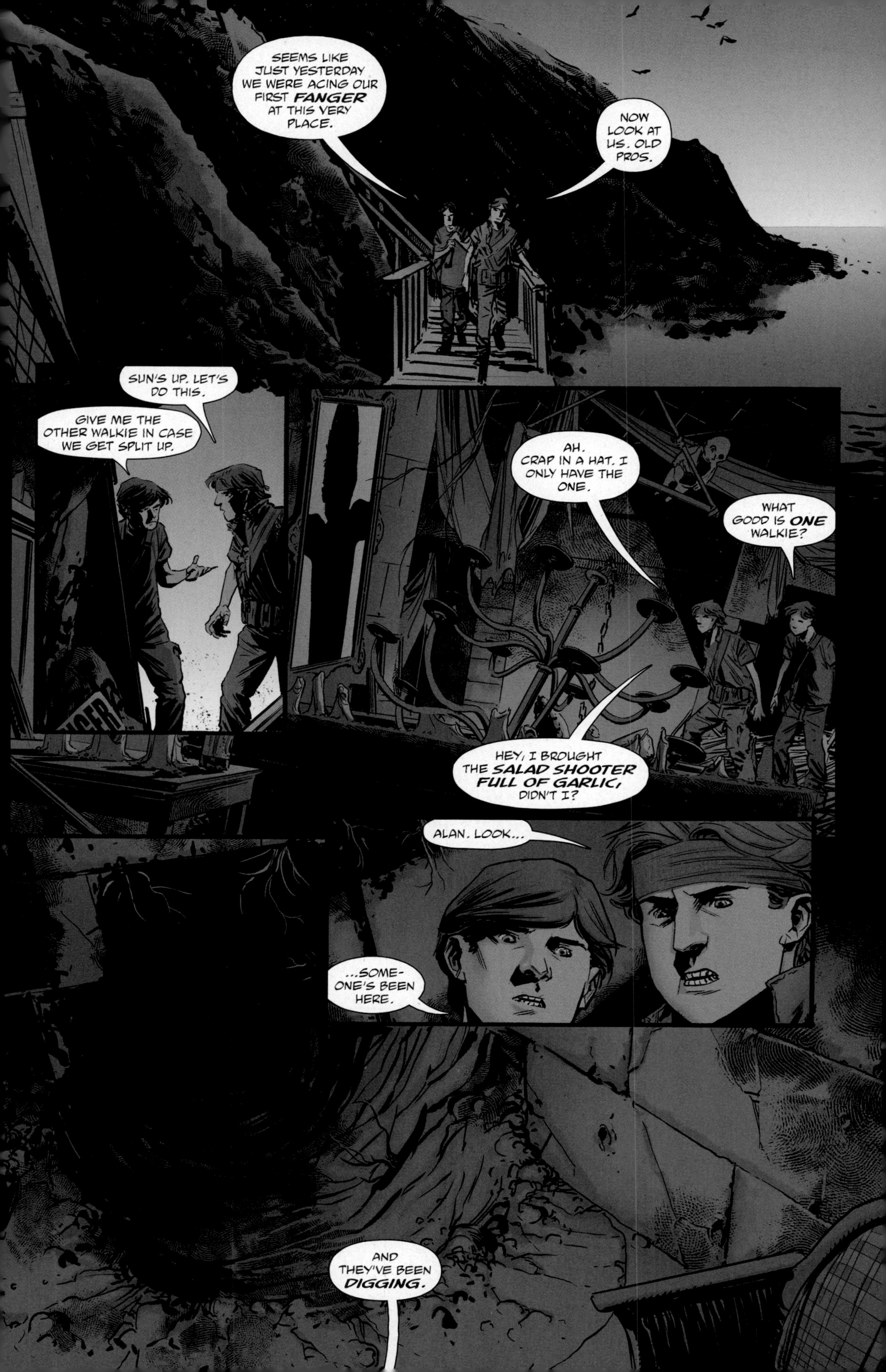
SEEMS LIKE JUST YESTERDAY WE WERE ACING OUR FIRST FANGER AT THIS VERY PLACE.
NOW LOOK AT US. OLD PROS.
SUN'S UP. LET'S DO THIS.
GIVE ME THE OTHER WALKIE IN CASE WE GET SPLIT UP.
AH. CRAP IN A HAT. I ONLY HAVE THE ONE.
WHAT GOOD IS ONE WALKIE?
HEY, I BROUGHT THE SALAD SHOOTER FULL OF GARLIC, DIDN'T I?
ALAN. LOOK...
...SOME-ONE'S BEEN HERE.
AND THEY'VE BEEN DIGGING.

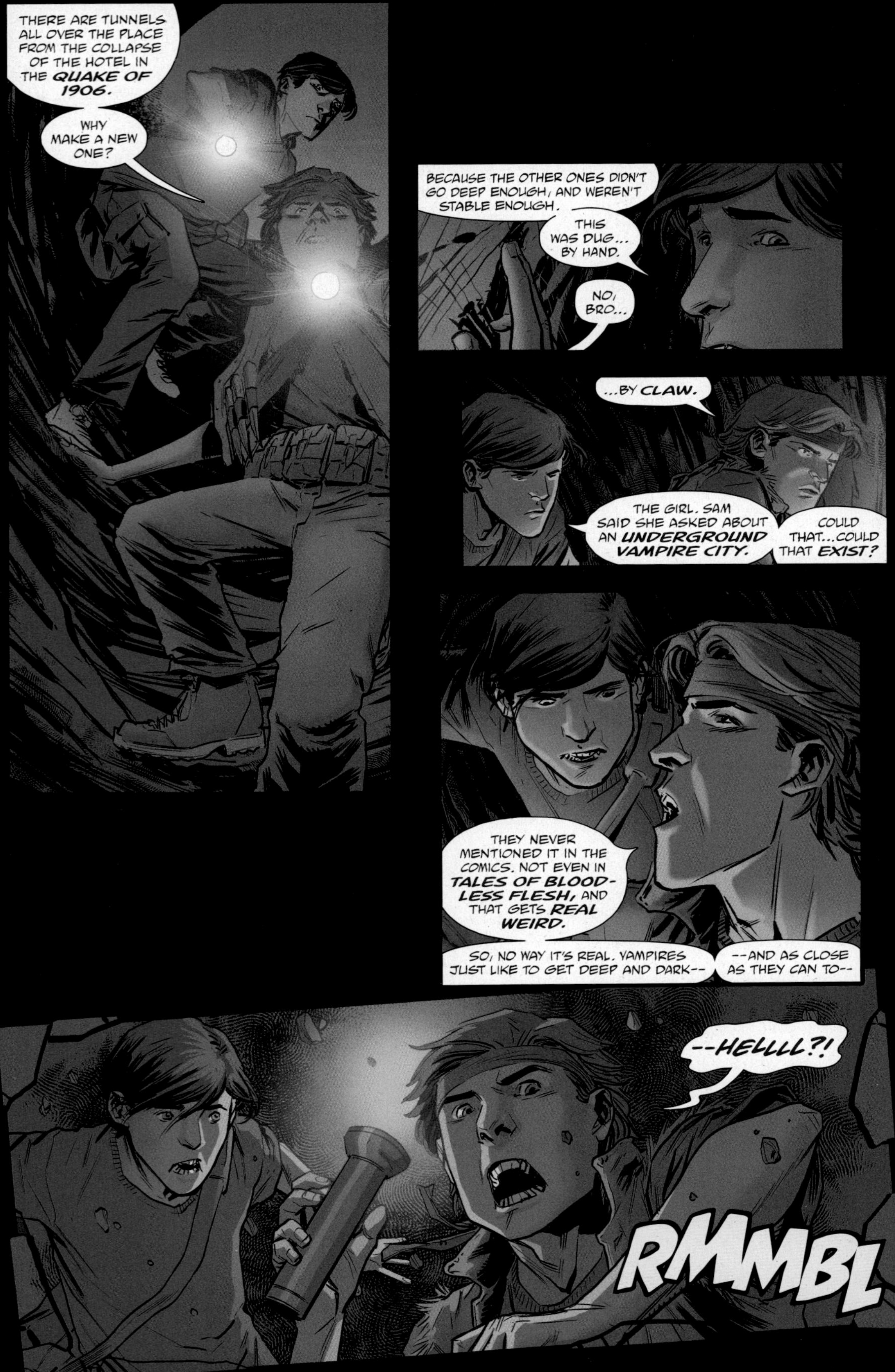
THERE ARE TUNNELS ALL OVER THE PLACE FROM THE COLLAPSE OF THE HOTEL IN THE QUAKE OF 1906.
WHY MAKE A NEW ONE?
BECAUSE THE OTHER ONES DIDN'T GO DEEP ENOUGH, AND WEREN'T STABLE ENOUGH.
THIS WAS DUG... BY HAND.
NO, BRO...
...BY CLAW.
THE GIRL. SAM SAID SHE ASKED ABOUT AN UNDERGROUND VAMPIRE CITY.
COULD THAT...COULD THAT EXIST?
THEY NEVER MENTIONED IT IN THE COMICS. NOT EVEN IN TALES OF BLOOD-LESS FLESH, AND THAT GETS REAL WEIRD.
SO, NO WAY IT'S REAL. VAMPIRES JUST LIKE TO GET DEEP AND DARK--
--AND AS CLOSE AS THEY CAN TO--
--HELLLL?!
RMMBL

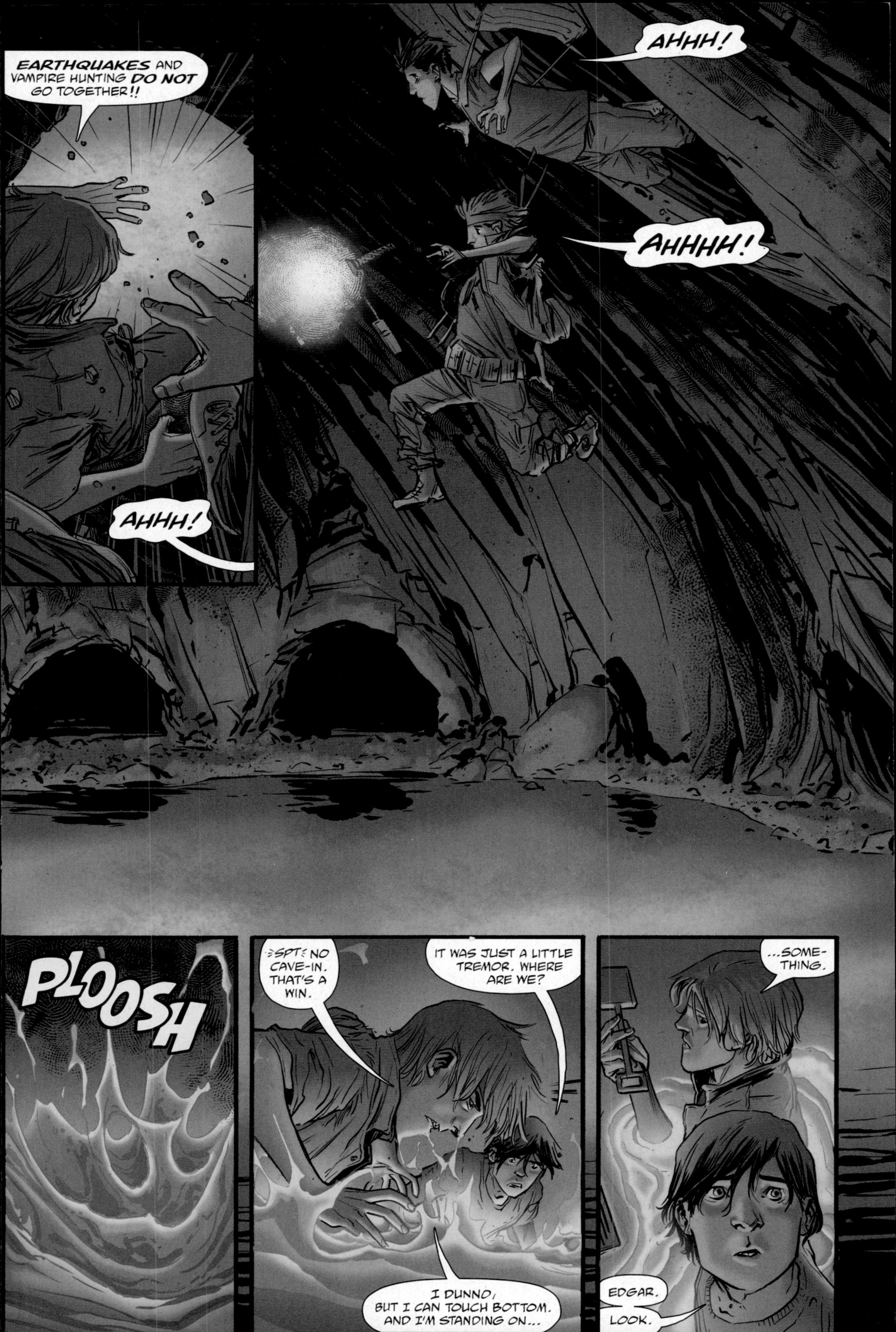
EARTHQUAKES AND VAMPIRE HUNTING DO NOT GO TOGETHER!!
AHHH!
AHHHH!
AHHH!
PLOOSH
SPT NO CAVE-IN. THAT'S A WIN.
IT WAS JUST A LITTLE TREMOR. WHERE ARE WE?
I DUNNO, BUT I CAN TOUCH BOTTOM. AND I'M STANDING ON...
...SOME-THING.
EDGAR.
LOOK.

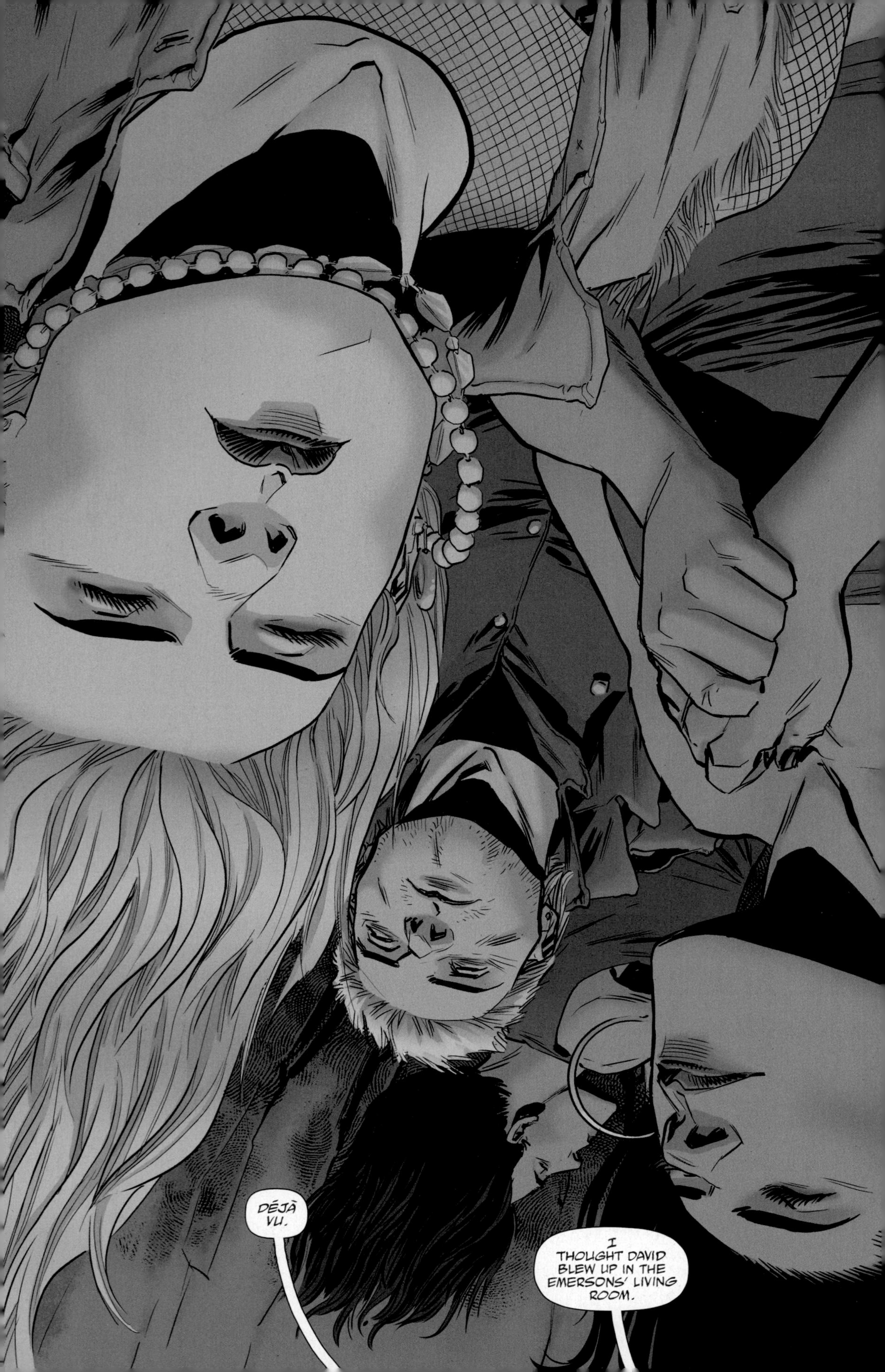
DÉJÀ VU.
I THOUGHT DAVID BLEW UP IN THE EMERSONS' LIVING ROOM.

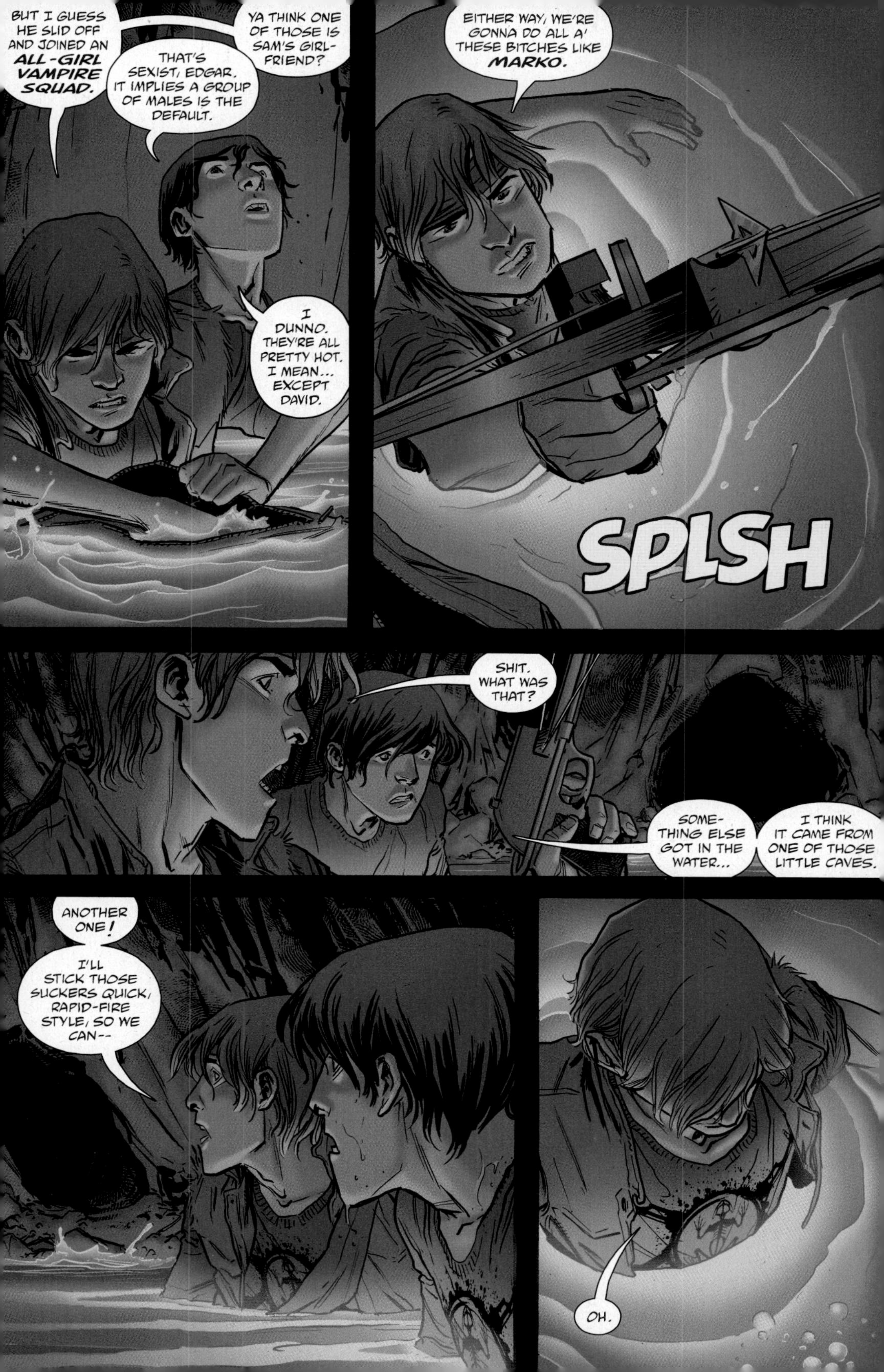

BUT I GUESS HE SLID OFF AND JOINED AN ALL-GIRL VAMPIRE SQUAD.
YA THINK ONE OF THOSE IS SAM'S GIRLFRIEND?
THAT'S SEXIST, EDGAR. IT IMPLIES A GROUP OF MALES IS THE DEFAULT.
I DUNNO. THEY'RE ALL PRETTY HOT. I MEAN... EXCEPT DAVID.
EITHER WAY, WE'RE GONNA DO ALL A' THESE BITCHES LIKE MARKO.
SPLSH
SHIT. WHAT WAS THAT?
SOMETHING ELSE GOT IN THE WATER...
I THINK IT CAME FROM ONE OF THOSE LITTLE CAVES.
ANOTHER ONE!
I'LL STICK THOSE SUCKERS QUICK, RAPID-FIRE STYLE, SO WE CAN--
OH.

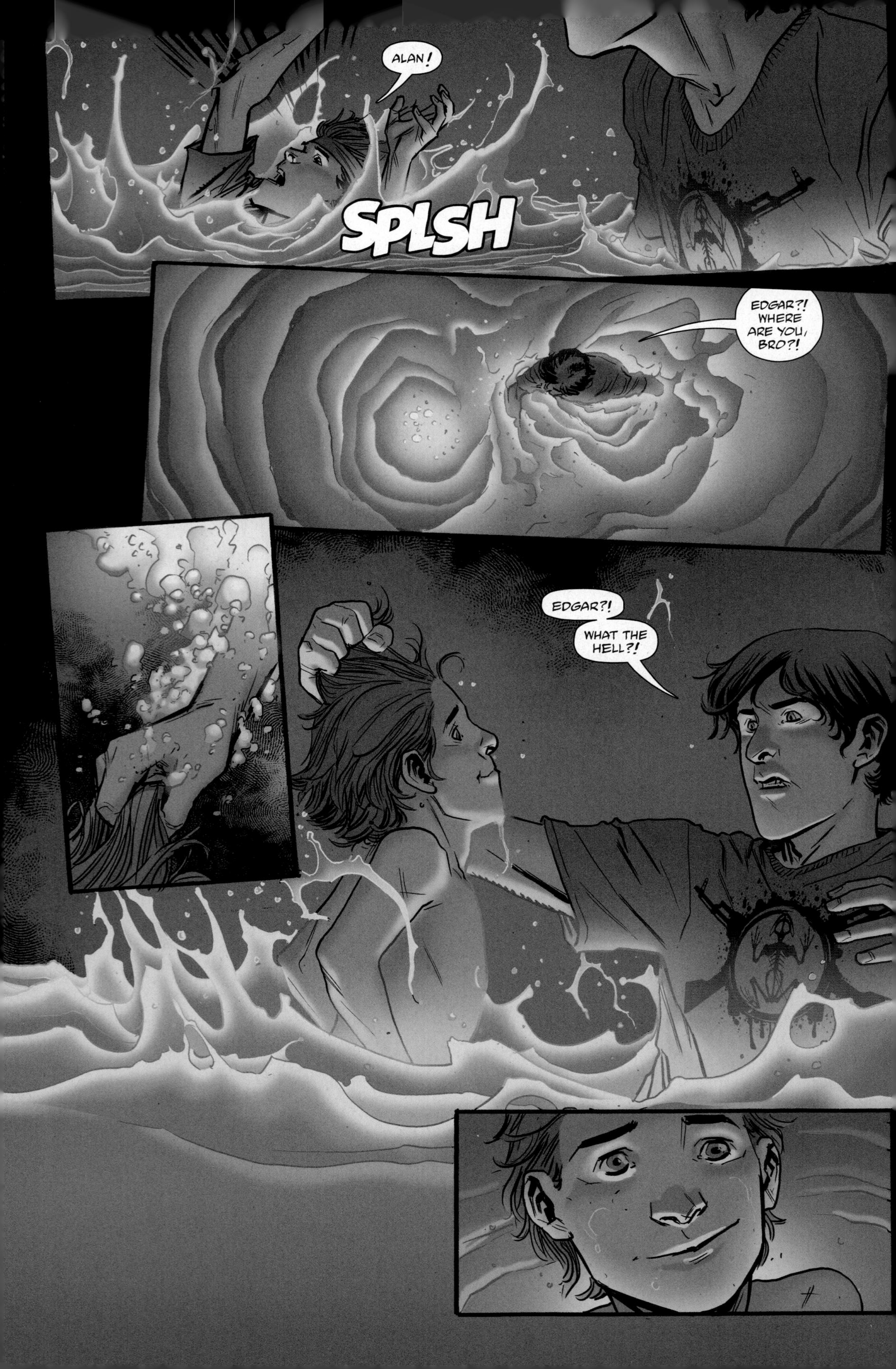
ALAN!
SPLSH
EDGAR?! WHERE ARE YOU, BRO?!
EDGAR?!
WHAT THE HELL?!

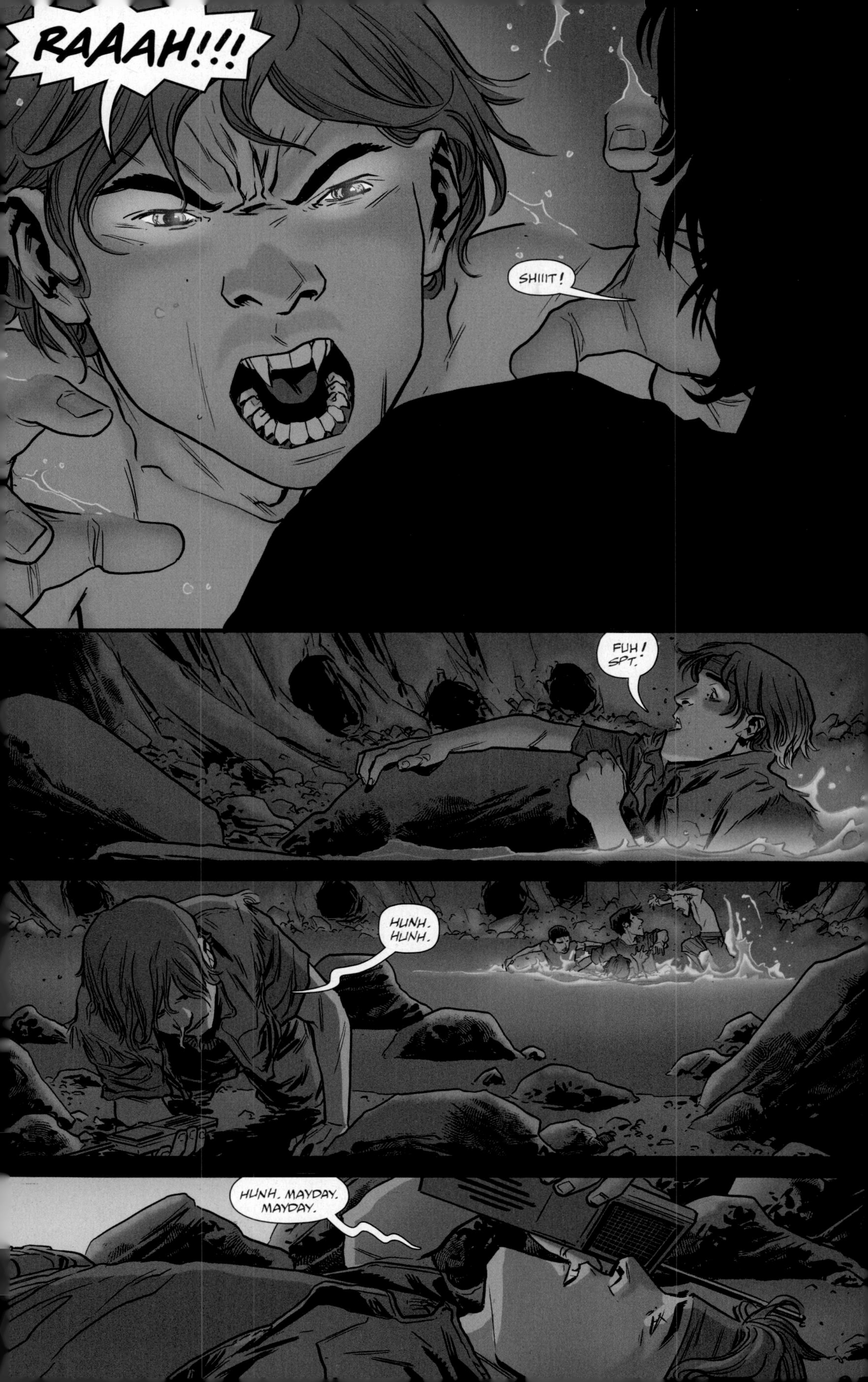
RAAAH!!!
SHIIIT!
FUH! SPT.
HUNH. HUNH.
HUNH. MAYDAY. MAYDAY.

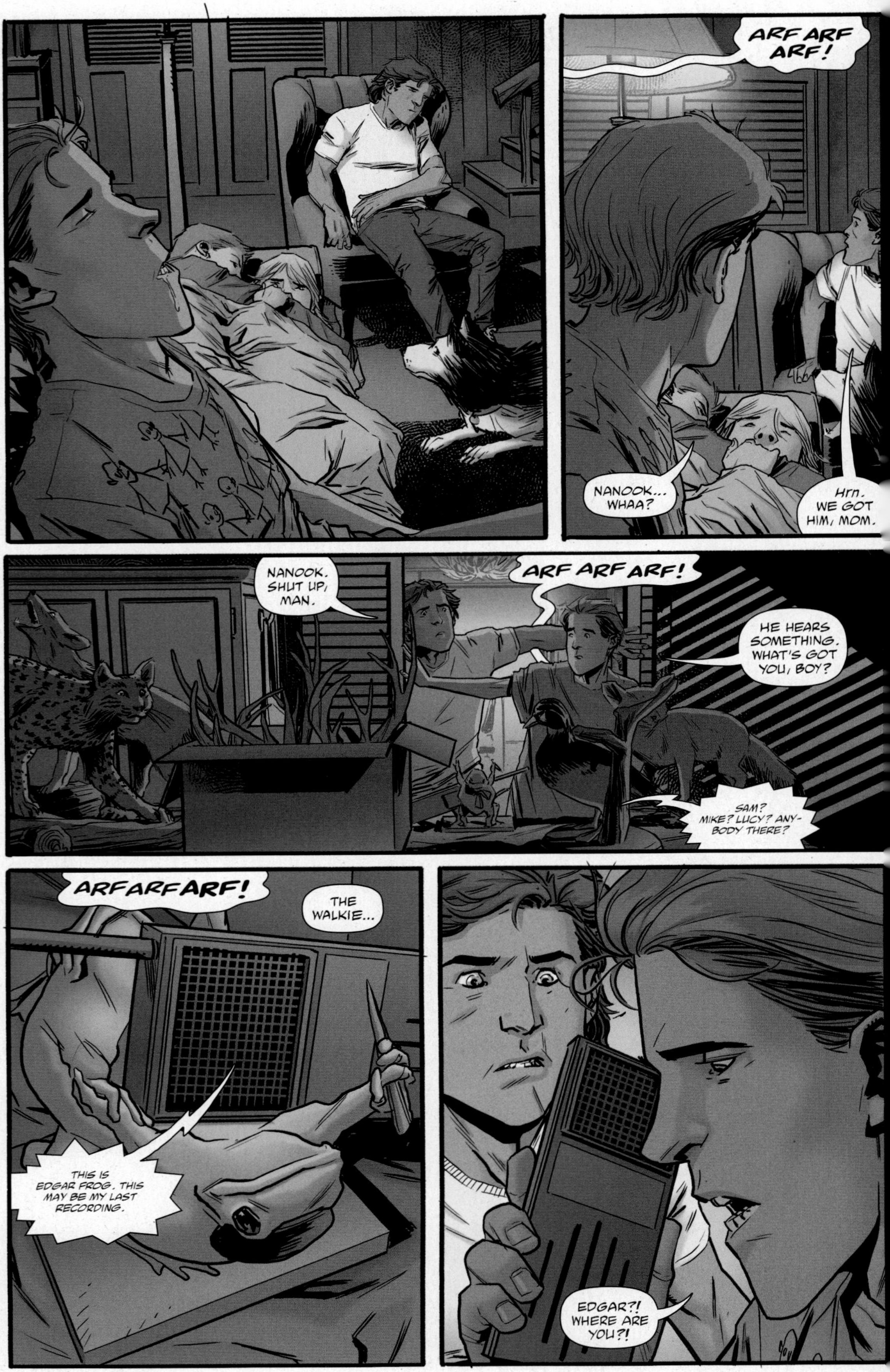
ARF ARF ARF!
NANOOK... WHAA?
Hrn. WE GOT HIM, MOM.
NANOOK. SHUT UP, MAN.
ARF ARF ARF!
HE HEARS SOMETHING. WHAT'S GOT YOU, BOY?
SAM? MIKE? LUCY? ANY-BODY THERE?
ARFARFARF!
THE WALKIE...
THIS IS EDGAR FROG. THIS MAY BE MY LAST RECORDING.
EDGAR?! WHERE ARE YOU?!

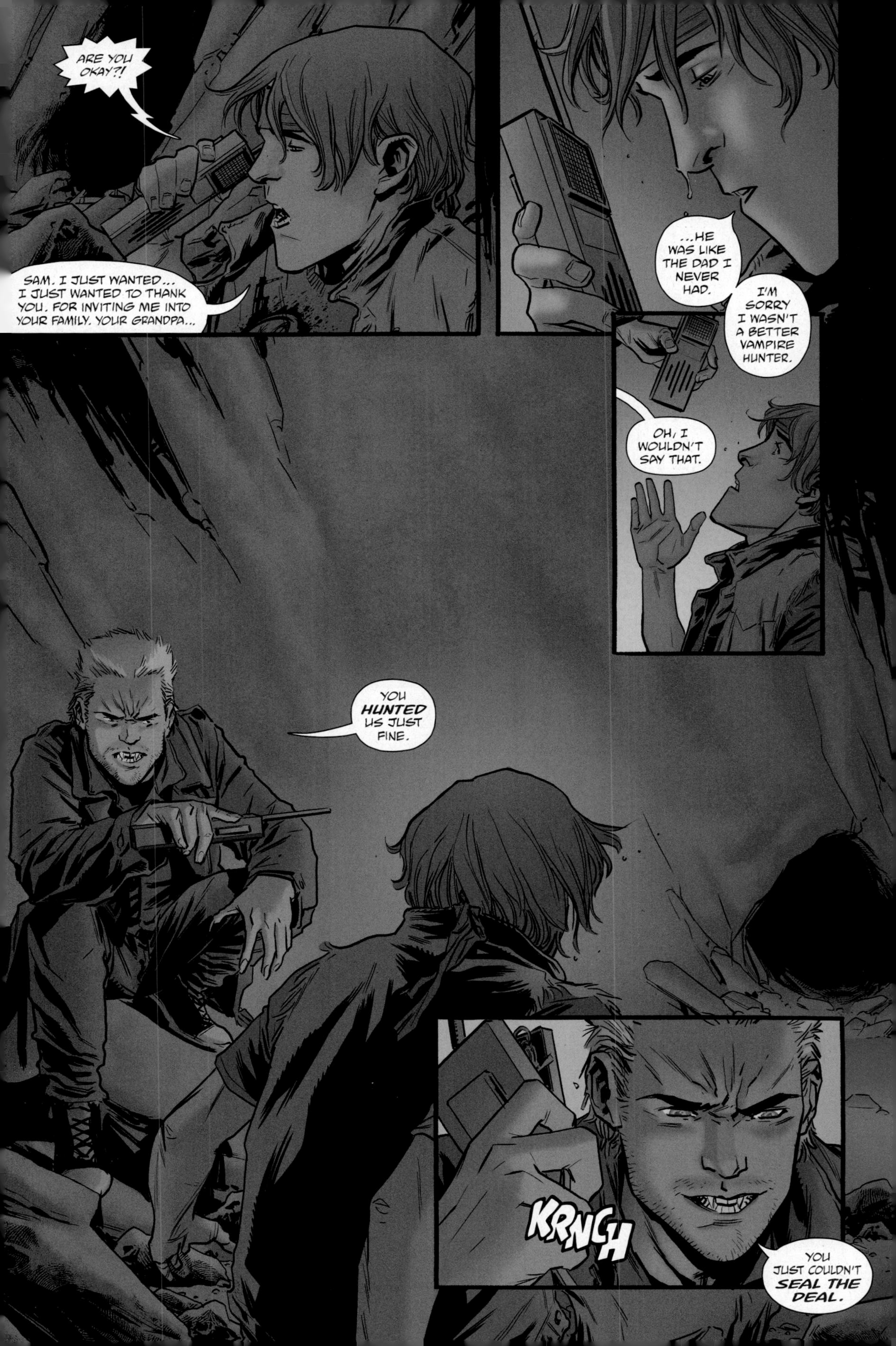
ARE YOU OKAY?!
SAM. I JUST WANTED... I JUST WANTED TO THANK YOU. FOR INVITING ME INTO YOUR FAMILY. YOUR GRANDPA...
...HE WAS LIKE THE DAD I NEVER HAD.
I'M SORRY I WASN'T A BETTER VAMPIRE HUNTER.
OH, I WOULDN'T SAY THAT.
YOU HUNTED US JUST FINE.
KRNCH
YOU JUST COULDN'T SEAL THE DEAL.

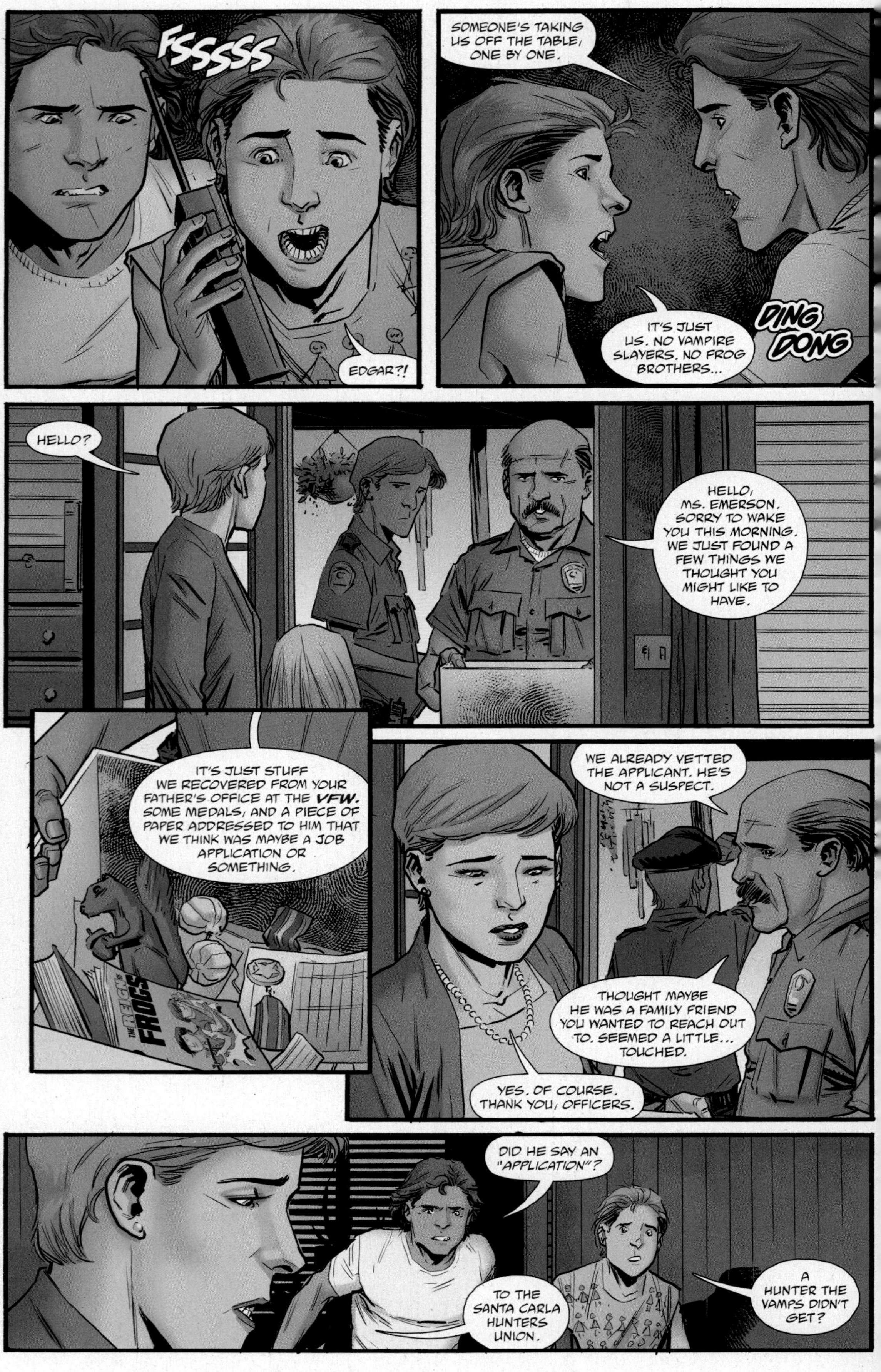
FSSSSS
EDGAR?!
SOMEONE'S TAKING US OFF THE TABLE, ONE BY ONE.
IT'S JUST US. NO VAMPIRE SLAYERS. NO FROG BROTHERS...
DING DONG
HELLO?
HELLO, MS. EMERSON. SORRY TO WAKE YOU THIS MORNING. WE JUST FOUND A FEW THINGS WE THOUGHT YOU MIGHT LIKE TO HAVE.
IT'S JUST STUFF WE RECOVERED FROM YOUR FATHER'S OFFICE AT THE VFW. SOME MEDALS, AND A PIECE OF PAPER ADDRESSED TO HIM THAT WE THINK WAS MAYBE A JOB APPLICATION OR SOMETHING.
THE REIGN OF THE FROGS
WE ALREADY VETTED THE APPLICANT. HE'S NOT A SUSPECT.
THOUGHT MAYBE HE WAS A FAMILY FRIEND YOU WANTED TO REACH OUT TO. SEEMED A LITTLE... TOUCHED.
YES. OF COURSE. THANK YOU, OFFICERS.
DID HE SAY AN "APPLICATION"?
TO THE SANTA CARLA HUNTERS UNION.
A HUNTER THE VAMPS DIDN'T GET?

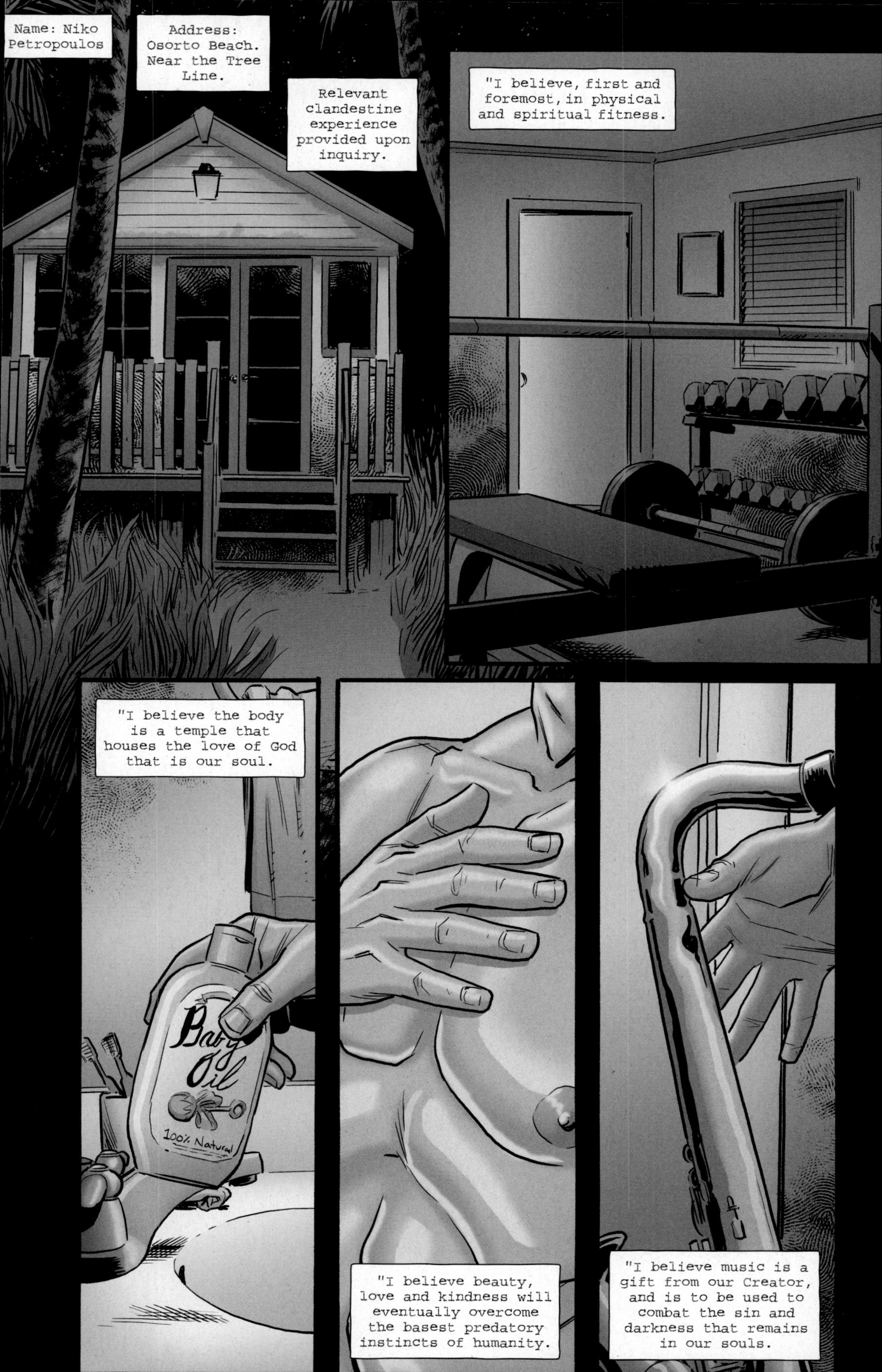
Name: Niko Petropoulos
Address: Osorto Beach. Near the Tree Line.
Relevant clandestine experience provided upon inquiry.
"I believe, first and foremost, in physical and spiritual fitness.
"I believe the body is a temple that houses the love of God that is our soul.
Baby Oil
100% Natural
"I believe beauty, love and kindness will eventually overcome the basest predatory instincts of humanity.
"I believe music is a gift from our Creator, and is to be used to combat the sin and darkness that remains in our souls.

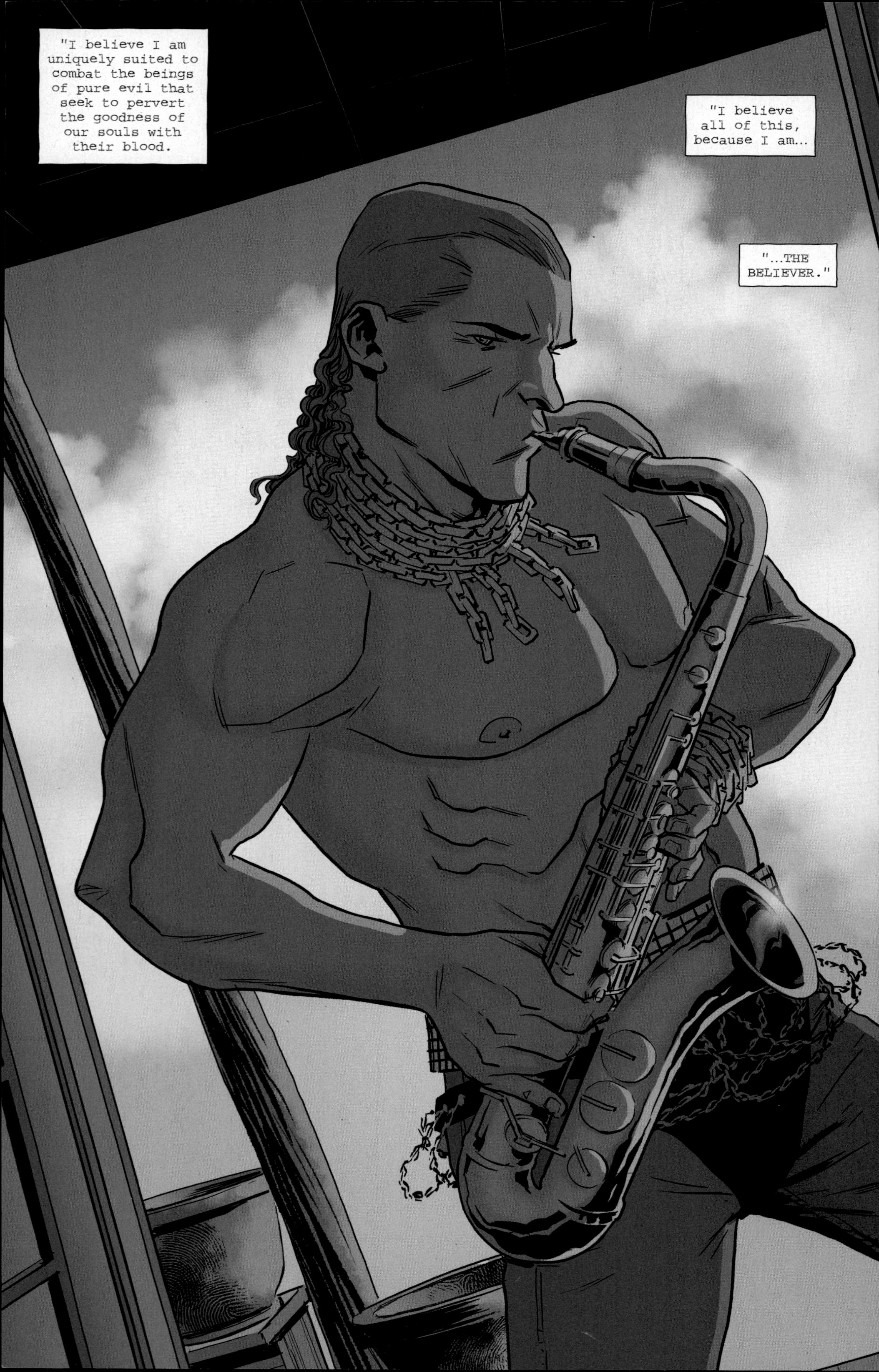
"I believe I am uniquely suited to combat the beings of pure evil that seek to pervert the goodness of our souls with their blood.
"I believe all of this, because I am...
"...THE BELIEVER."

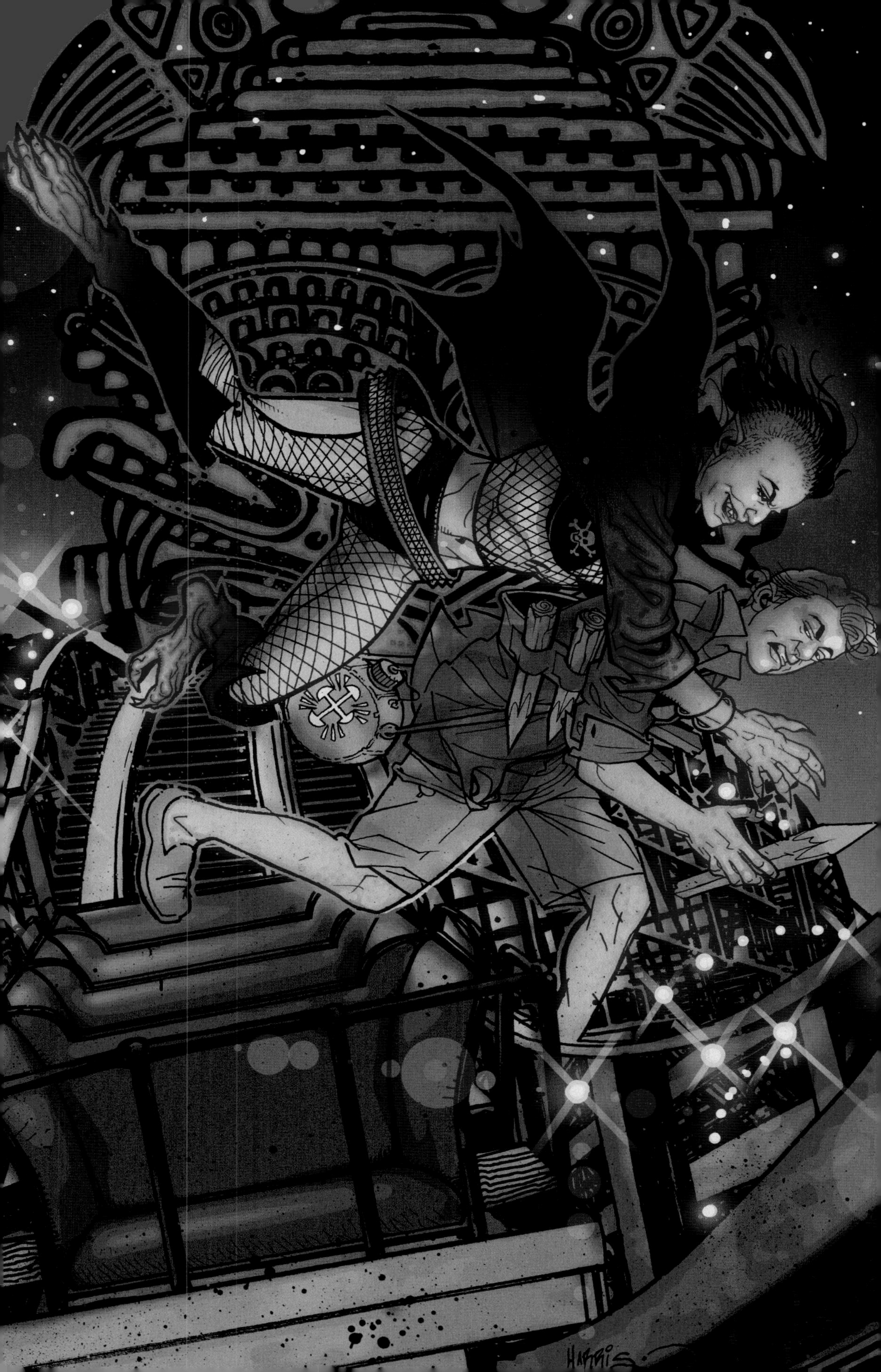
HARRIS

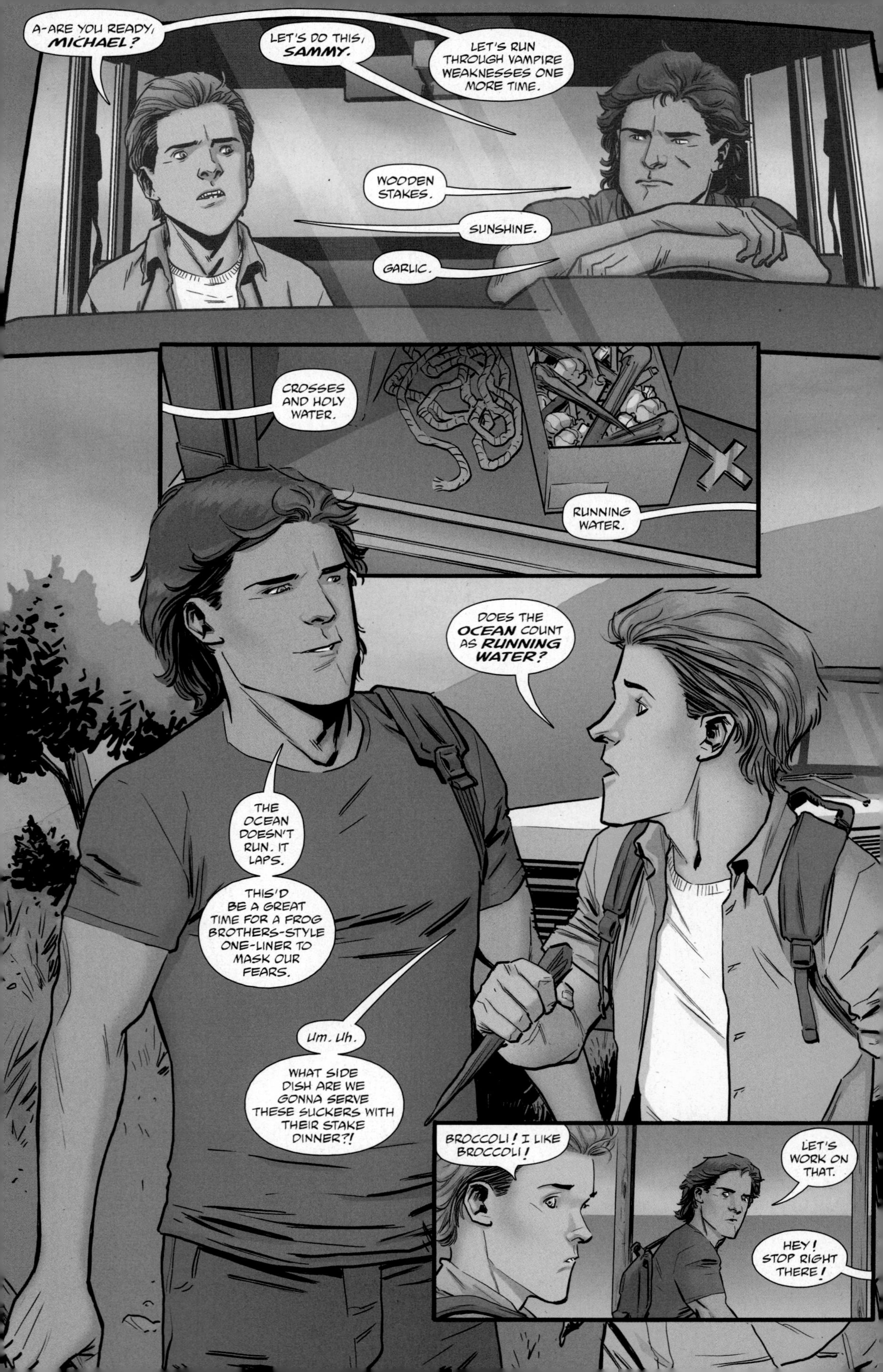
A-ARE YOU READY, **MICHAEL?**
LET'S DO THIS, **SAMMY.**
LET'S RUN THROUGH VAMPIRE WEAKNESSES ONE MORE TIME.
WOODEN STAKES.
SUNSHINE.
GARLIC.
CROSSES AND HOLY WATER.
RUNNING WATER.
DOES THE **OCEAN** COUNT AS **RUNNING WATER?**
THE OCEAN DOESN'T RUN. IT LAPS.
THIS'D BE A GREAT TIME FOR A FROG BROTHERS-STYLE ONE-LINER TO MASK OUR FEARS.
UM. UH.
WHAT SIDE DISH ARE WE GONNA SERVE THESE SUCKERS WITH THEIR STAKE DINNER?!
BROCCOLI! I LIKE BROCCOLI!
LET'S WORK ON THAT.
HEY! STOP RIGHT THERE!

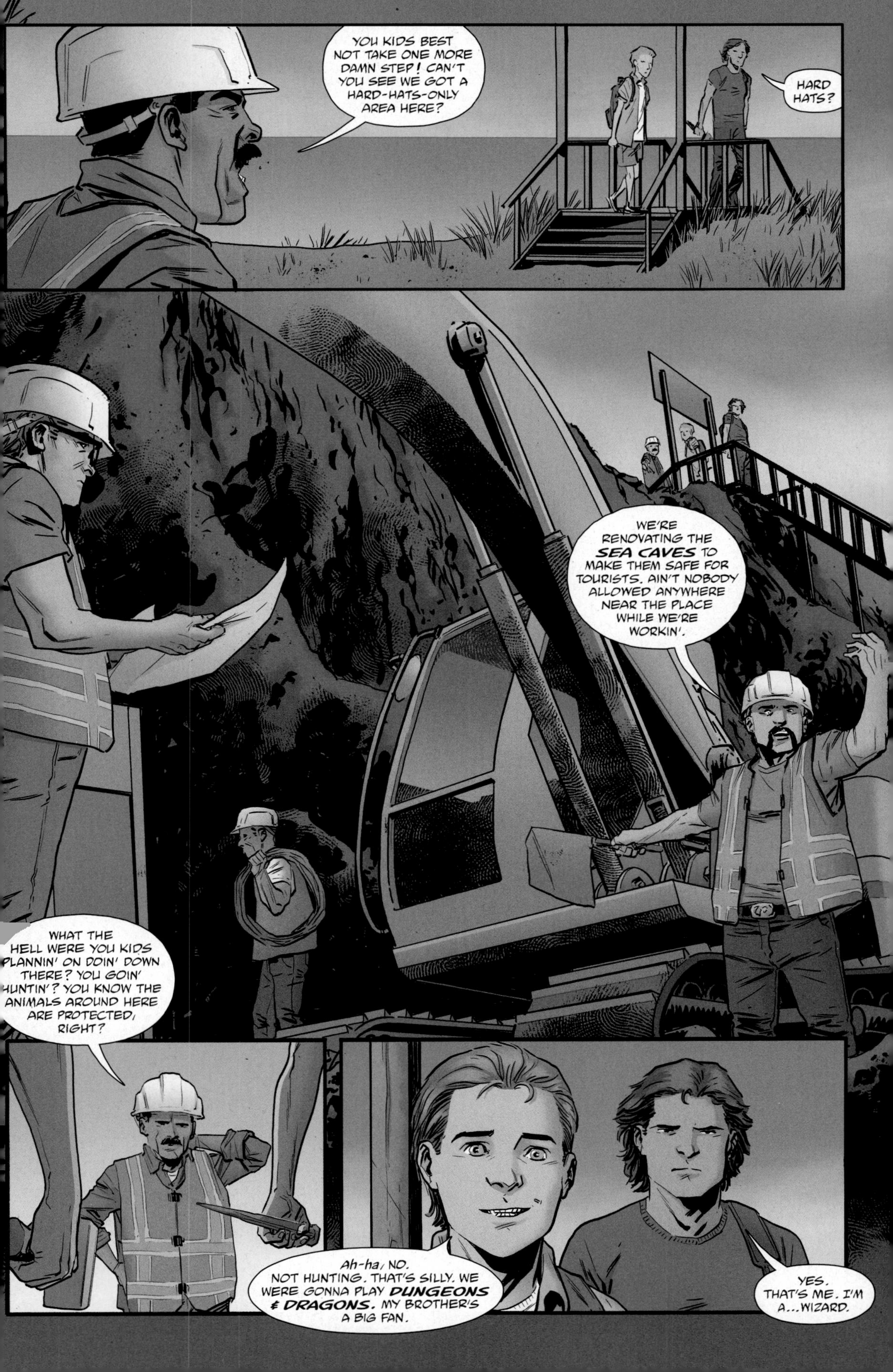
YOU KIDS BEST NOT TAKE ONE MORE DAMN STEP! CAN'T YOU SEE WE GOT A HARD-HATS-ONLY AREA HERE?
HARD HATS?
WE'RE RENOVATING THE SEA CAVES TO MAKE THEM SAFE FOR TOURISTS. AIN'T NOBODY ALLOWED ANYWHERE NEAR THE PLACE WHILE WE'RE WORKIN'.
WHAT THE HELL WERE YOU KIDS PLANNIN' ON DOIN' DOWN THERE? YOU GOIN' HUNTIN'? YOU KNOW THE ANIMALS AROUND HERE ARE PROTECTED, RIGHT?
Ah-ha, NO. NOT HUNTING. THAT'S SILLY. WE WERE GONNA PLAY DUNGEONS & DRAGONS. MY BROTHER'S A BIG FAN.
YES. THAT'S ME. I'M A...WIZARD.

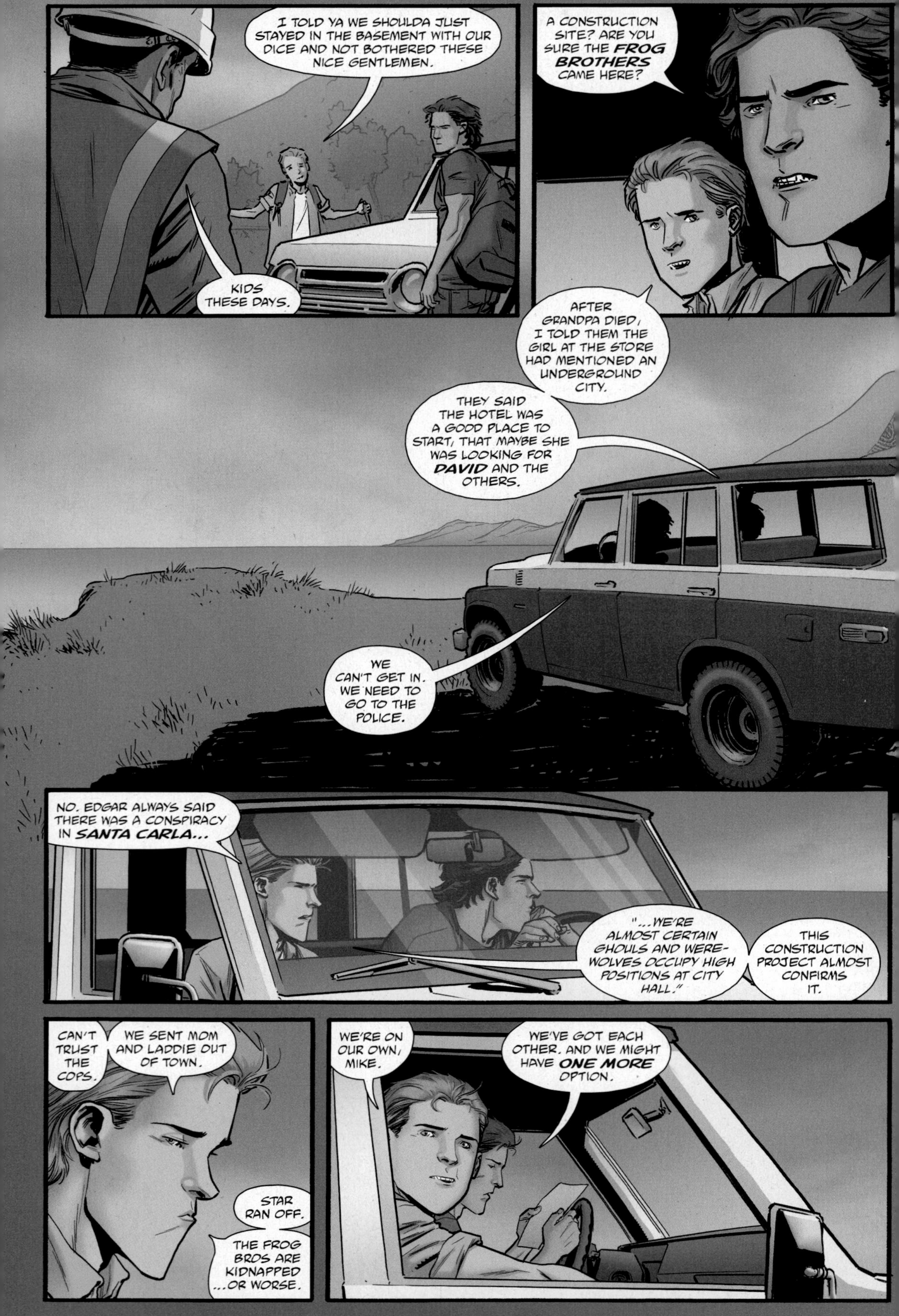
I TOLD YA WE SHOULDA JUST STAYED IN THE BASEMENT WITH OUR DICE AND NOT BOTHERED THESE NICE GENTLEMEN.
KIDS THESE DAYS.
A CONSTRUCTION SITE? ARE YOU SURE THE FROG BROTHERS CAME HERE?
AFTER GRANDPA DIED, I TOLD THEM THE GIRL AT THE STORE HAD MENTIONED AN UNDERGROUND CITY.
THEY SAID THE HOTEL WAS A GOOD PLACE TO START, THAT MAYBE SHE WAS LOOKING FOR DAVID AND THE OTHERS.
WE CAN'T GET IN. WE NEED TO GO TO THE POLICE.
NO. EDGAR ALWAYS SAID THERE WAS A CONSPIRACY IN SANTA CARLA...
"...WE'RE ALMOST CERTAIN GHOULS AND WERE-WOLVES OCCUPY HIGH POSITIONS AT CITY HALL."
THIS CONSTRUCTION PROJECT ALMOST CONFIRMS IT.
CAN'T TRUST THE COPS.
WE SENT MOM AND LADDIE OUT OF TOWN.
STAR RAN OFF.
THE FROG BROS ARE KIDNAPPED ...OR WORSE.
WE'RE ON OUR OWN, MIKE.
WE'VE GOT EACH OTHER. AND WE MIGHT HAVE ONE MORE OPTION.

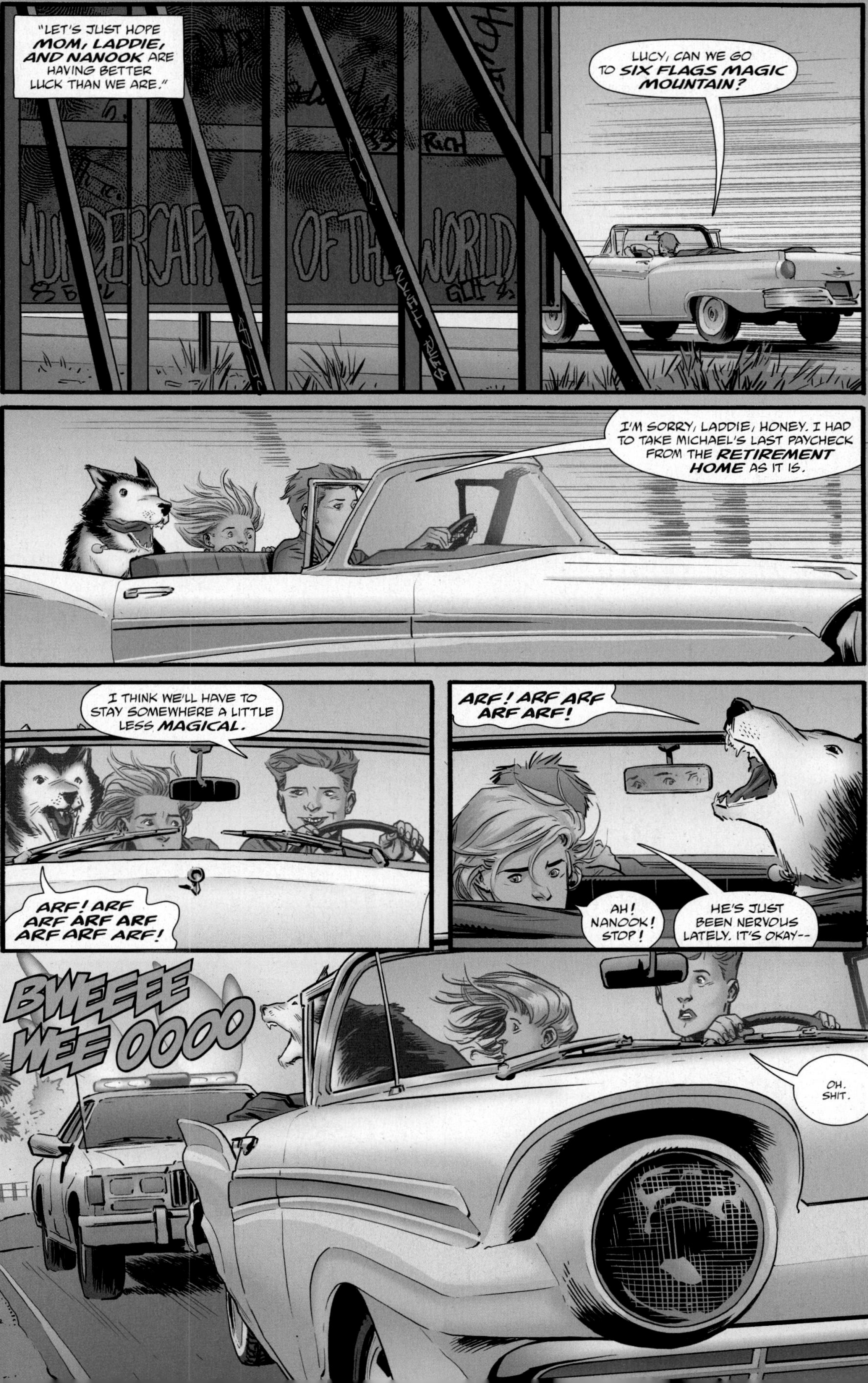
"LET'S JUST HOPE MOM, LADDIE, AND NANOOK ARE HAVING BETTER LUCK THAN WE ARE."
LUCY, CAN WE GO TO SIX FLAGS MAGIC MOUNTAIN?
I'M SORRY, LADDIE, HONEY. I HAD TO TAKE MICHAEL'S LAST PAYCHECK FROM THE RETIREMENT HOME AS IT IS.
I THINK WE'LL HAVE TO STAY SOMEWHERE A LITTLE LESS MAGICAL.
ARF! ARF ARF ARF ARF ARF ARF ARF ARF!
ARF! ARF ARF ARF ARF!
AH! NANOOK! STOP!
HE'S JUST BEEN NERVOUS LATELY. IT'S OKAY--
BWEEEE WEE OOOO
OH. SHIT.

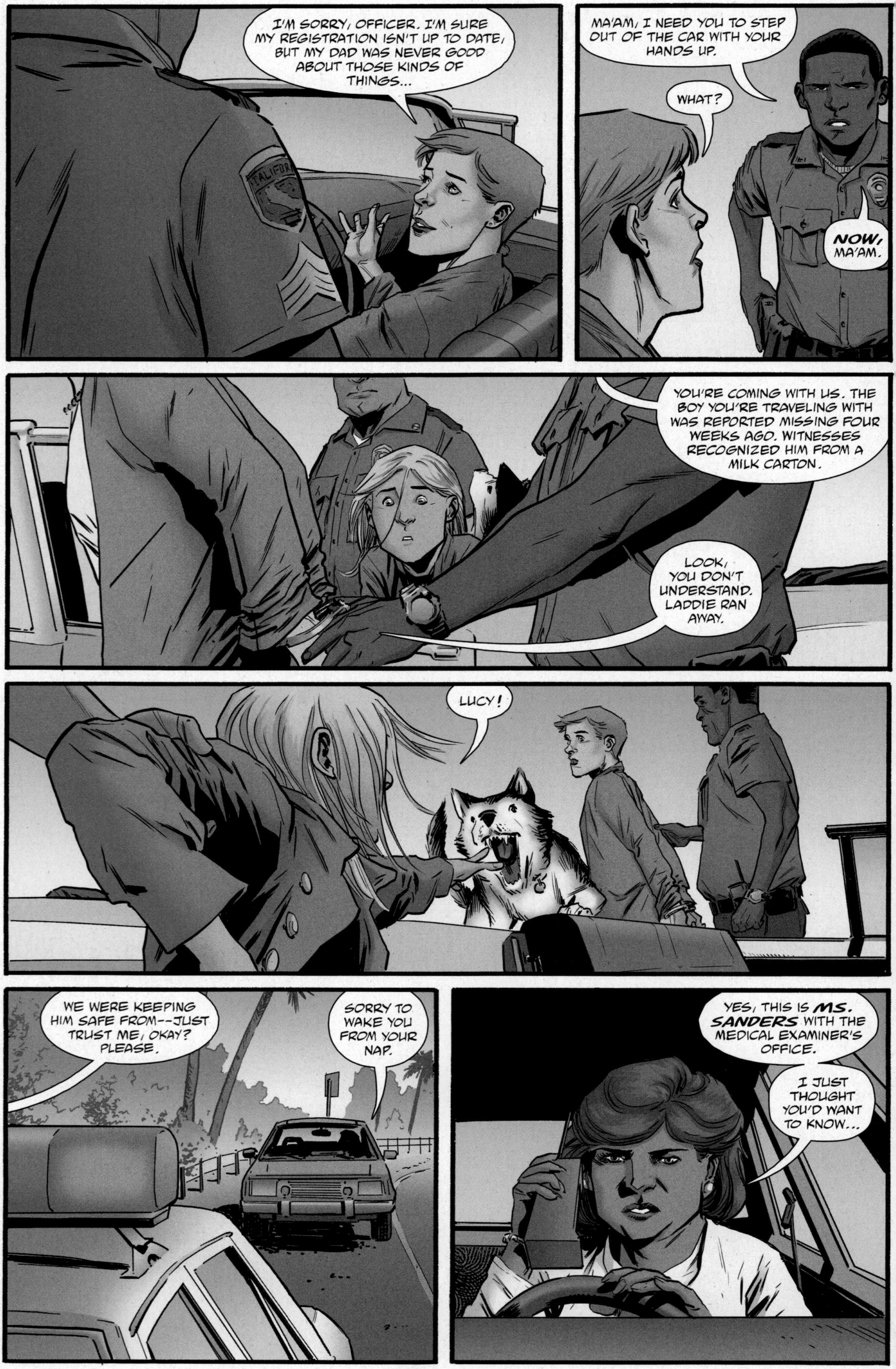
I'M SORRY, OFFICER. I'M SURE MY REGISTRATION ISN'T UP TO DATE, BUT MY DAD WAS NEVER GOOD ABOUT THOSE KINDS OF THINGS...
MA'AM, I NEED YOU TO STEP OUT OF THE CAR WITH YOUR HANDS UP.
WHAT?
NOW, MA'AM.
YOU'RE COMING WITH US. THE BOY YOU'RE TRAVELING WITH WAS REPORTED MISSING FOUR WEEKS AGO. WITNESSES RECOGNIZED HIM FROM A MILK CARTON.
LOOK, YOU DON'T UNDERSTAND. LADDIE RAN AWAY.
LUCY!
WE WERE KEEPING HIM SAFE FROM--JUST TRUST ME, OKAY? PLEASE.
SORRY TO WAKE YOU FROM YOUR NAP.
YES, THIS IS MS. SANDERS WITH THE MEDICAL EXAMINER'S OFFICE.
I JUST THOUGHT YOU'D WANT TO KNOW...

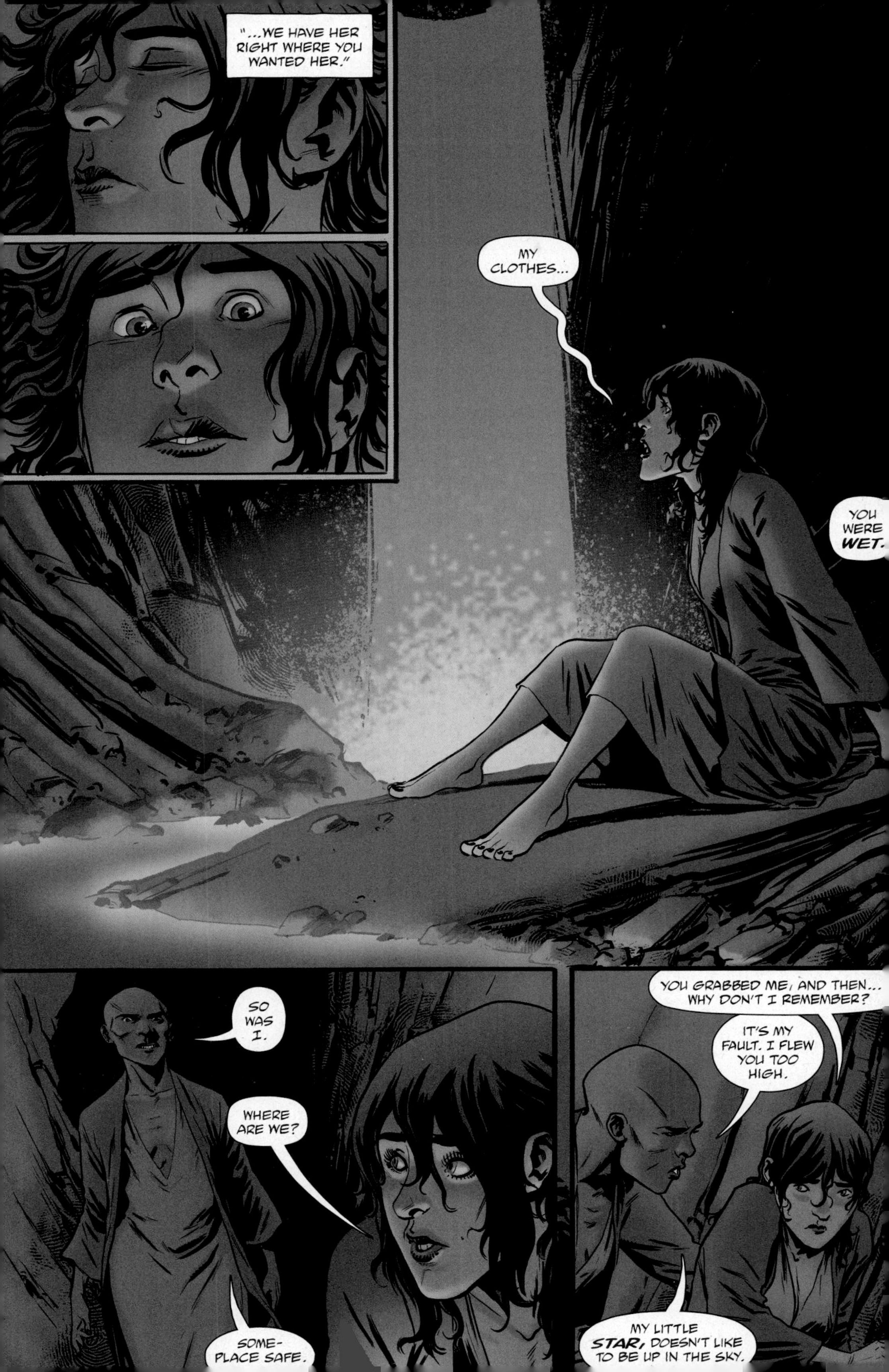
"...WE HAVE HER RIGHT WHERE YOU WANTED HER."
MY CLOTHES...
YOU WERE *WET.*
SO WAS I.
WHERE ARE WE?
SOME- PLACE SAFE.
YOU GRABBED ME, AND THEN... WHY DON'T I REMEMBER?
IT'S MY FAULT. I FLEW YOU TOO HIGH.
MY LITTLE *STAR,* DOESN'T LIKE TO BE UP IN THE SKY.

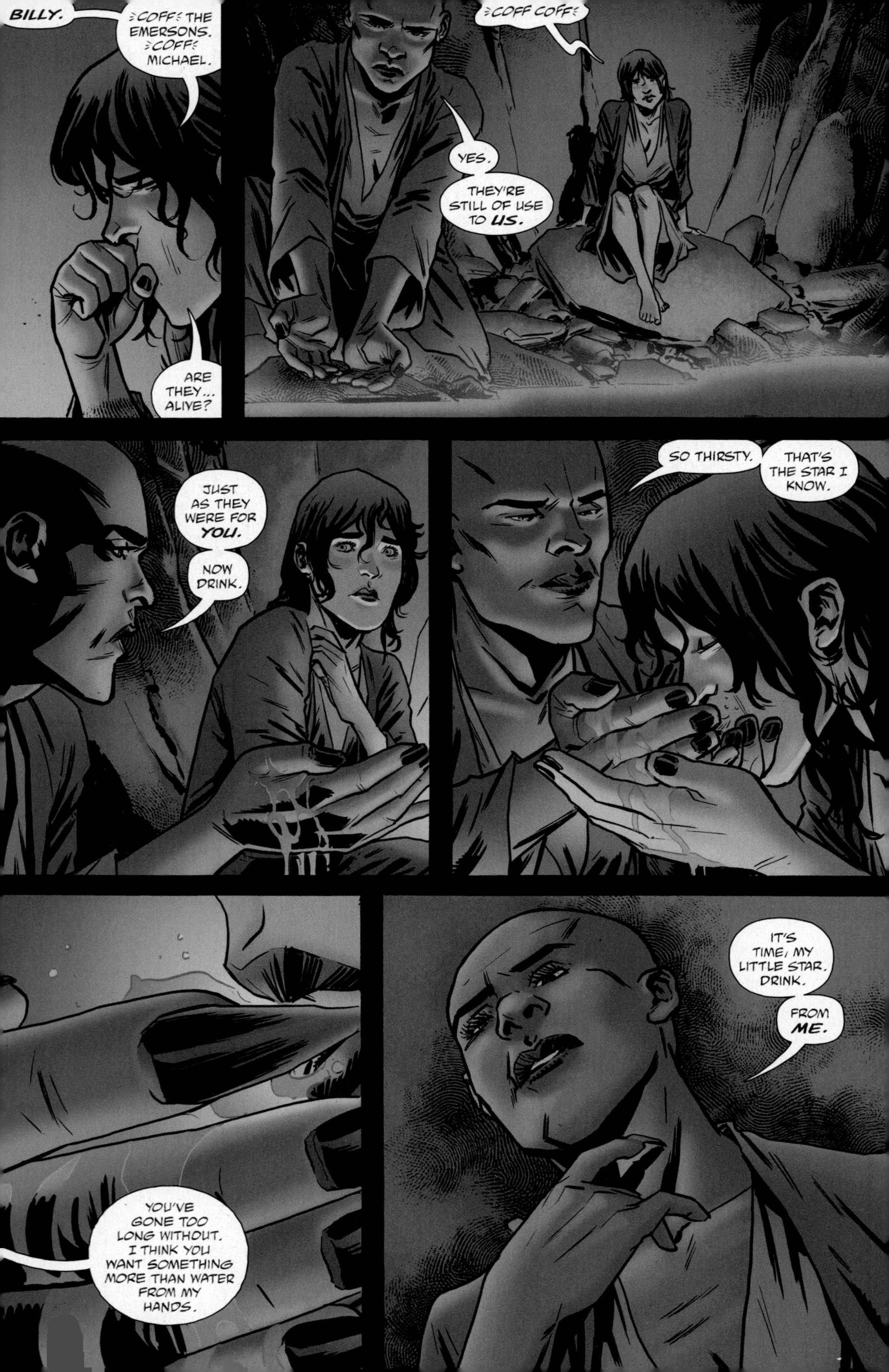
BILLY.
COFF THE EMERSONS. COFF MICHAEL.
COFF COFF
YES.
THEY'RE STILL OF USE TO US.
ARE THEY... ALIVE?
JUST AS THEY WERE FOR YOU.
NOW DRINK.
SO THIRSTY.
THAT'S THE STAR I KNOW.
YOU'VE GONE TOO LONG WITHOUT. I THINK YOU WANT SOMETHING MORE THAN WATER FROM MY HANDS.
IT'S TIME, MY LITTLE STAR. DRINK.
FROM ME.

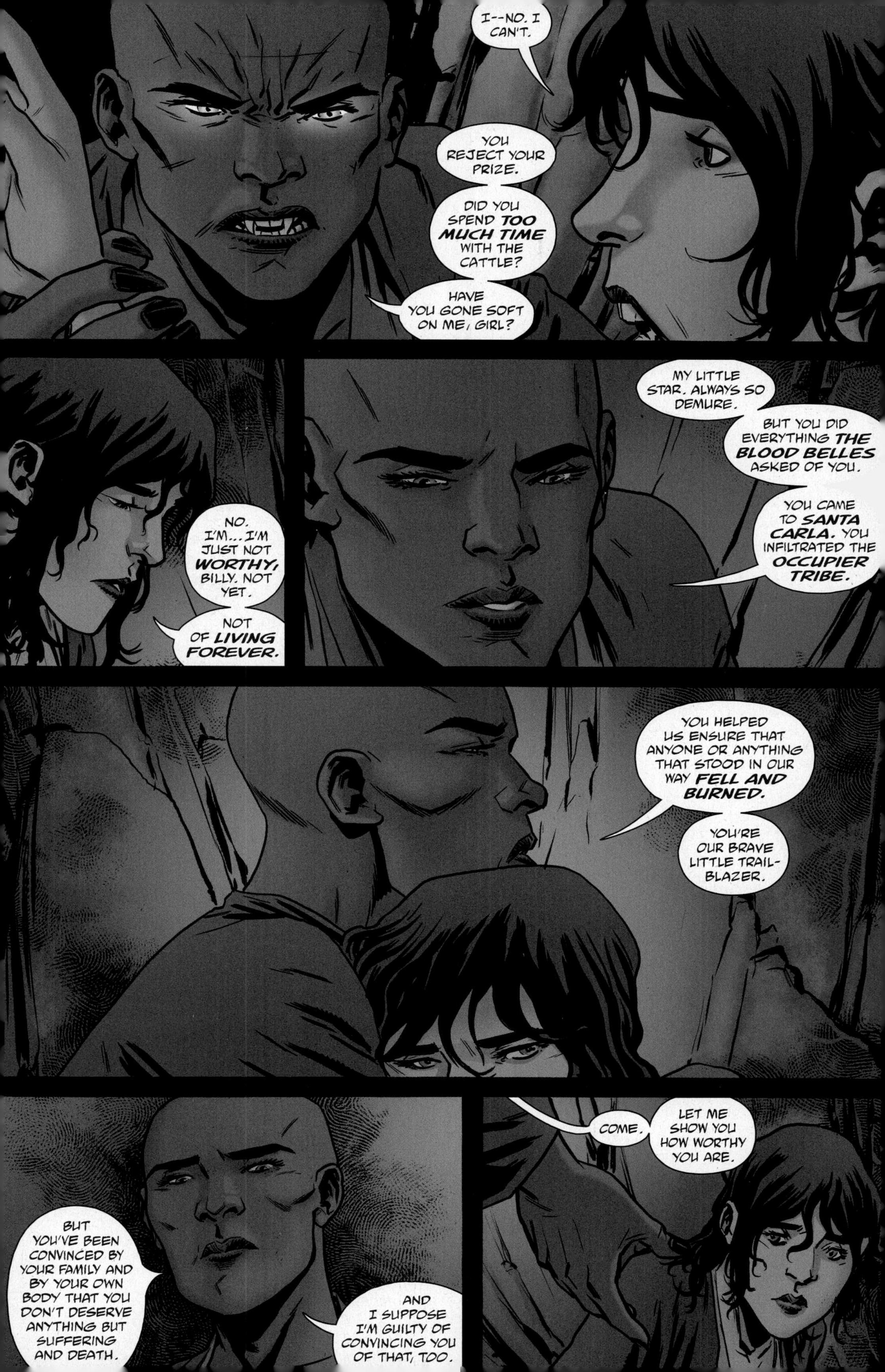
I--NO. I CAN'T.
YOU REJECT YOUR PRIZE.
DID YOU SPEND TOO MUCH TIME WITH THE CATTLE?
HAVE YOU GONE SOFT ON ME, GIRL?
NO. I'M... I'M JUST NOT WORTHY, BILLY. NOT YET.
NOT OF LIVING FOREVER.
MY LITTLE STAR. ALWAYS SO DEMURE.
BUT YOU DID EVERYTHING THE BLOOD BELLES ASKED OF YOU.
YOU CAME TO SANTA CARLA. YOU INFILTRATED THE OCCUPIER TRIBE.
YOU HELPED US ENSURE THAT ANYONE OR ANYTHING THAT STOOD IN OUR WAY FELL AND BURNED.
YOU'RE OUR BRAVE LITTLE TRAIL-BLAZER.
BUT YOU'VE BEEN CONVINCED BY YOUR FAMILY AND BY YOUR OWN BODY THAT YOU DON'T DESERVE ANYTHING BUT SUFFERING AND DEATH.
AND I SUPPOSE I'M GUILTY OF CONVINCING YOU OF THAT, TOO.
COME.
LET ME SHOW YOU HOW WORTHY YOU ARE.

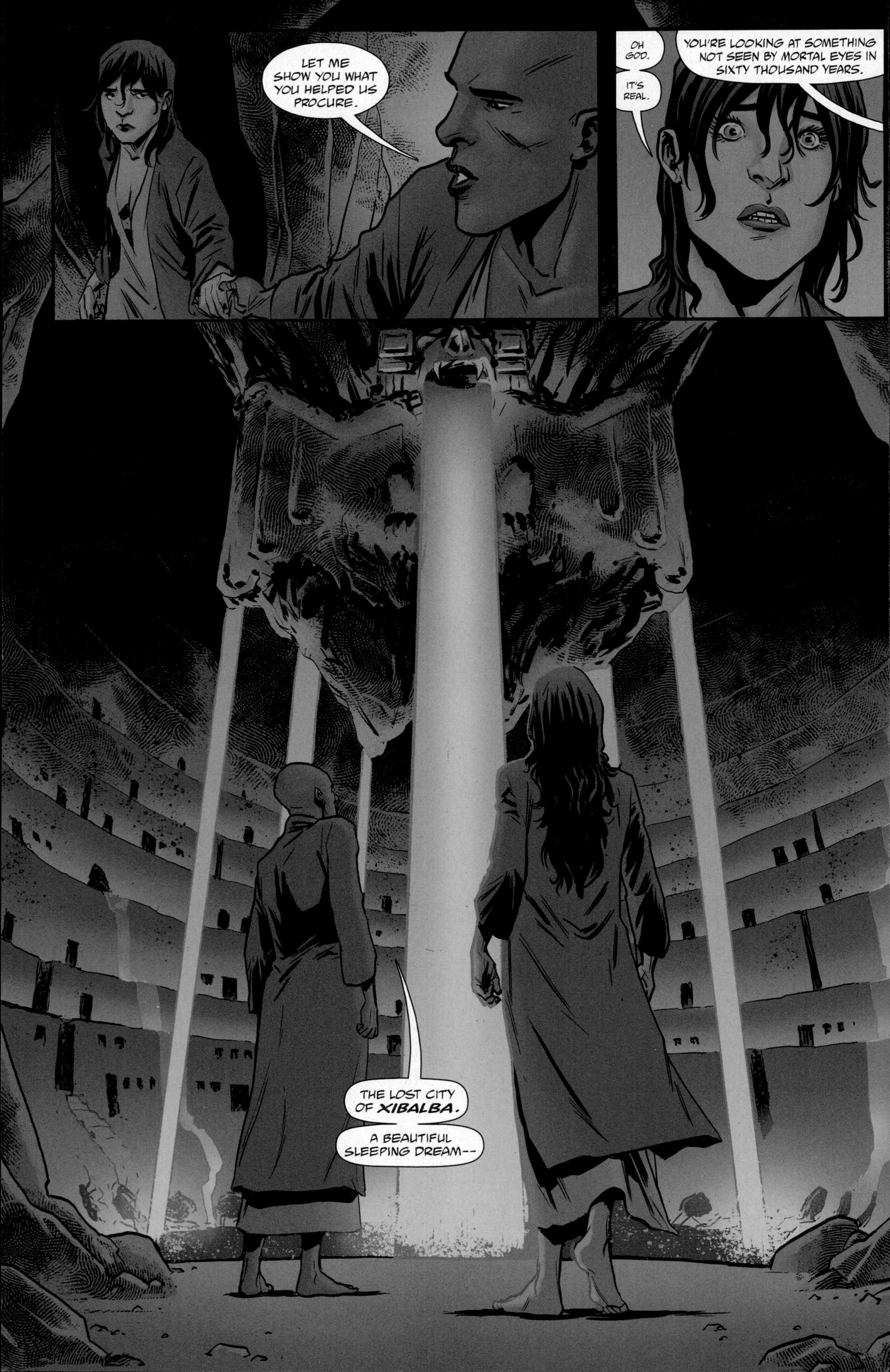

LET ME SHOW YOU WHAT YOU HELPED US PROCURE.
OH GOD.
IT'S REAL.
YOU'RE LOOKING AT SOMETHING NOT SEEN BY MORTAL EYES IN SIXTY THOUSAND YEARS.
THE LOST CITY OF XIBALBA.
A BEAUTIFUL SLEEPING DREAM--

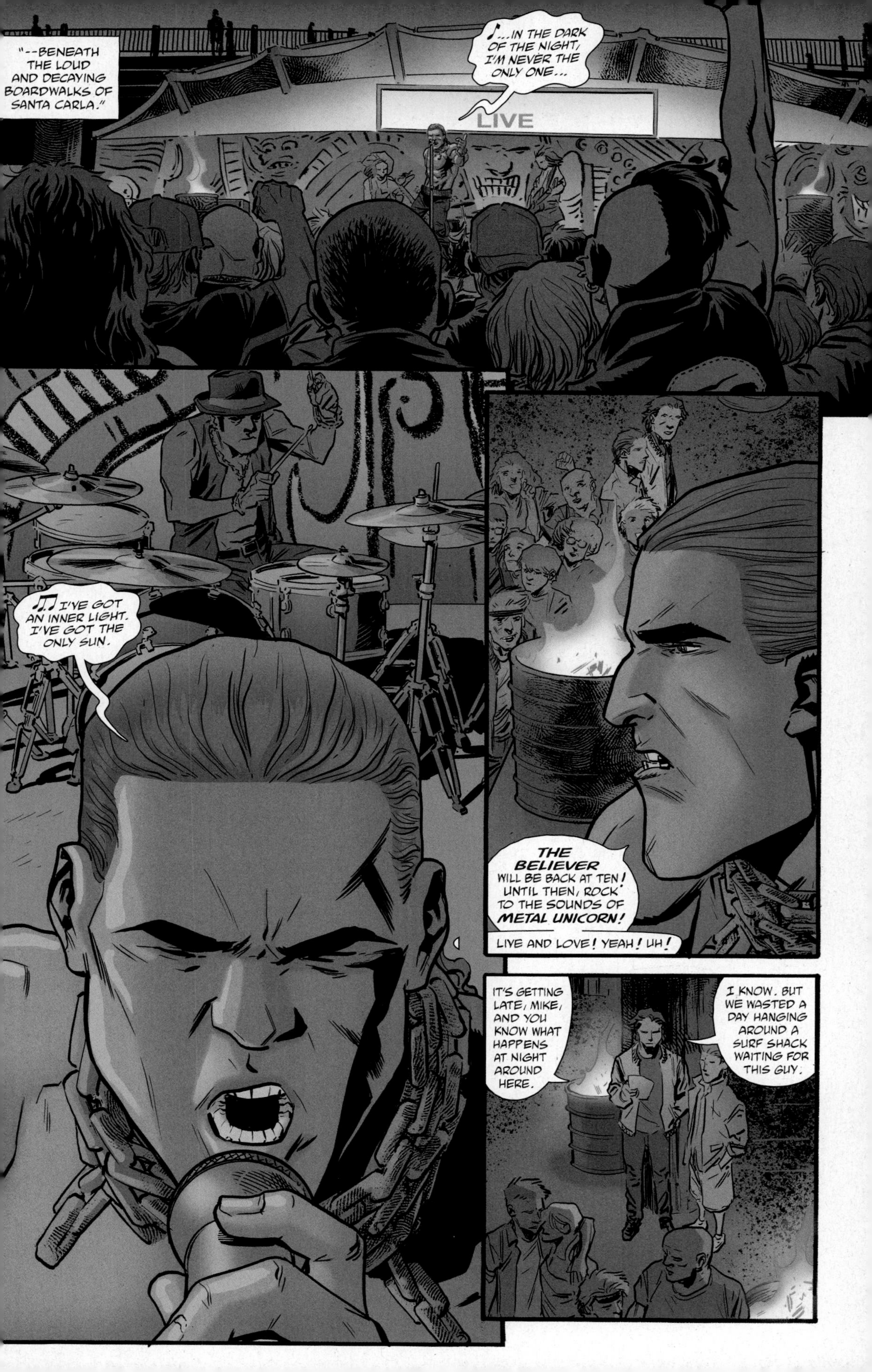
"--BENEATH THE LOUD AND DECAYING BOARDWALKS OF SANTA CARLA."
♪...IN THE DARK OF THE NIGHT, I'M NEVER THE ONLY ONE...
LIVE
♫ I'VE GOT AN INNER LIGHT. I'VE GOT THE ONLY SUN.
THE BELIEVER WILL BE BACK AT TEN! UNTIL THEN, ROCK TO THE SOUNDS OF METAL UNICORN!
LIVE AND LOVE! YEAH! UH!
IT'S GETTING LATE, MIKE, AND YOU KNOW WHAT HAPPENS AT NIGHT AROUND HERE.
I KNOW. BUT WE WASTED A DAY HANGING AROUND A SURF SHACK WAITING FOR THIS GUY.

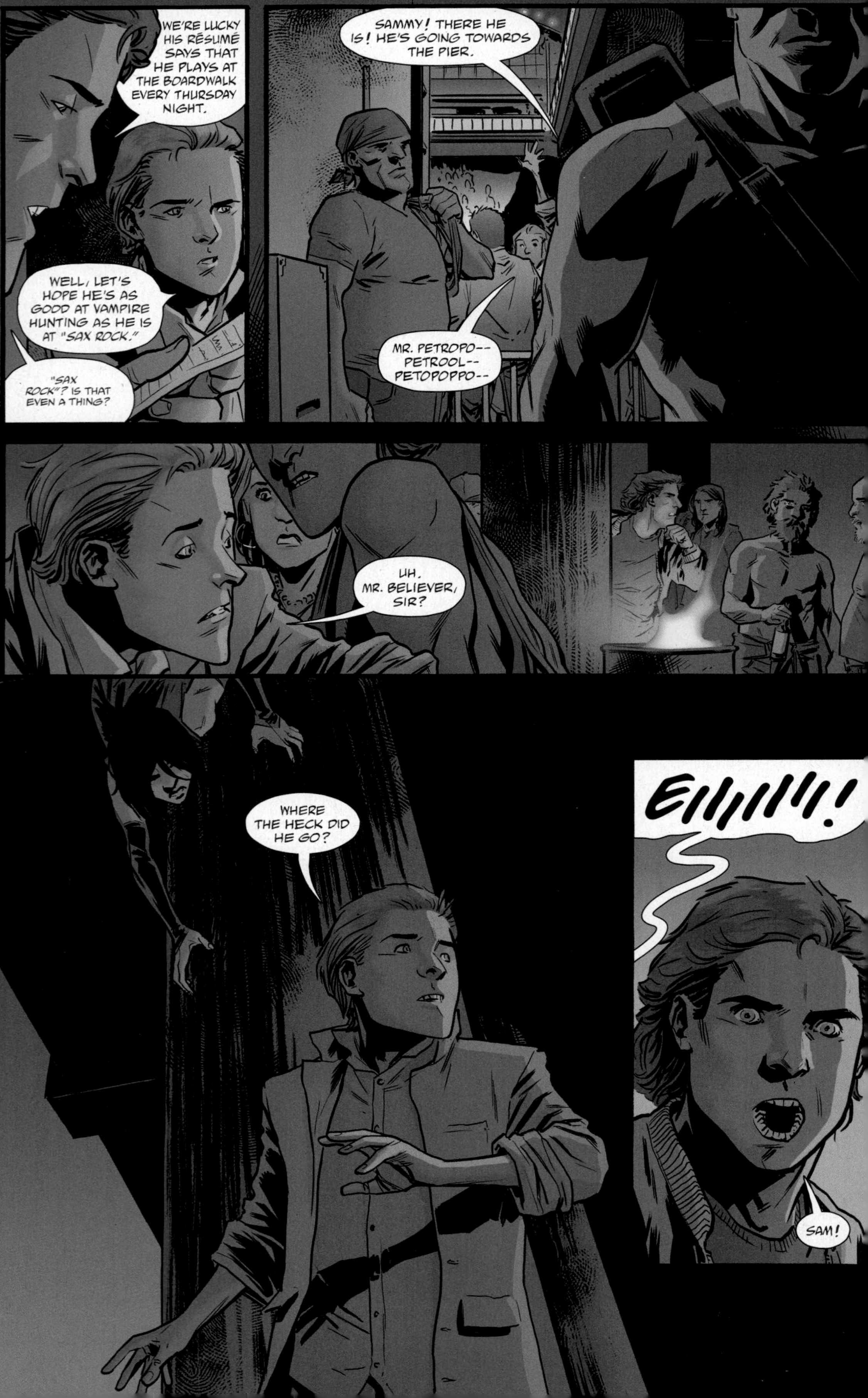
WE'RE LUCKY HIS RÉSUMÉ SAYS THAT HE PLAYS AT THE BOARDWALK EVERY THURSDAY NIGHT.
WELL, LET'S HOPE HE'S AS GOOD AT VAMPIRE HUNTING AS HE IS AT "SAX ROCK."
"SAX ROCK"? IS THAT EVEN A THING?
SAMMY! THERE HE IS! HE'S GOING TOWARDS THE PIER.
MR. PETROPO-- PETROOL-- PETOPOPPO--
UH. MR. BELIEVER, SIR?
WHERE THE HECK DID HE GO?
EIIIIII!
SAM!

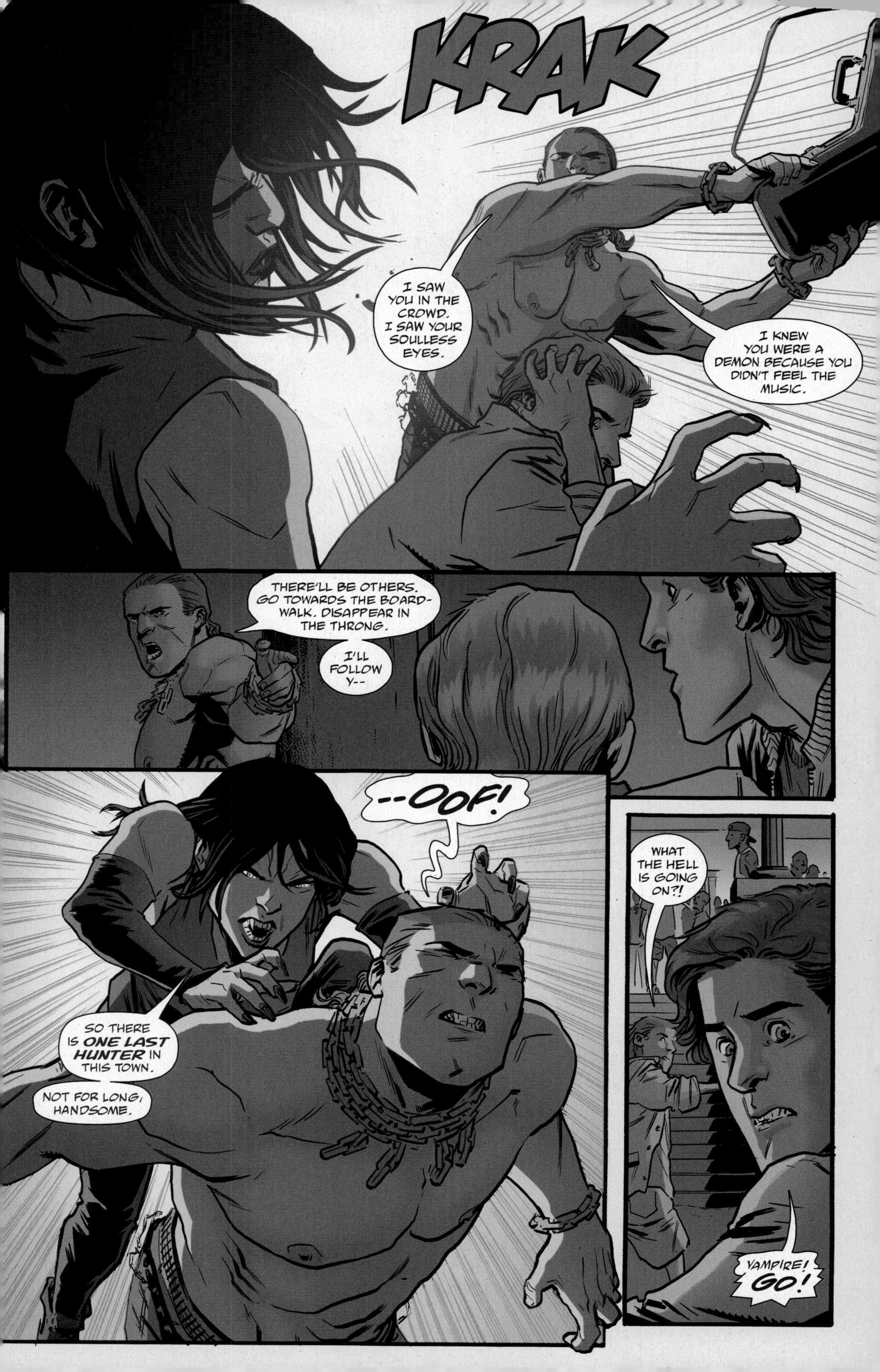
KRAK
I SAW YOU IN THE CROWD. I SAW YOUR SOULLESS EYES.
I KNEW YOU WERE A DEMON BECAUSE YOU DIDN'T FEEL THE MUSIC.
THERE'LL BE OTHERS. GO TOWARDS THE BOARD-WALK. DISAPPEAR IN THE THRONG.
I'LL FOLLOW Y--
--OOF!
SO THERE IS ONE LAST HUNTER IN THIS TOWN.
NOT FOR LONG, HANDSOME.
WHAT THE HELL IS GOING ON?!
VAMPIRE! GO!

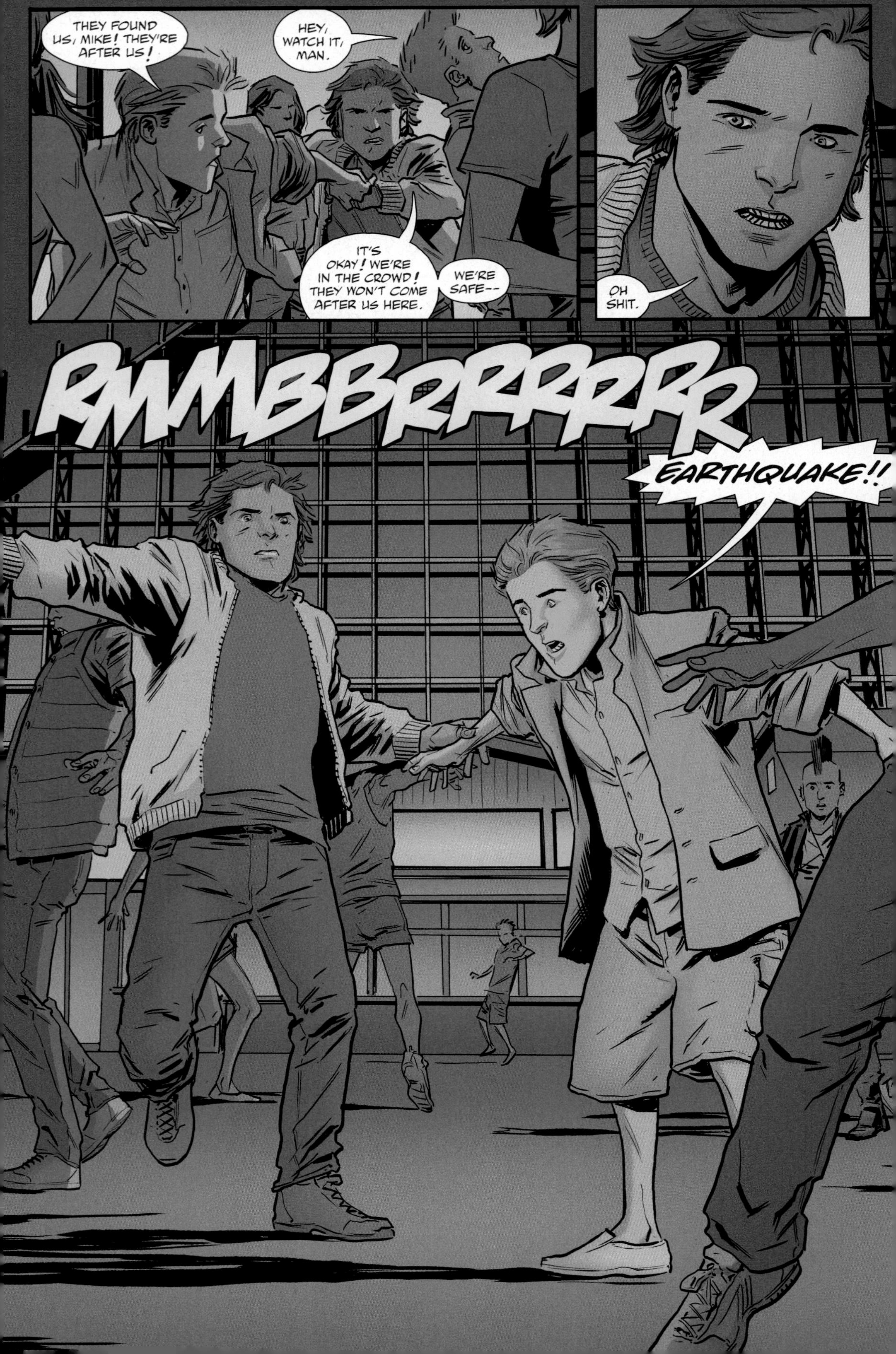

THEY FOUND US, MIKE! THEY'RE AFTER US!
HEY, WATCH IT, MAN.
IT'S OKAY! WE'RE IN THE CROWD! THEY WON'T COME AFTER US HERE.
WE'RE SAFE--
OH SHIT.
RMMBBRRRRRR
EARTHQUAKE!!

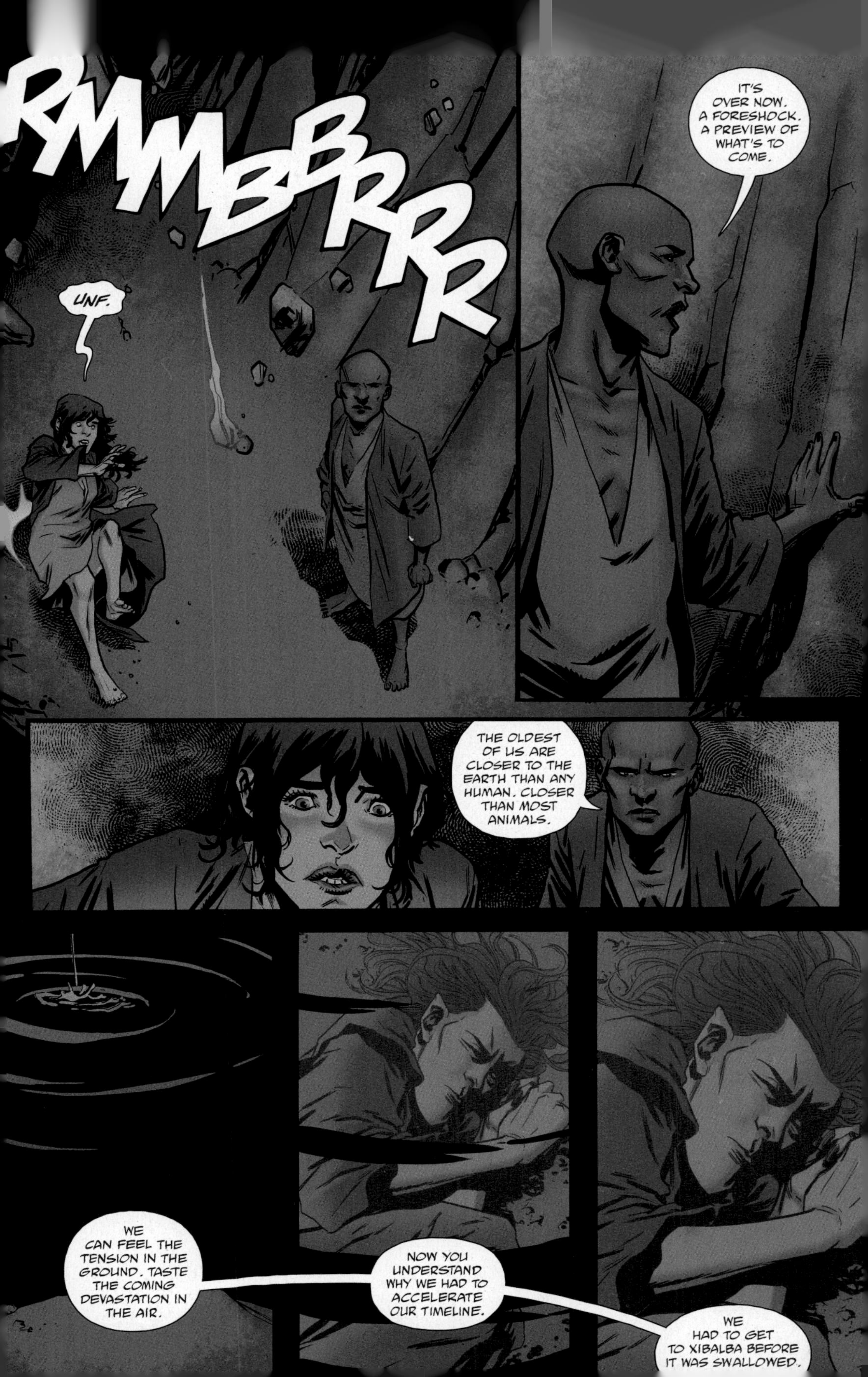
RMMBBRRR
UNF.
IT'S OVER NOW. A FORESHOCK. A PREVIEW OF WHAT'S TO COME.
THE OLDEST OF US ARE CLOSER TO THE EARTH THAN ANY HUMAN. CLOSER THAN MOST ANIMALS.
WE CAN FEEL THE TENSION IN THE GROUND. TASTE THE COMING DEVASTATION IN THE AIR.
NOW YOU UNDERSTAND WHY WE HAD TO ACCELERATE OUR TIMELINE.
WE HAD TO GET TO XIBALBA BEFORE IT WAS SWALLOWED.

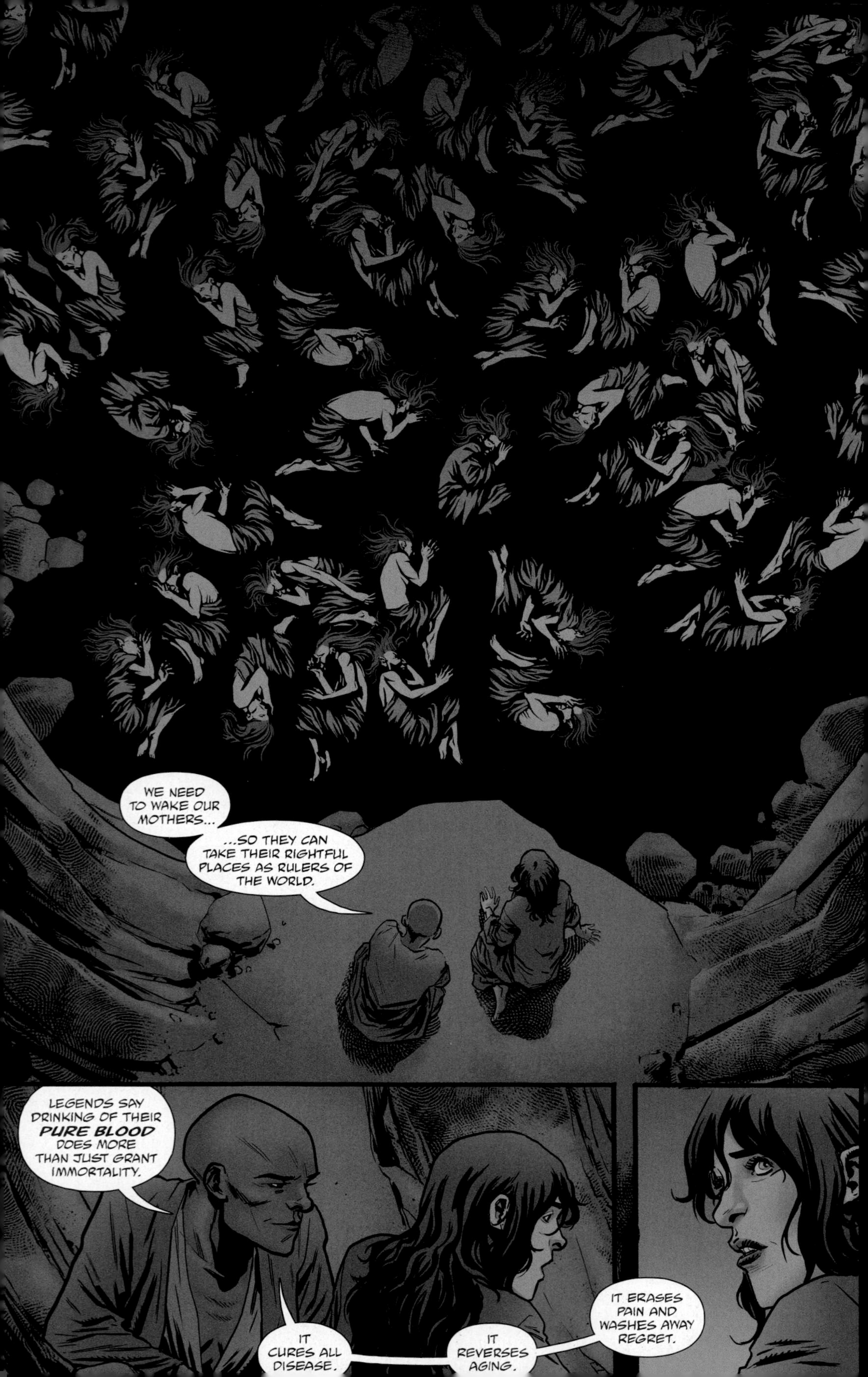
WE NEED TO WAKE OUR MOTHERS...
...SO THEY CAN TAKE THEIR RIGHTFUL PLACES AS RULERS OF THE WORLD.
LEGENDS SAY DRINKING OF THEIR PURE BLOOD DOES MORE THAN JUST GRANT IMMORTALITY.
IT CURES ALL DISEASE.
IT REVERSES AGING.
IT ERASES PAIN AND WASHES AWAY REGRET.

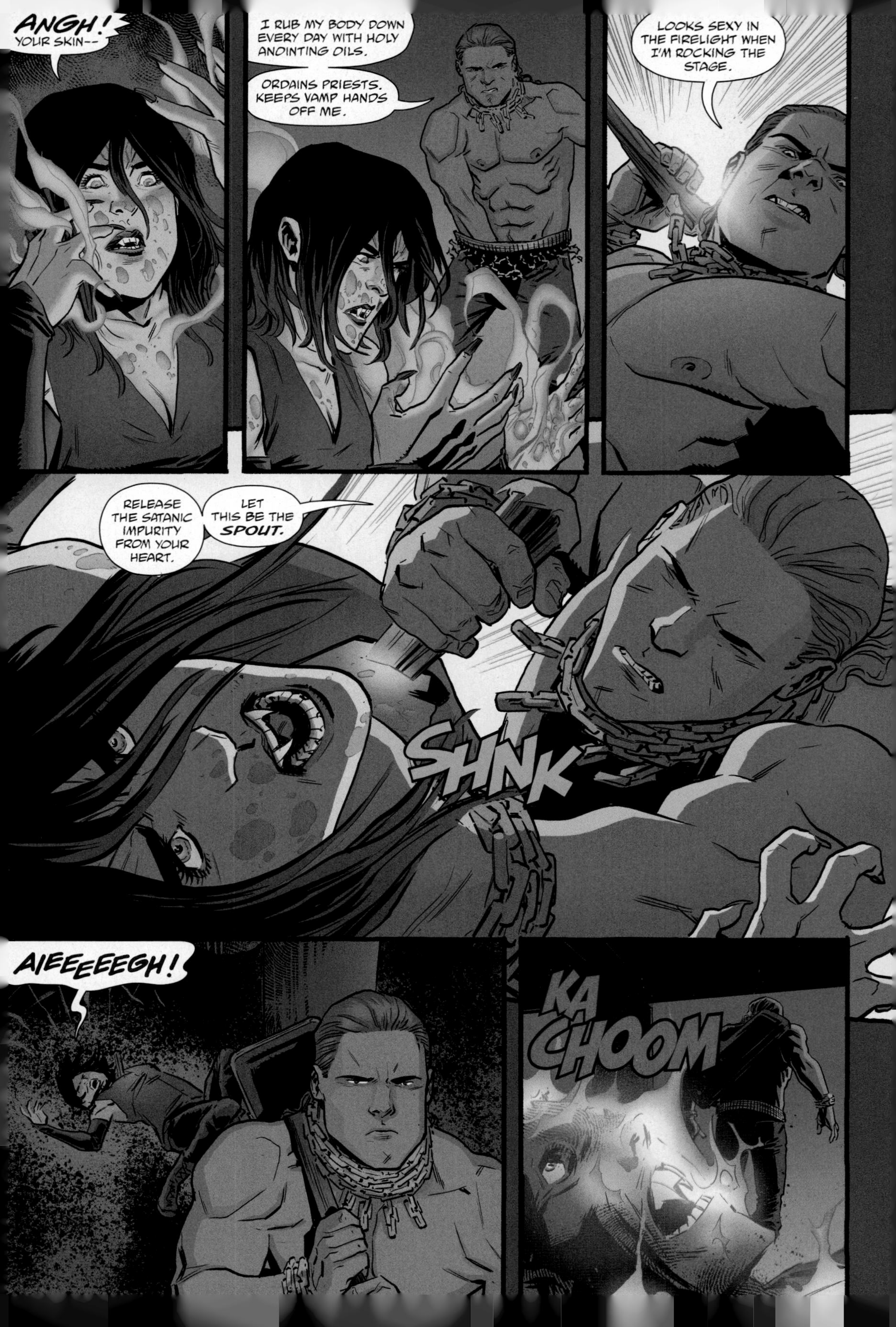
ANGH! YOUR SKIN--
I RUB MY BODY DOWN EVERY DAY WITH HOLY ANOINTING OILS.
ORDAINS PRIESTS. KEEPS VAMP HANDS OFF ME.
LOOKS SEXY IN THE FIRELIGHT WHEN I'M ROCKING THE STAGE.
RELEASE THE SATANIC IMPURITY FROM YOUR HEART.
LET THIS BE THE SPOUT.
SHNK
AIEEEEEGH!
KA CHOOM

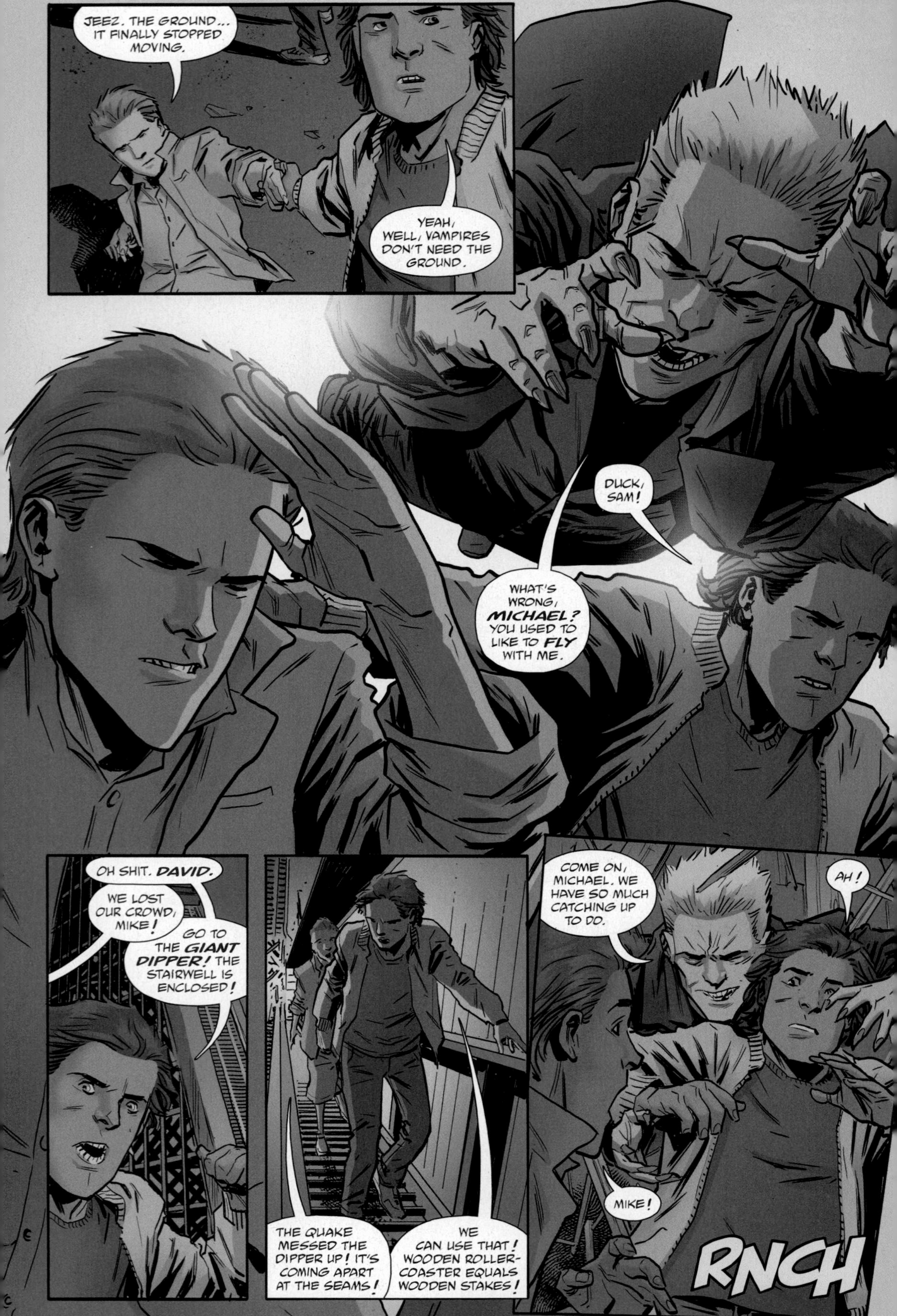
JEEZ. THE GROUND... IT FINALLY STOPPED MOVING.
YEAH, WELL, VAMPIRES DON'T NEED THE GROUND.
DUCK, SAM!
WHAT'S WRONG, MICHAEL? YOU USED TO LIKE TO FLY WITH ME.
OH SHIT. DAVID.
WE LOST OUR CROWD, MIKE!
GO TO THE GIANT DIPPER! THE STAIRWELL IS ENCLOSED!
THE QUAKE MESSED THE DIPPER UP! IT'S COMING APART AT THE SEAMS!
WE CAN USE THAT! WOODEN ROLLER-COASTER EQUALS WOODEN STAKES!
COME ON, MICHAEL. WE HAVE SO MUCH CATCHING UP TO DO.
AH!
MIKE!
RNCH

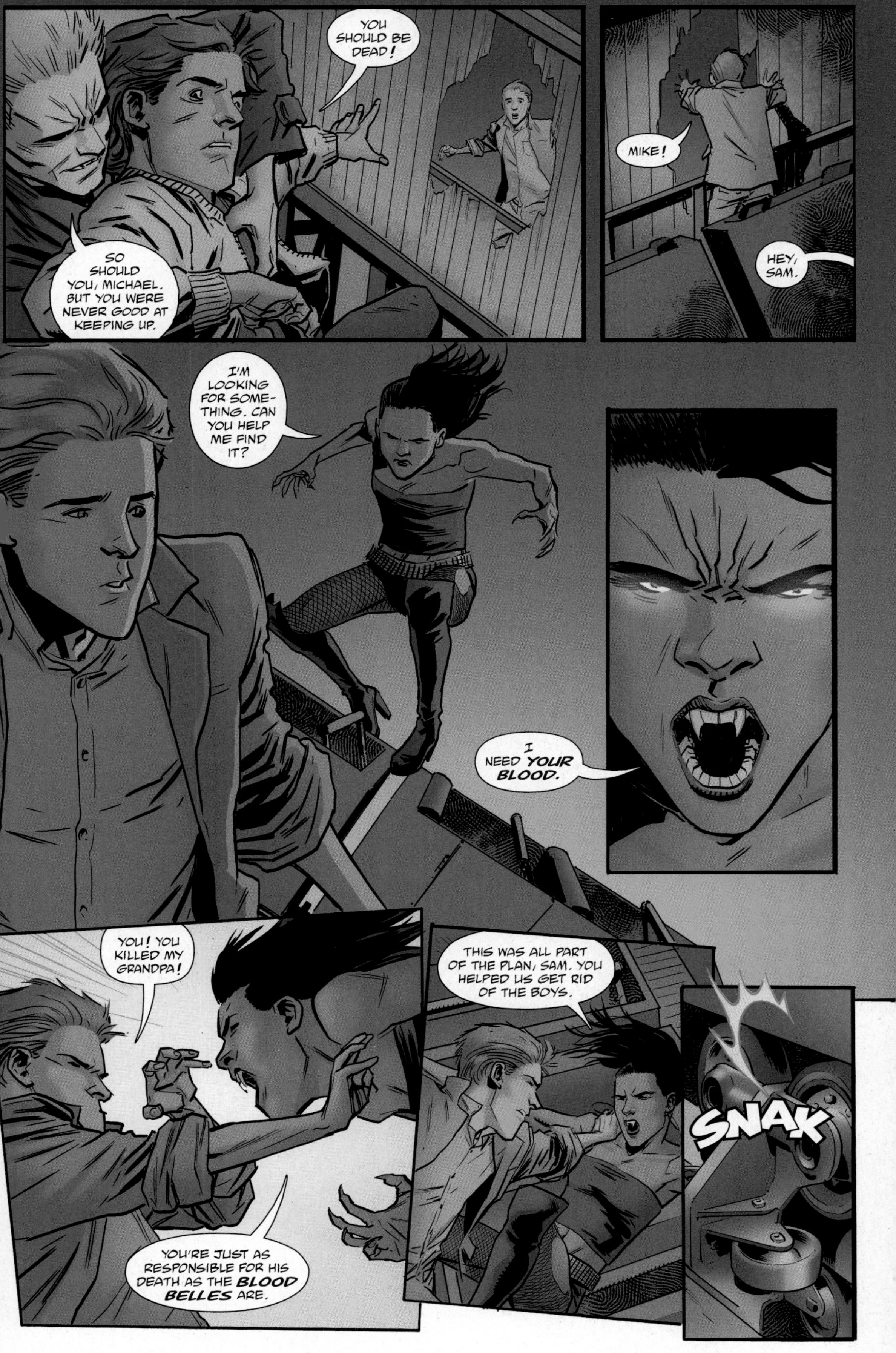

YOU SHOULD BE DEAD!
SO SHOULD YOU, MICHAEL. BUT YOU WERE NEVER GOOD AT KEEPING UP.
MIKE!
HEY, SAM.
I'M LOOKING FOR SOME-THING. CAN YOU HELP ME FIND IT?
I NEED YOUR BLOOD.
YOU! YOU KILLED MY GRANDPA!
YOU'RE JUST AS RESPONSIBLE FOR HIS DEATH AS THE BLOOD BELLES ARE.
THIS WAS ALL PART OF THE PLAN, SAM. YOU HELPED US GET RID OF THE BOYS.
SNAK

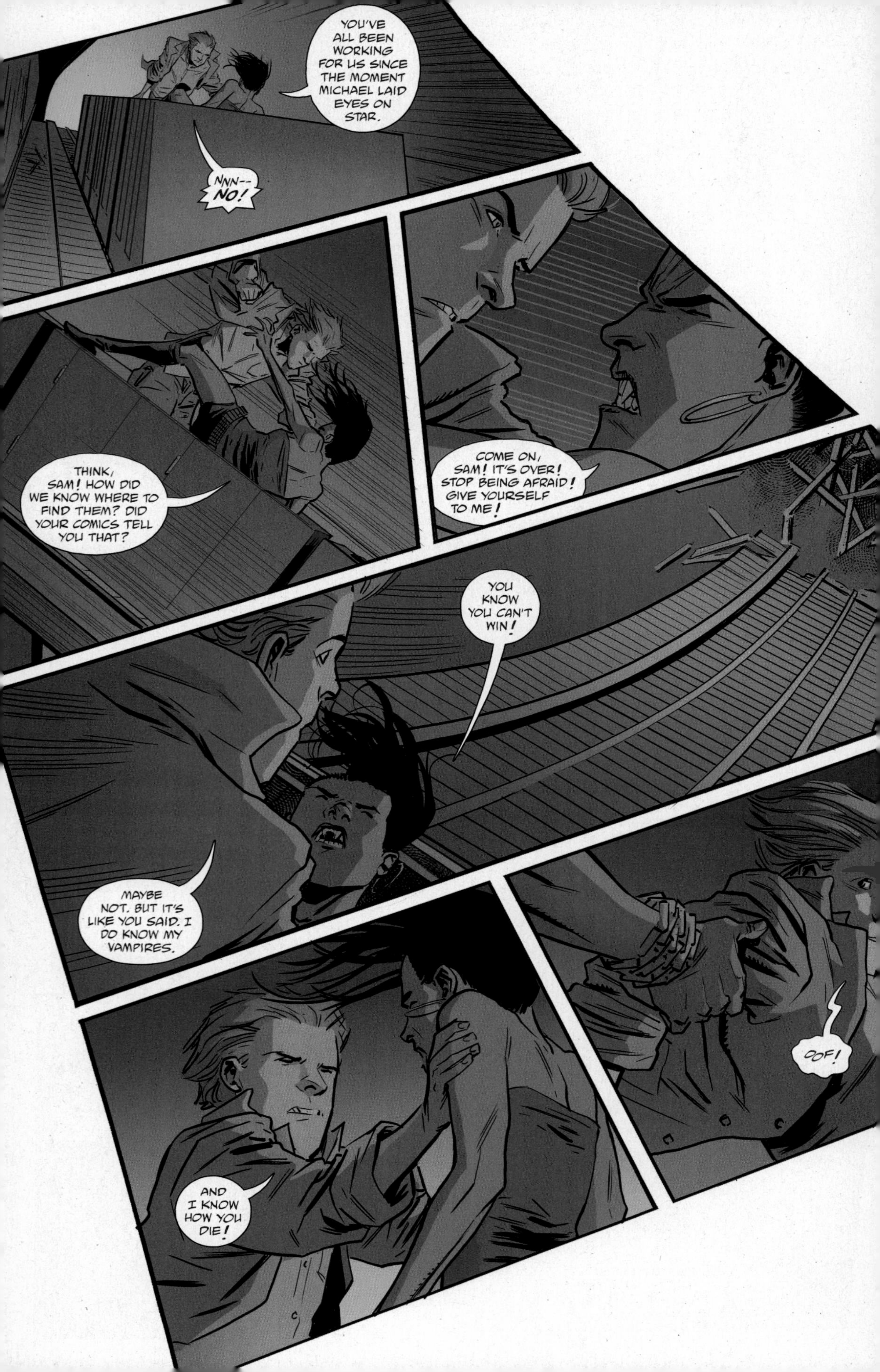
YOU'VE ALL BEEN WORKING FOR US SINCE THE MOMENT MICHAEL LAID EYES ON STAR.
NNN-- NO!
THINK, SAM! HOW DID WE KNOW WHERE TO FIND THEM? DID YOUR COMICS TELL YOU THAT?
COME ON, SAM! IT'S OVER! STOP BEING AFRAID! GIVE YOURSELF TO ME!
YOU KNOW YOU CAN'T WIN!
MAYBE NOT. BUT IT'S LIKE YOU SAID. I DO KNOW MY VAMPIRES.
AND I KNOW HOW YOU DIE!
OOF!

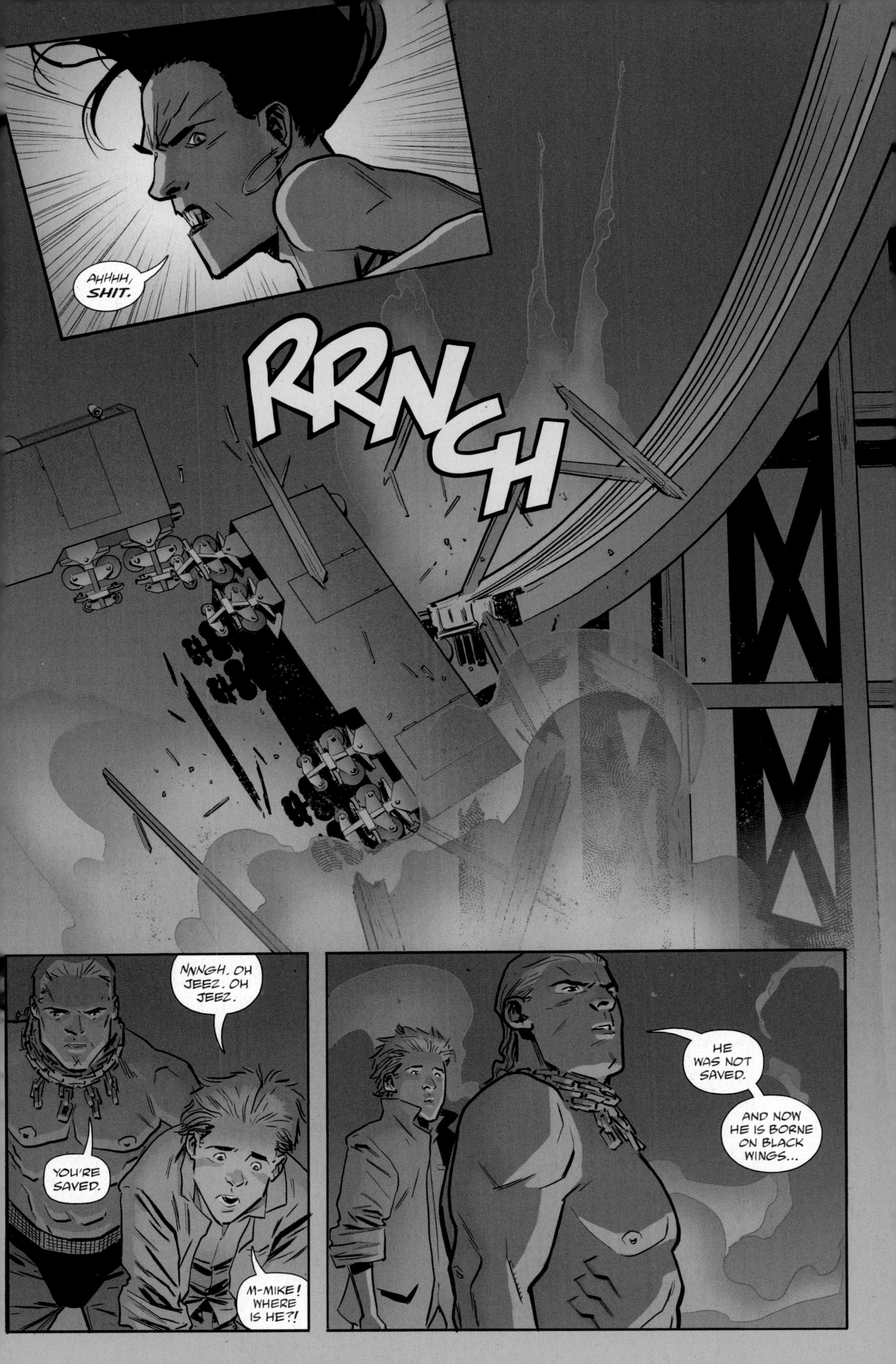
AHHHH, SHIT.
RRNCH
NNNGH. OH JEEZ. OH JEEZ.
YOU'RE SAVED.
M-MIKE! WHERE IS HE?!
HE WAS NOT SAVED.
AND NOW HE IS BORNE ON BLACK WINGS...

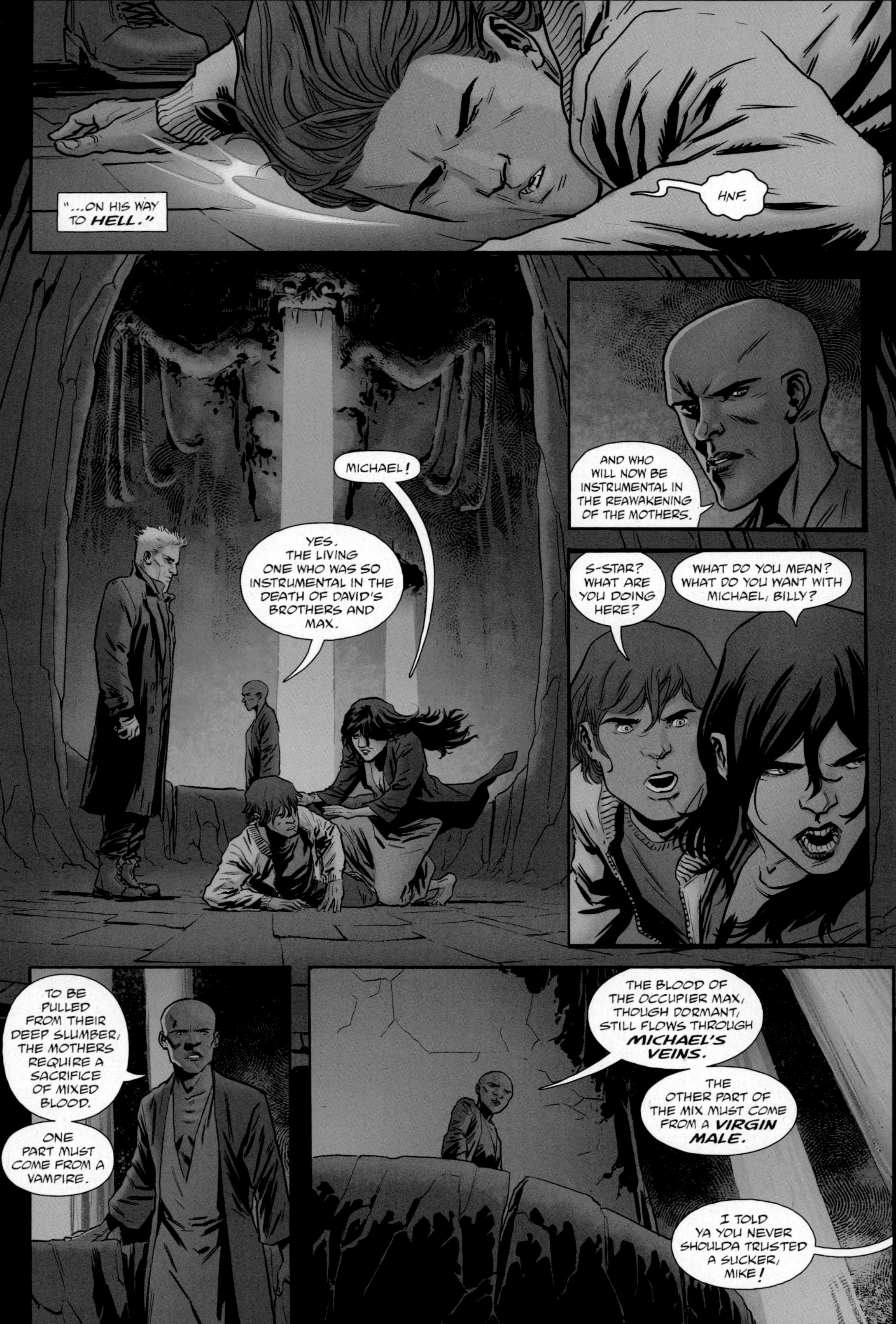
"...ON HIS WAY TO HELL."
HNF.
MICHAEL!
YES. THE LIVING ONE WHO WAS SO INSTRUMENTAL IN THE DEATH OF DAVID'S BROTHERS AND MAX.
AND WHO WILL NOW BE INSTRUMENTAL IN THE REAWAKENING OF THE MOTHERS.
S-STAR? WHAT ARE YOU DOING HERE?
WHAT DO YOU MEAN? WHAT DO YOU WANT WITH MICHAEL, BILLY?
TO BE PULLED FROM THEIR DEEP SLUMBER, THE MOTHERS REQUIRE A SACRIFICE OF MIXED BLOOD.
ONE PART MUST COME FROM A VAMPIRE.
THE BLOOD OF THE OCCUPIER MAX, THOUGH DORMANT, STILL FLOWS THROUGH MICHAEL'S VEINS.
THE OTHER PART OF THE MIX MUST COME FROM A VIRGIN MALE.
I TOLD YA YOU NEVER SHOULDA TRUSTED A SUCKER, MIKE!

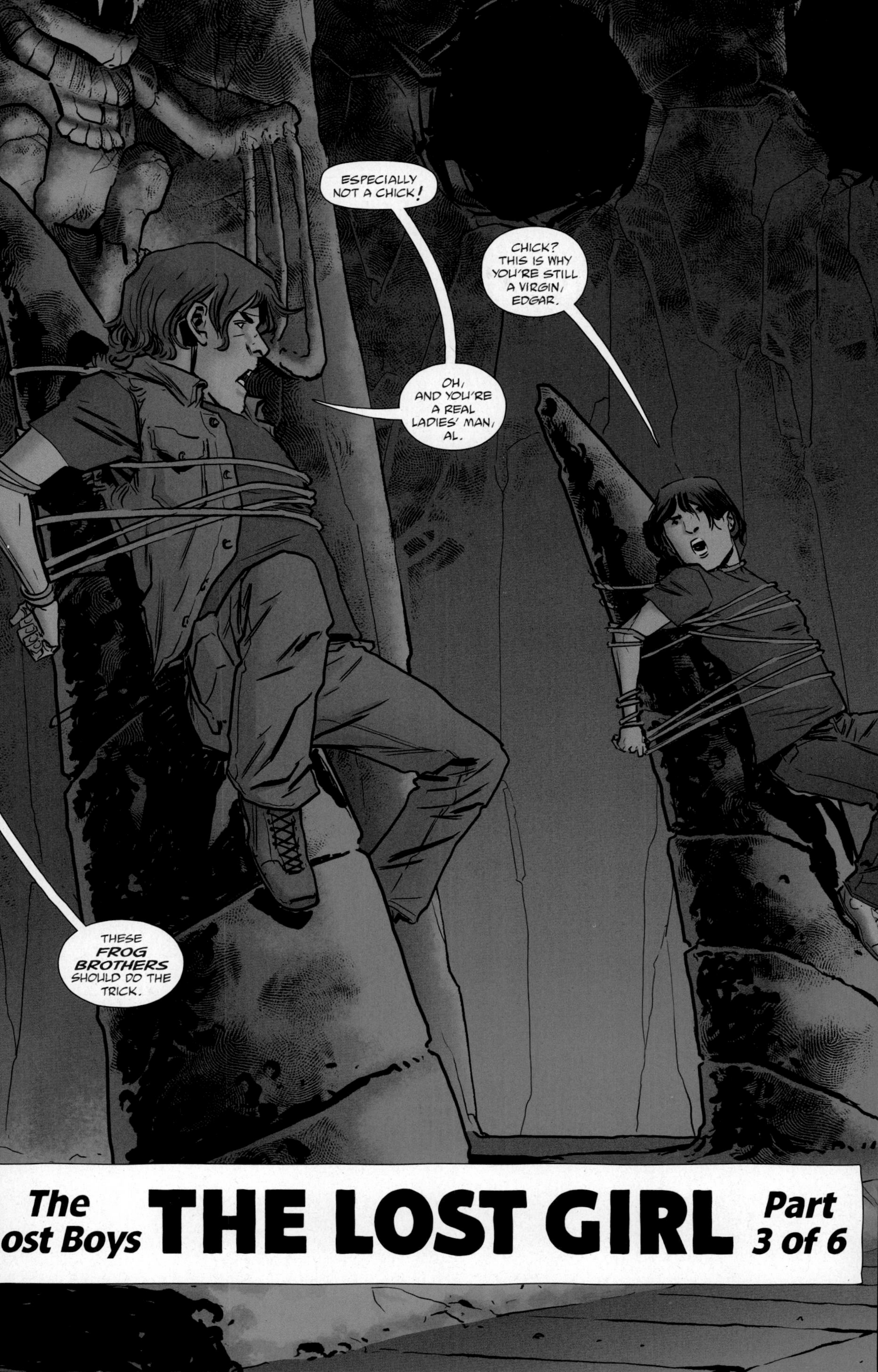
ESPECIALLY NOT A CHICK!
CHICK? THIS IS WHY YOU'RE STILL A VIRGIN, EDGAR.
OH, AND YOU'RE A REAL LADIES' MAN, AL.
THESE *FROG BROTHERS* SHOULD DO THE TRICK.
The
ost Boys
THE LOST GIRL
Part 3 of 6

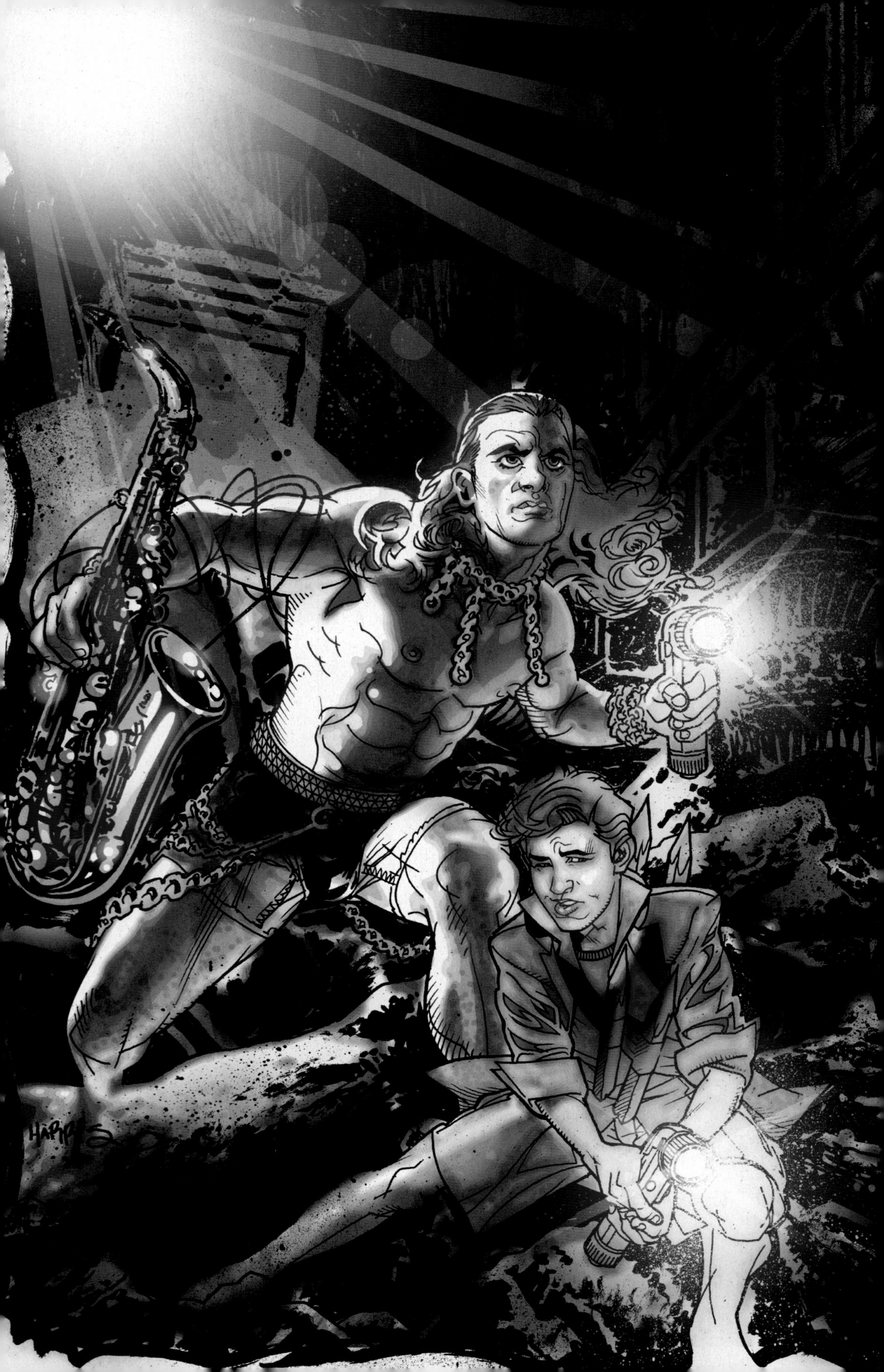

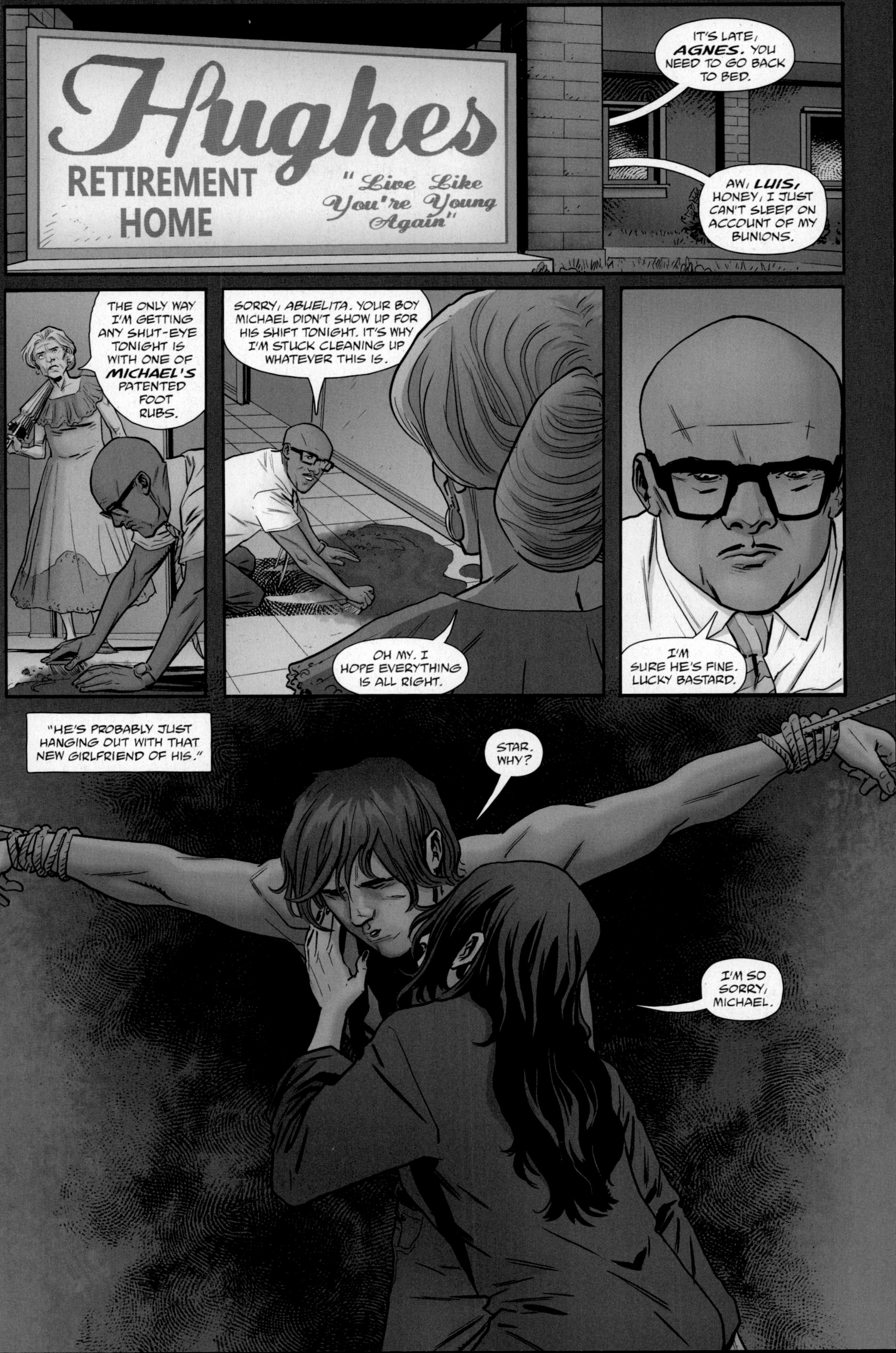
Hughes
RETIREMENT HOME
"Live Like You're Young Again"
IT'S LATE, AGNES. YOU NEED TO GO BACK TO BED.
AW, LUIS, HONEY, I JUST CAN'T SLEEP ON ACCOUNT OF MY BUNIONS.
THE ONLY WAY I'M GETTING ANY SHUT-EYE TONIGHT IS WITH ONE OF MICHAEL'S PATENTED FOOT RUBS.
SORRY, ABUELITA. YOUR BOY MICHAEL DIDN'T SHOW UP FOR HIS SHIFT TONIGHT. IT'S WHY I'M STUCK CLEANING UP WHATEVER THIS IS.
OH MY. I HOPE EVERYTHING IS ALL RIGHT.
I'M SURE HE'S FINE. LUCKY BASTARD.
"HE'S PROBABLY JUST HANGING OUT WITH THAT NEW GIRLFRIEND OF HIS."
STAR. WHY?
I'M SO SORRY, MICHAEL.

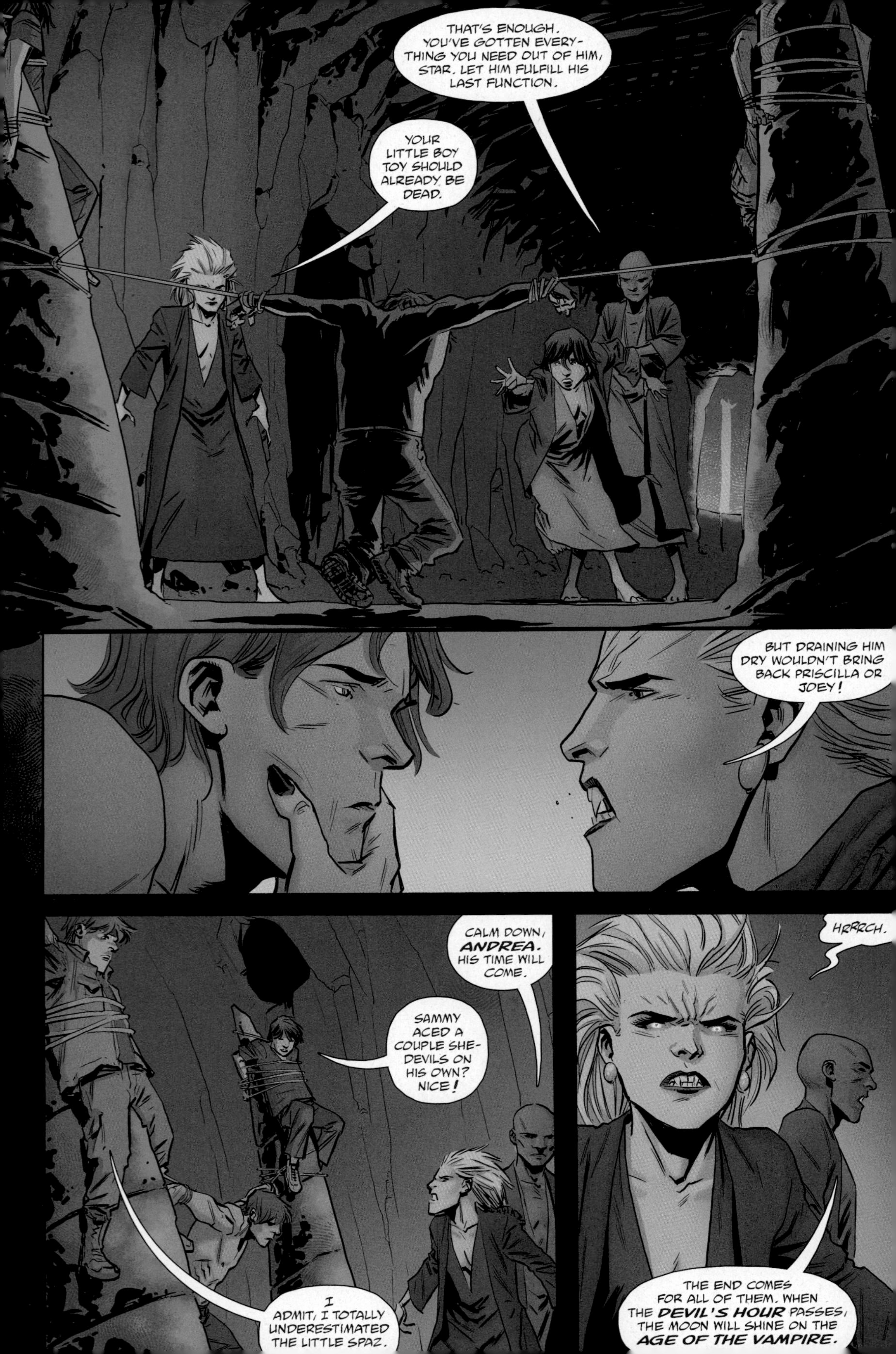
THAT'S ENOUGH. YOU'VE GOTTEN EVERY-THING YOU NEED OUT OF HIM, STAR. LET HIM FULFILL HIS LAST FUNCTION.
YOUR LITTLE BOY TOY SHOULD ALREADY BE DEAD.
BUT DRAINING HIM DRY WOULDN'T BRING BACK PRISCILLA OR JOEY!
CALM DOWN, ANDREA. HIS TIME WILL COME.
SAMMY ACED A COUPLE SHE-DEVILS ON HIS OWN? NICE!
I ADMIT, I TOTALLY UNDERESTIMATED THE LITTLE SPAZ.
HRRRCH.
THE END COMES FOR ALL OF THEM. WHEN THE DEVIL'S HOUR PASSES, THE MOON WILL SHINE ON THE AGE OF THE VAMPIRE.

BUT FIRST, WE MUST PREPARE FOR THE **AWAKENING OF THE MOTHERS.**

TO ENSURE THEY ARE AS STRONG AS POSSIBLE WHEN THEY OPEN THEIR EYES TO THE NIGHT ONCE AGAIN.

THEY HAVE DEMANDED CERTAIN RITUALS.

...AS ILL-ADVISED AS THEY MAY SEEM.

HNH.

YOU SAID MAX'S BOYS WERE OCCUPIERS. YOU SENT ME TO INFILTRATE THEM. YOU WANTED THEM DEAD.

I DID. BUT THERE ARE CERTAIN THINGS YOU WOULDN'T DO.

WE NEEDED SOMEONE TO TRACK DOWN THE REST OF THE HUNTERS IN SANTA CARLA. TO FIND OUT WHERE THEY GATHERED.

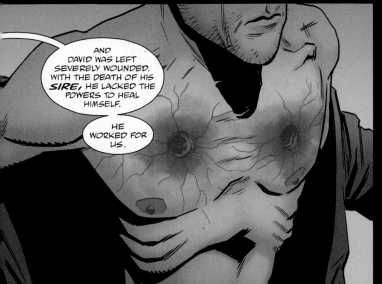

AND DAVID WAS LEFT SEVERELY WOUNDED. WITH THE DEATH OF HIS *SIRE*, HE LACKED THE POWERS TO HEAL HIMSELF.

HE WORKED FOR US.

NOW HE'S HERE TO RECEIVE **HIS** REWARD.

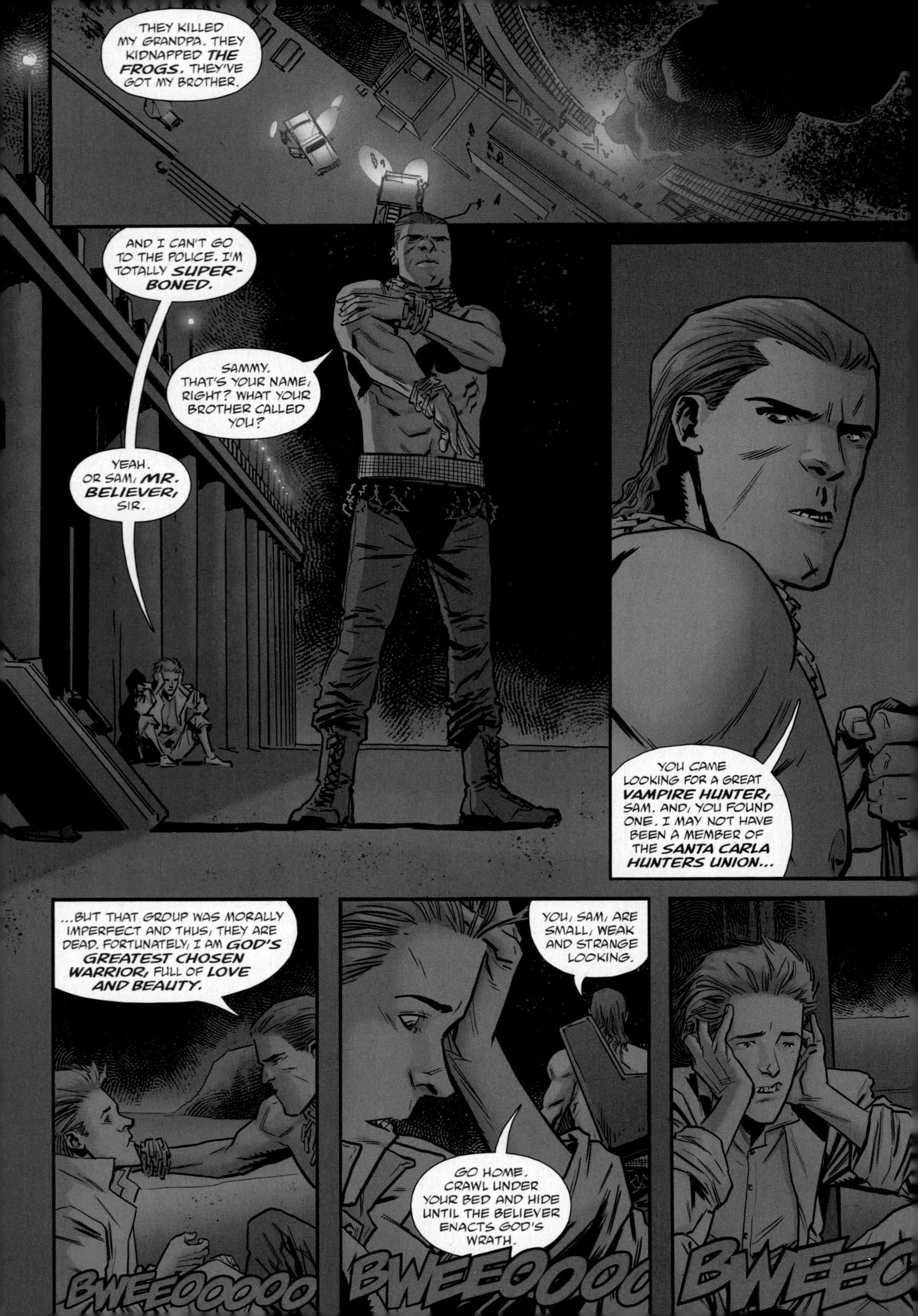
THEY KILLED MY GRANDPA. THEY KIDNAPPED THE FROGS. THEY'VE GOT MY BROTHER.
AND I CAN'T GO TO THE POLICE. I'M TOTALLY SUPER-BONED.
SAMMY. THAT'S YOUR NAME, RIGHT? WHAT YOUR BROTHER CALLED YOU?
YEAH. OR SAM, MR. BELIEVER, SIR.
YOU CAME LOOKING FOR A GREAT VAMPIRE HUNTER, SAM. AND, YOU FOUND ONE. I MAY NOT HAVE BEEN A MEMBER OF THE SANTA CARLA HUNTERS UNION...
...BUT THAT GROUP WAS MORALLY IMPERFECT AND THUS, THEY ARE DEAD. FORTUNATELY, I AM GOD'S GREATEST CHOSEN WARRIOR, FULL OF LOVE AND BEAUTY.
YOU, SAM, ARE SMALL, WEAK AND STRANGE LOOKING.
GO HOME. CRAWL UNDER YOUR BED AND HIDE UNTIL THE BELIEVER ENACTS GOD'S WRATH.
BWEEOOOOOO
BWEEOOOOO
BWEEO

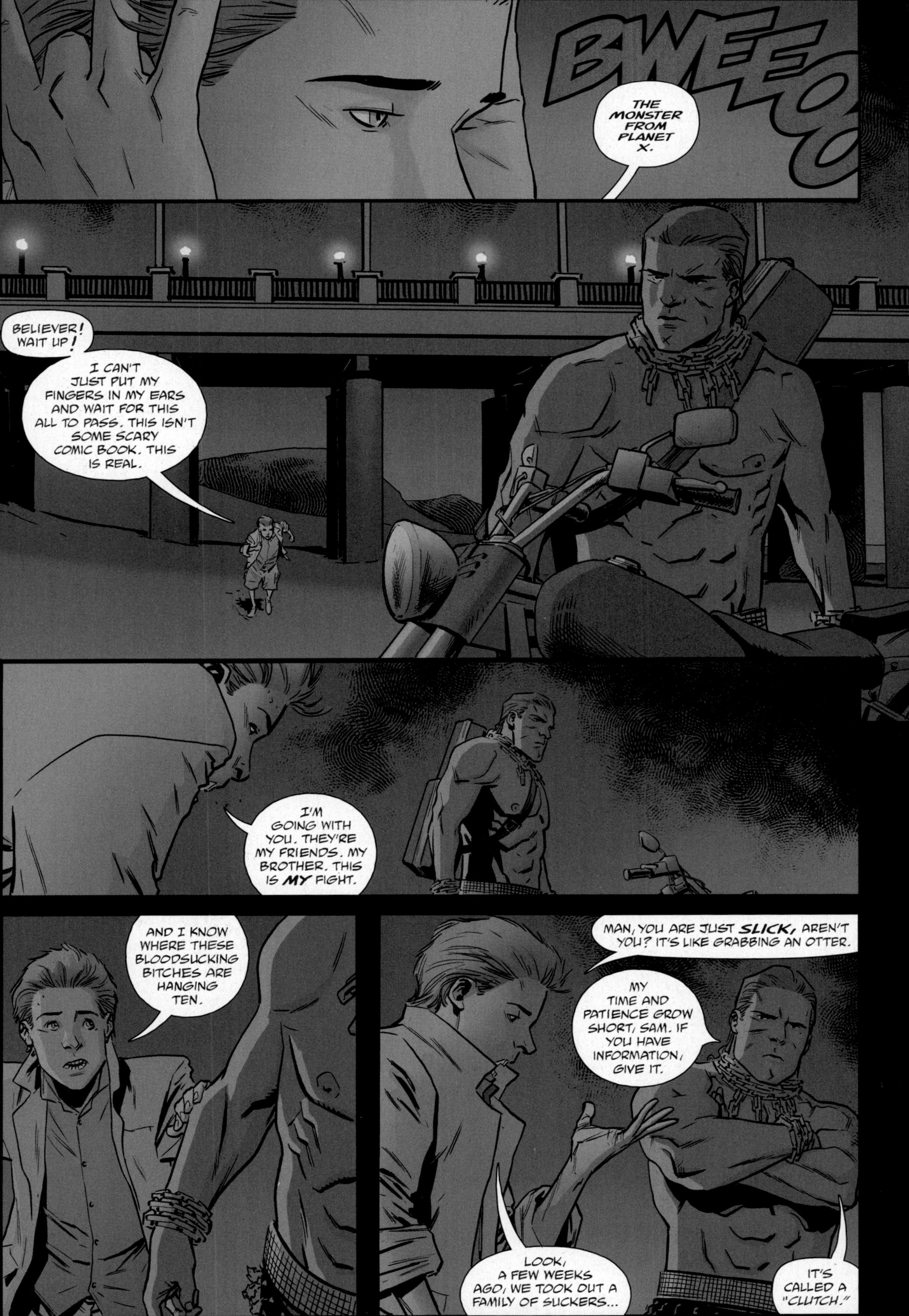
BWEEOOO
THE MONSTER FROM PLANET X.
BELIEVER! WAIT UP!
I CAN'T JUST PUT MY FINGERS IN MY EARS AND WAIT FOR THIS ALL TO PASS. THIS ISN'T SOME SCARY COMIC BOOK. THIS IS REAL.
I'M GOING WITH YOU. THEY'RE MY FRIENDS. MY BROTHER. THIS IS MY FIGHT.
AND I KNOW WHERE THESE BLOODSUCKING BITCHES ARE HANGING TEN.
MAN, YOU ARE JUST SLICK, AREN'T YOU? IT'S LIKE GRABBING AN OTTER.
MY TIME AND PATIENCE GROW SHORT, SAM. IF YOU HAVE INFORMATION, GIVE IT.
LOOK, A FEW WEEKS AGO, WE TOOK OUT A FAMILY OF SUCKERS...
IT'S CALLED A "CLUTCH."

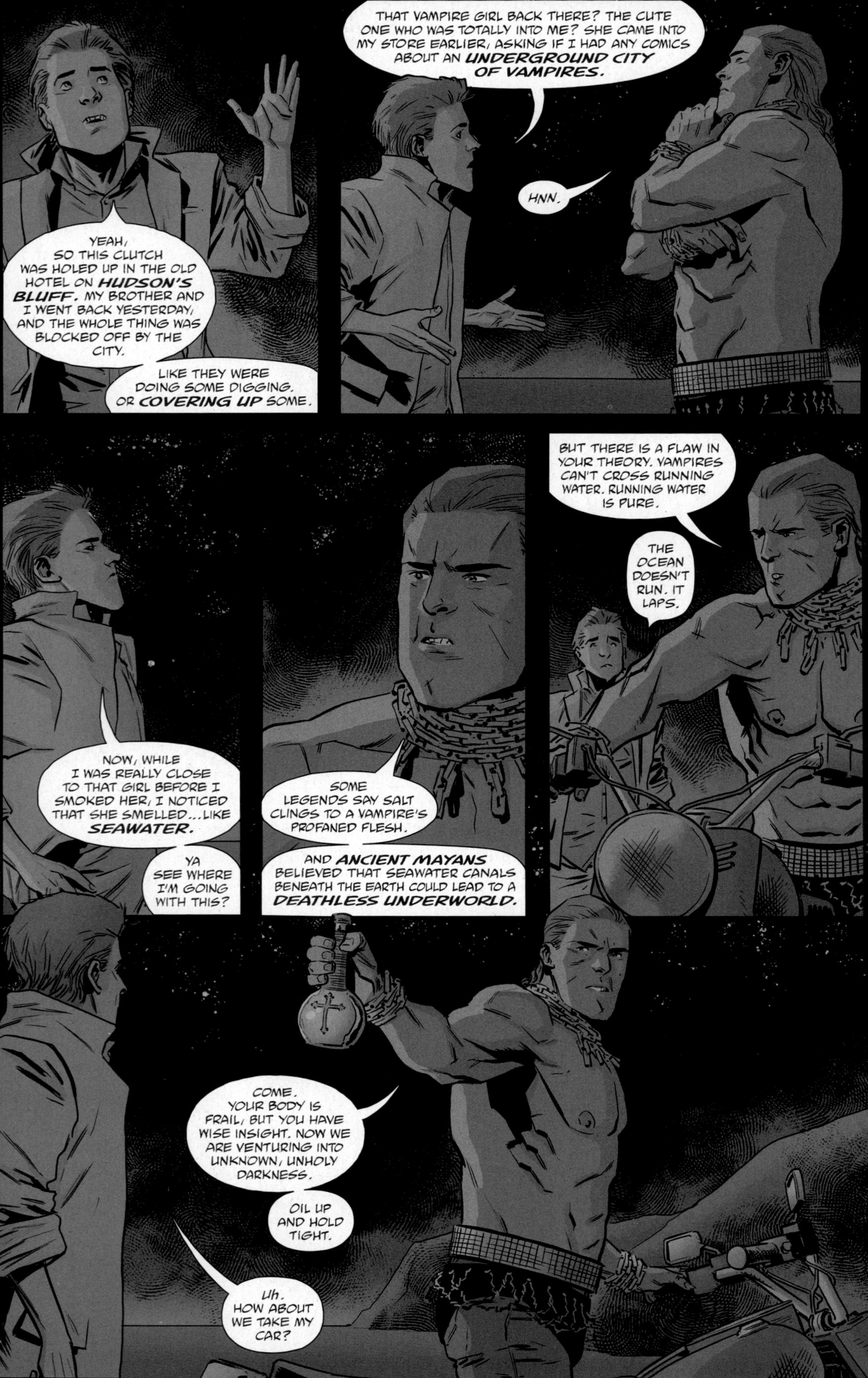
YEAH, SO THIS CLUTCH WAS HOLED UP IN THE OLD HOTEL ON HUDSON'S BLUFF. MY BROTHER AND I WENT BACK YESTERDAY, AND THE WHOLE THING WAS BLOCKED OFF BY THE CITY.
LIKE THEY WERE DOING SOME DIGGING. OR COVERING UP SOME.
THAT VAMPIRE GIRL BACK THERE? THE CUTE ONE WHO WAS TOTALLY INTO ME? SHE CAME INTO MY STORE EARLIER, ASKING IF I HAD ANY COMICS ABOUT AN UNDERGROUND CITY OF VAMPIRES.
HNN.
NOW, WHILE I WAS REALLY CLOSE TO THAT GIRL BEFORE I SMOKED HER, I NOTICED THAT SHE SMELLED...LIKE SEAWATER.
YA SEE WHERE I'M GOING WITH THIS?
SOME LEGENDS SAY SALT CLINGS TO A VAMPIRE'S PROFANED FLESH.
AND ANCIENT MAYANS BELIEVED THAT SEAWATER CANALS BENEATH THE EARTH COULD LEAD TO A DEATHLESS UNDERWORLD.
BUT THERE IS A FLAW IN YOUR THEORY. VAMPIRES CAN'T CROSS RUNNING WATER. RUNNING WATER IS PURE.
THE OCEAN DOESN'T RUN. IT LAPS.
COME. YOUR BODY IS FRAIL, BUT YOU HAVE WISE INSIGHT. NOW WE ARE VENTURING INTO UNKNOWN, UNHOLY DARKNESS.
OIL UP AND HOLD TIGHT.
UH. HOW ABOUT WE TAKE MY CAR?

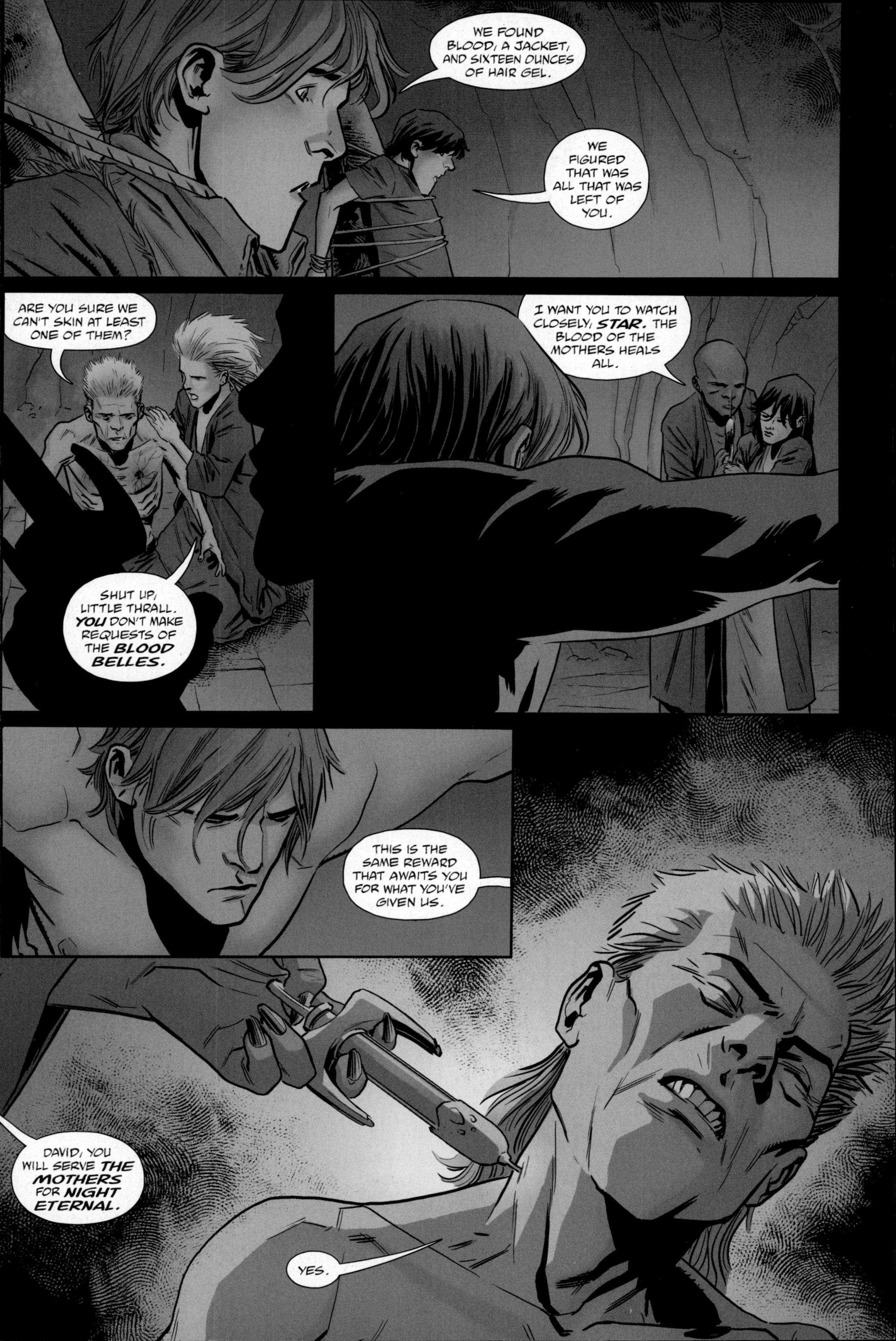
WE FOUND BLOOD, A JACKET, AND SIXTEEN OUNCES OF HAIR GEL.
WE FIGURED THAT WAS ALL THAT WAS LEFT OF YOU.
ARE YOU SURE WE CAN'T SKIN AT LEAST ONE OF THEM?
SHUT UP, LITTLE THRALL. YOU DON'T MAKE REQUESTS OF THE BLOOD BELLES.
I WANT YOU TO WATCH CLOSELY, STAR. THE BLOOD OF THE MOTHERS HEALS ALL.
THIS IS THE SAME REWARD THAT AWAITS YOU FOR WHAT YOU'VE GIVEN US.
DAVID, YOU WILL SERVE THE MOTHERS FOR NIGHT ETERNAL.
YES.

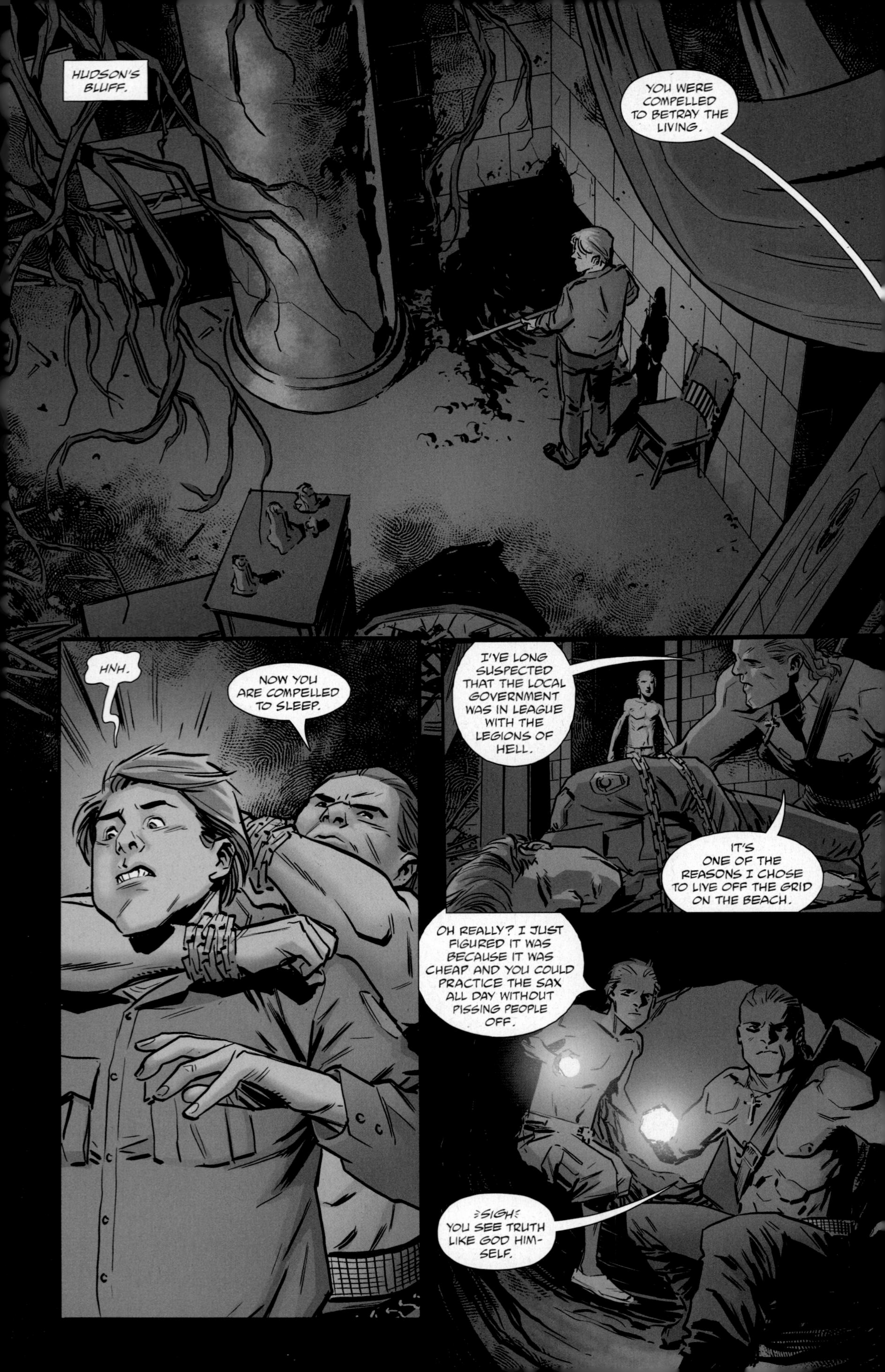
HUDSON'S BLUFF.
YOU WERE COMPELLED TO BETRAY THE LIVING.
HNH.
NOW YOU ARE COMPELLED TO SLEEP.
I'VE LONG SUSPECTED THAT THE LOCAL GOVERNMENT WAS IN LEAGUE WITH THE LEGIONS OF HELL.
IT'S ONE OF THE REASONS I CHOSE TO LIVE OFF THE GRID ON THE BEACH.
OH REALLY? I JUST FIGURED IT WAS BECAUSE IT WAS CHEAP AND YOU COULD PRACTICE THE SAX ALL DAY WITHOUT PISSING PEOPLE OFF.
SIGH
YOU SEE TRUTH LIKE GOD HIM-SELF.

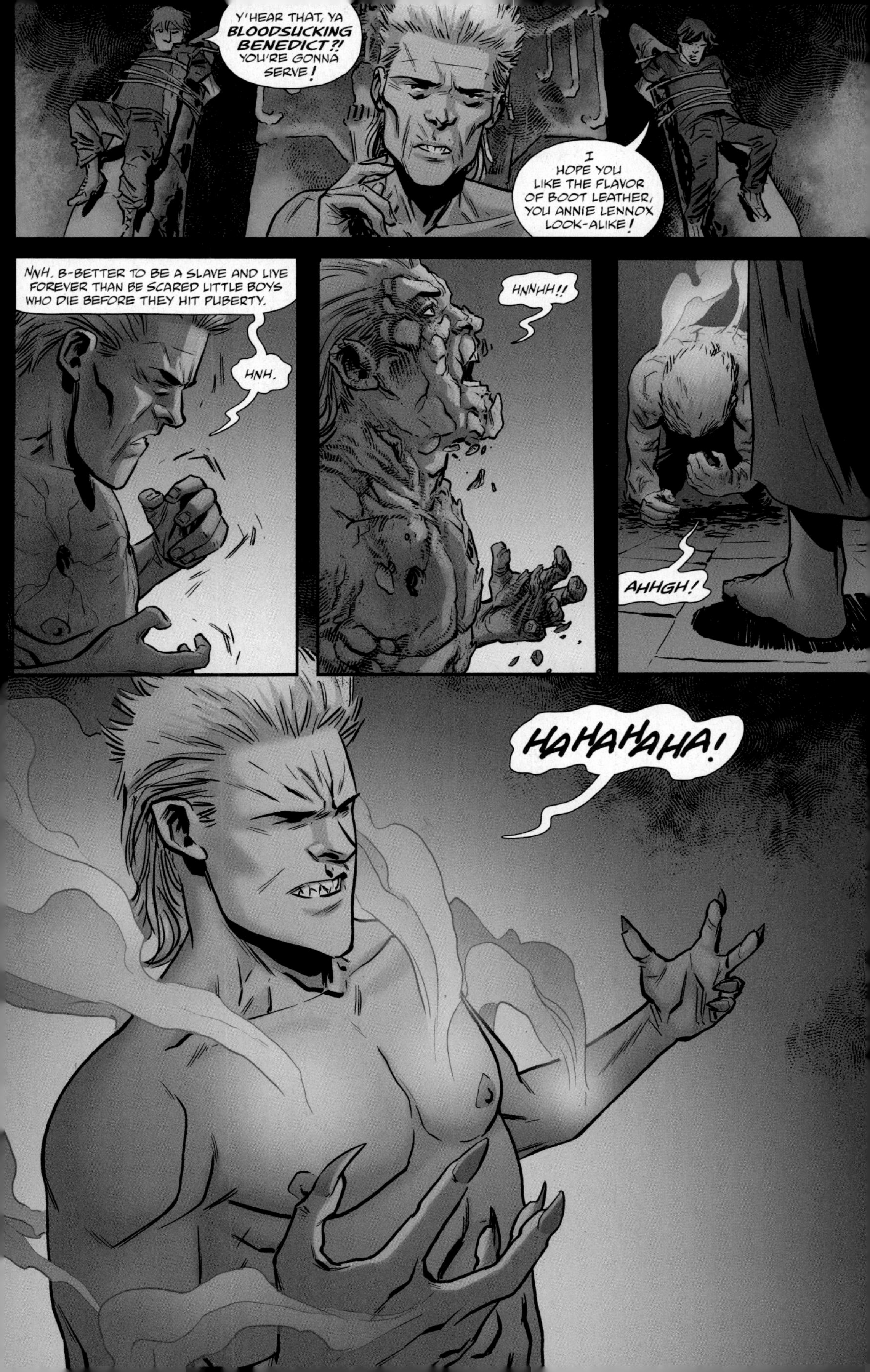

Y'HEAR THAT, YA BLOODSUCKING BENEDICT?! YOU'RE GONNA SERVE!
I HOPE YOU LIKE THE FLAVOR OF BOOT LEATHER, YOU ANNIE LENNOX LOOK-ALIKE!
NNH. B-BETTER TO BE A SLAVE AND LIVE FOREVER THAN BE SCARED LITTLE BOYS WHO DIE BEFORE THEY HIT PUBERTY.
HNH.
HNNHH!!
AHHGH!
HAHAHAHA!

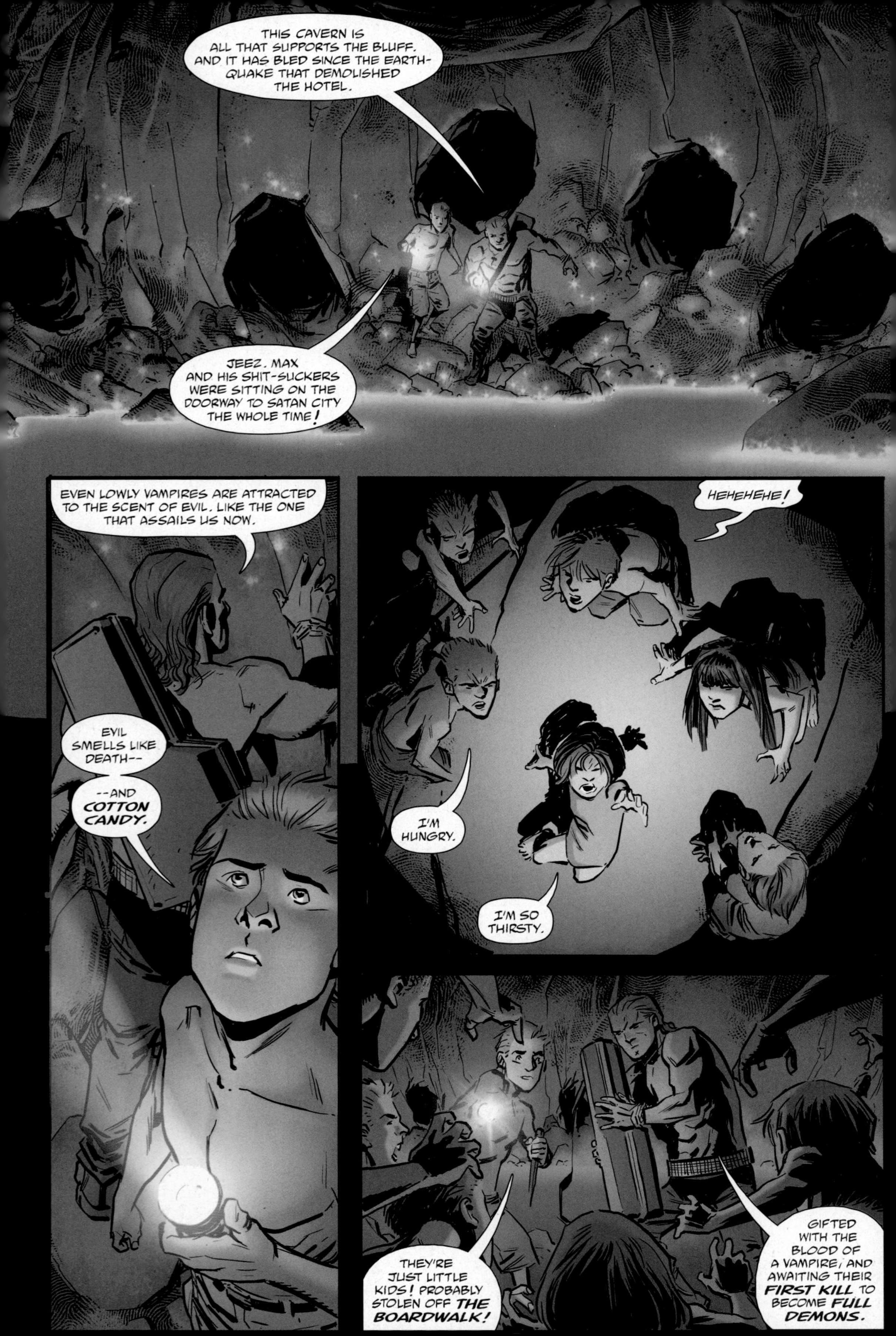
THIS CAVERN IS ALL THAT SUPPORTS THE BLUFF. AND IT HAS BLED SINCE THE EARTH-QUAKE THAT DEMOLISHED THE HOTEL.
JEEZ. MAX AND HIS SHIT-SUCKERS WERE SITTING ON THE DOORWAY TO SATAN CITY THE WHOLE TIME!
EVEN LOWLY VAMPIRES ARE ATTRACTED TO THE SCENT OF EVIL. LIKE THE ONE THAT ASSAILS US NOW.
EVIL SMELLS LIKE DEATH--
--AND COTTON CANDY.
HEHEHEHE!
I'M HUNGRY.
I'M SO THIRSTY.
THEY'RE JUST LITTLE KIDS! PROBABLY STOLEN OFF THE BOARDWALK!
GIFTED WITH THE BLOOD OF A VAMPIRE, AND AWAITING THEIR FIRST KILL TO BECOME FULL DEMONS.

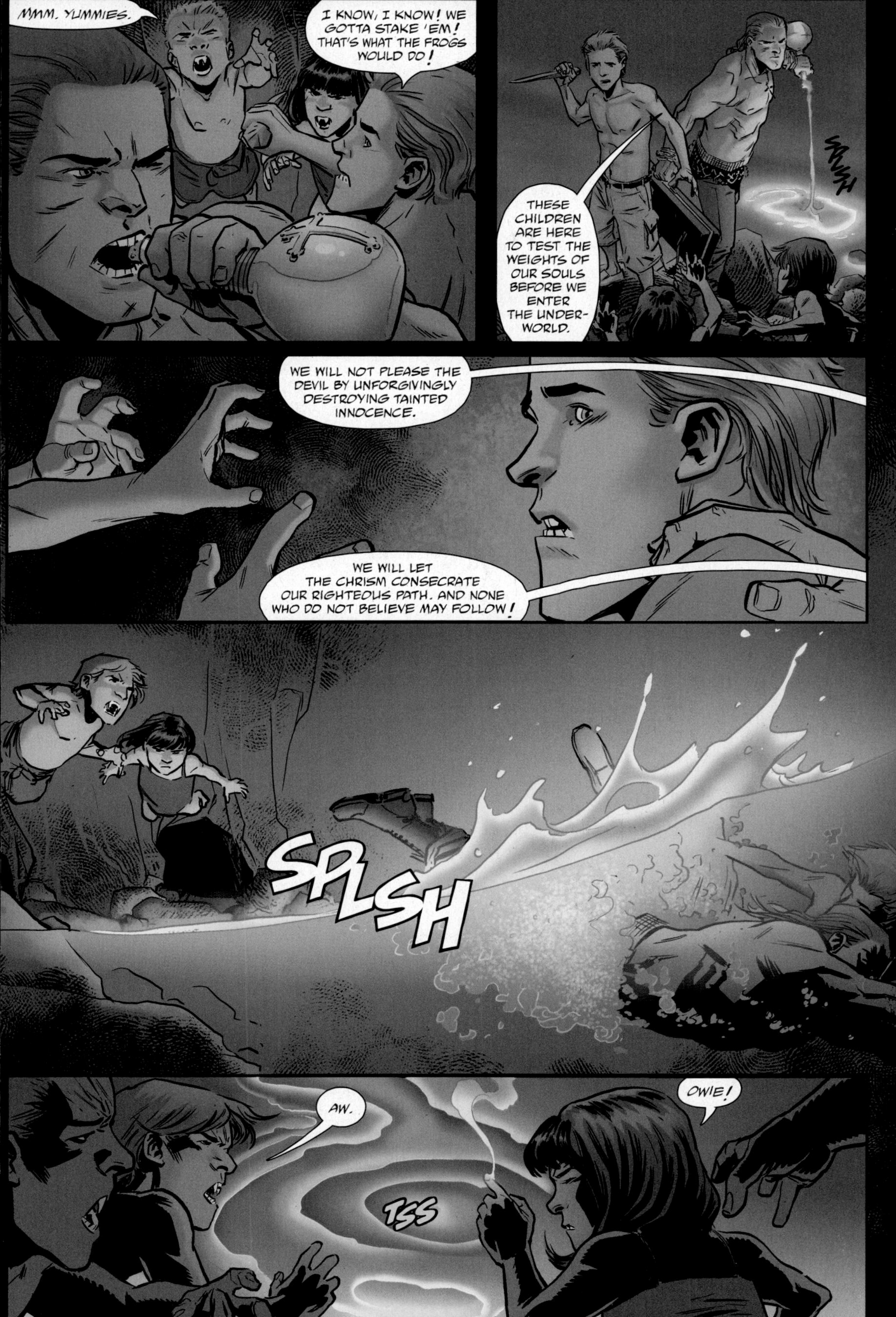
MMM. YUMMIES.
I KNOW, I KNOW! WE GOTTA STAKE 'EM! THAT'S WHAT THE FROGS WOULD DO!
SPLSH
THESE CHILDREN ARE HERE TO TEST THE WEIGHTS OF OUR SOULS BEFORE WE ENTER THE UNDER-WORLD.
WE WILL NOT PLEASE THE DEVIL BY UNFORGIVINGLY DESTROYING TAINTED INNOCENCE.
WE WILL LET THE CHRISM CONSECRATE OUR RIGHTEOUS PATH. AND NONE WHO DO NOT BELIEVE MAY FOLLOW!
SPLSH
AW.
OWIE!
TSS

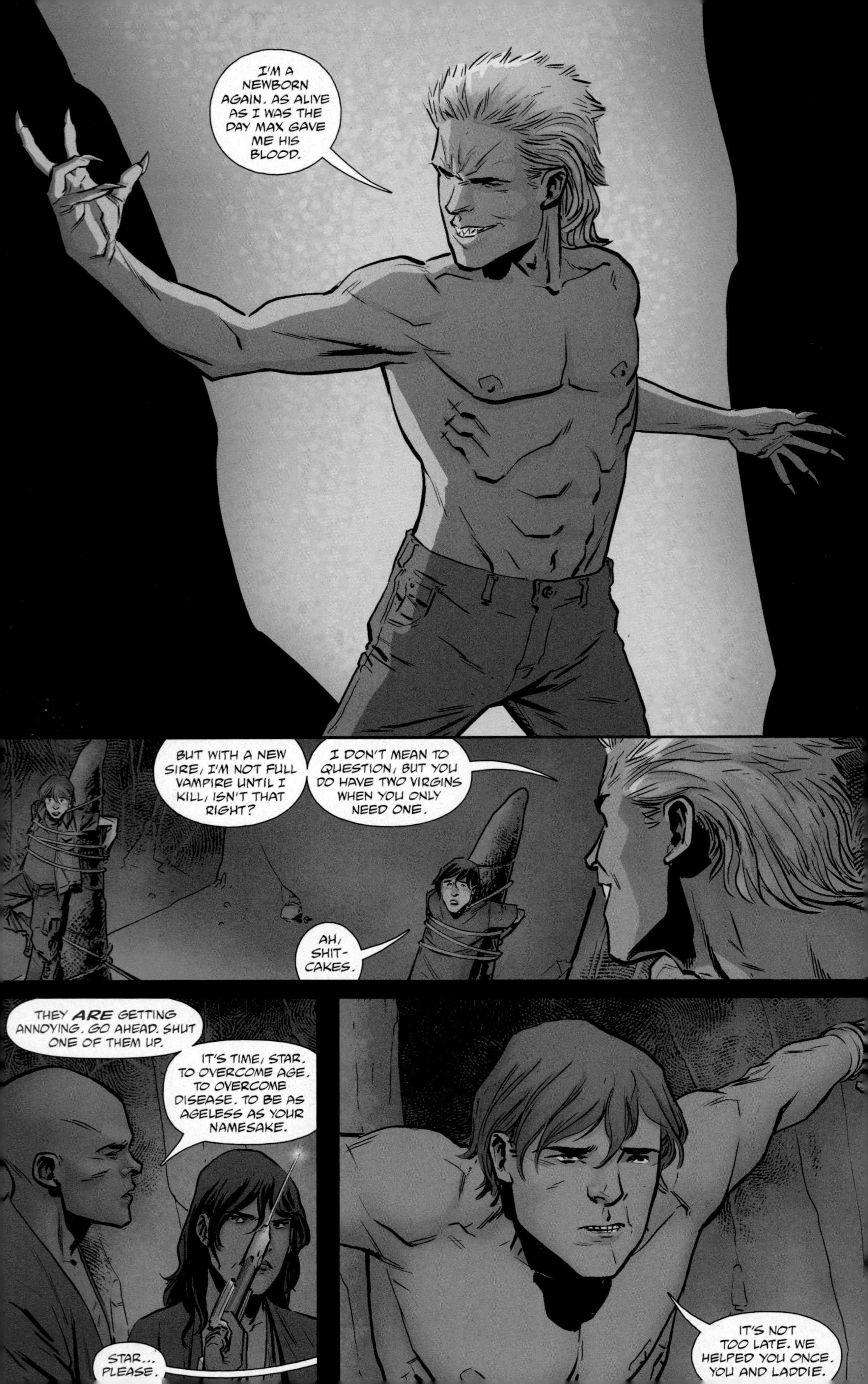
I'M A NEWBORN AGAIN. AS ALIVE AS I WAS THE DAY MAX GAVE ME HIS BLOOD.
BUT WITH A NEW SIRE, I'M NOT FULL VAMPIRE UNTIL I KILL, ISN'T THAT RIGHT?
I DON'T MEAN TO QUESTION, BUT YOU DO HAVE TWO VIRGINS WHEN YOU ONLY NEED ONE.
AH, SHIT-CAKES.
THEY ARE GETTING ANNOYING. GO AHEAD. SHUT ONE OF THEM UP.
IT'S TIME, STAR. TO OVERCOME AGE. TO OVERCOME DISEASE. TO BE AS AGELESS AS YOUR NAMESAKE.
STAR... PLEASE.
IT'S NOT TOO LATE. WE HELPED YOU ONCE. YOU AND LADDIE.

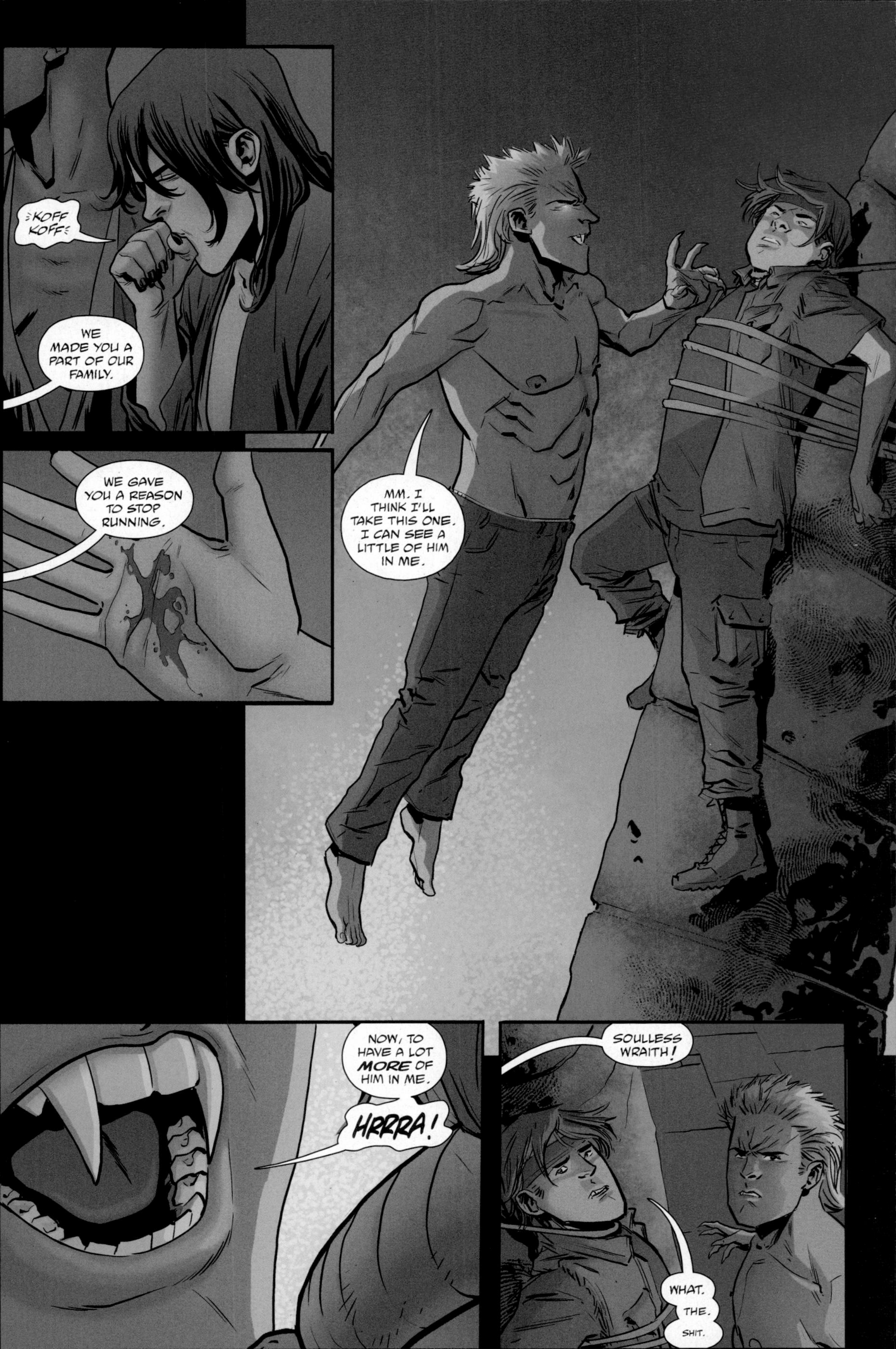
KOFF KOFF
WE MADE YOU A PART OF OUR FAMILY.
WE GAVE YOU A REASON TO STOP RUNNING.
MM. I THINK I'LL TAKE THIS ONE. I CAN SEE A LITTLE OF HIM IN ME.
NOW, TO HAVE A LOT MORE OF HIM IN ME.
HRRRA!
SOULLESS WRAITH!
WHAT.
THE.
SHIT.

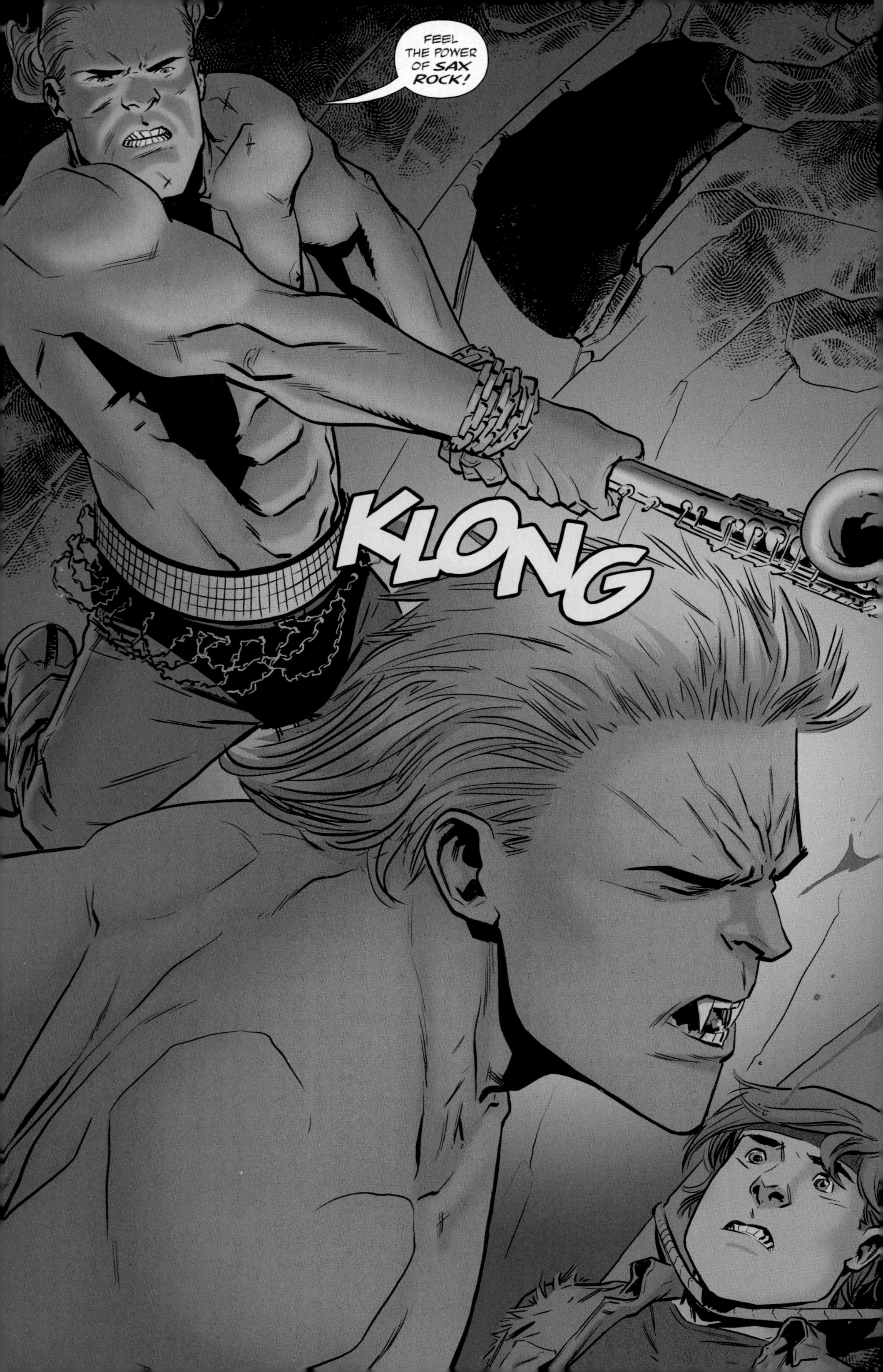
FEEL THE POWER OF SAX ROCK!
KLONG

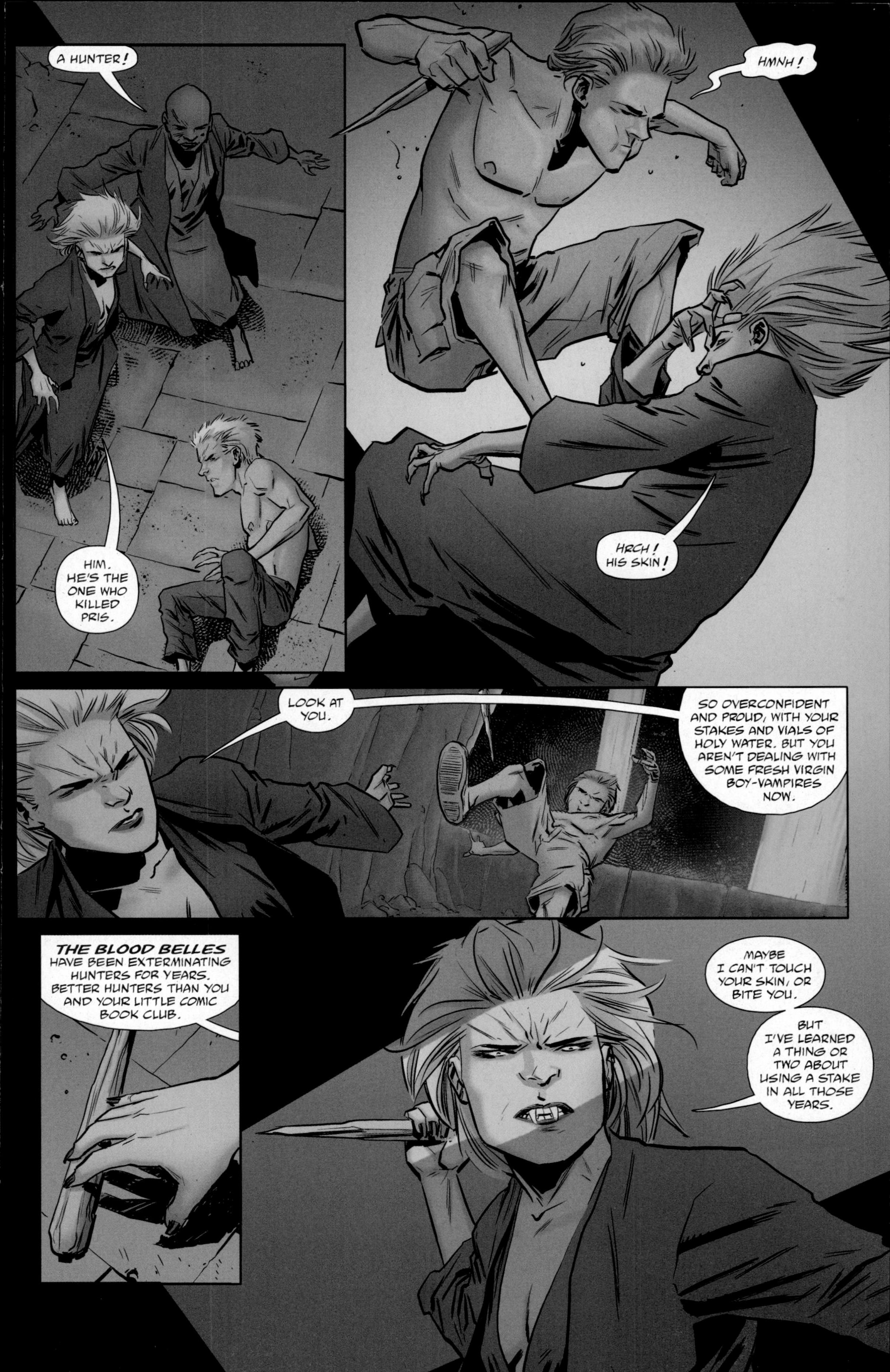
A HUNTER!
HIM. HE'S THE ONE WHO KILLED PRIS.
HMNH!
HRCH! HIS SKIN!
LOOK AT YOU.
SO OVERCONFIDENT AND PROUD, WITH YOUR STAKES AND VIALS OF HOLY WATER. BUT YOU AREN'T DEALING WITH SOME FRESH VIRGIN BOY-VAMPIRES NOW.
THE BLOOD BELLES HAVE BEEN EXTERMINATING HUNTERS FOR YEARS. BETTER HUNTERS THAN YOU AND YOUR LITTLE COMIC BOOK CLUB.
MAYBE I CAN'T TOUCH YOUR SKIN, OR BITE YOU.
BUT I'VE LEARNED A THING OR TWO ABOUT USING A STAKE IN ALL THOSE YEARS.

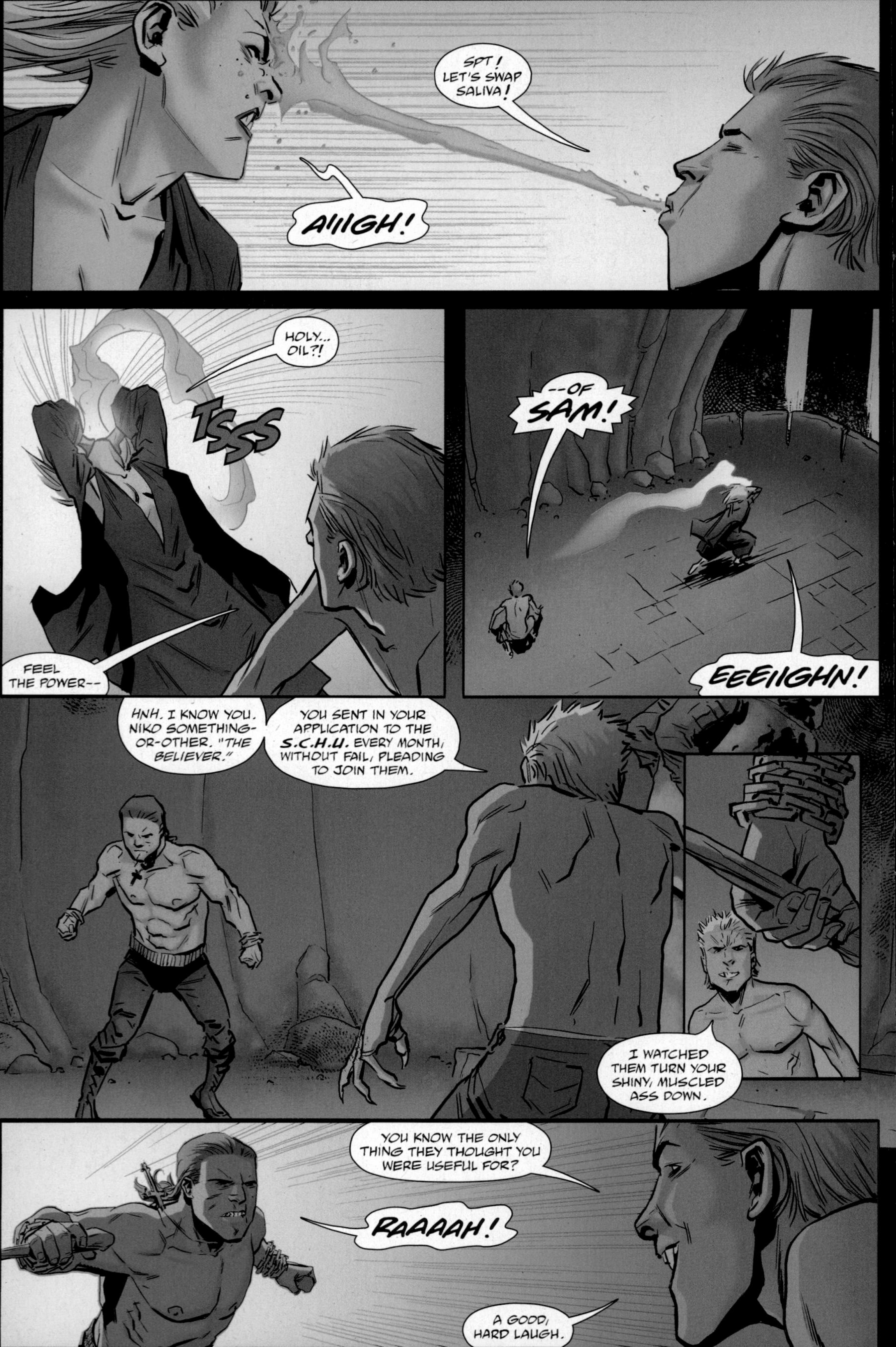
SPT! LET'S SWAP SALIVA!
AIIIGH!
HOLY... OIL?!
TSSS
FEEL THE POWER--
--OF SAM!
EEEIIGHN!
HNH. I KNOW YOU. NIKO SOMETHING-OR-OTHER. "THE BELIEVER."
YOU SENT IN YOUR APPLICATION TO THE S.C.H.U. EVERY MONTH, WITHOUT FAIL, PLEADING TO JOIN THEM.
I WATCHED THEM TURN YOUR SHINY, MUSCLED ASS DOWN.
YOU KNOW THE ONLY THING THEY THOUGHT YOU WERE USEFUL FOR?
RAAAAH!
A GOOD, HARD LAUGH.

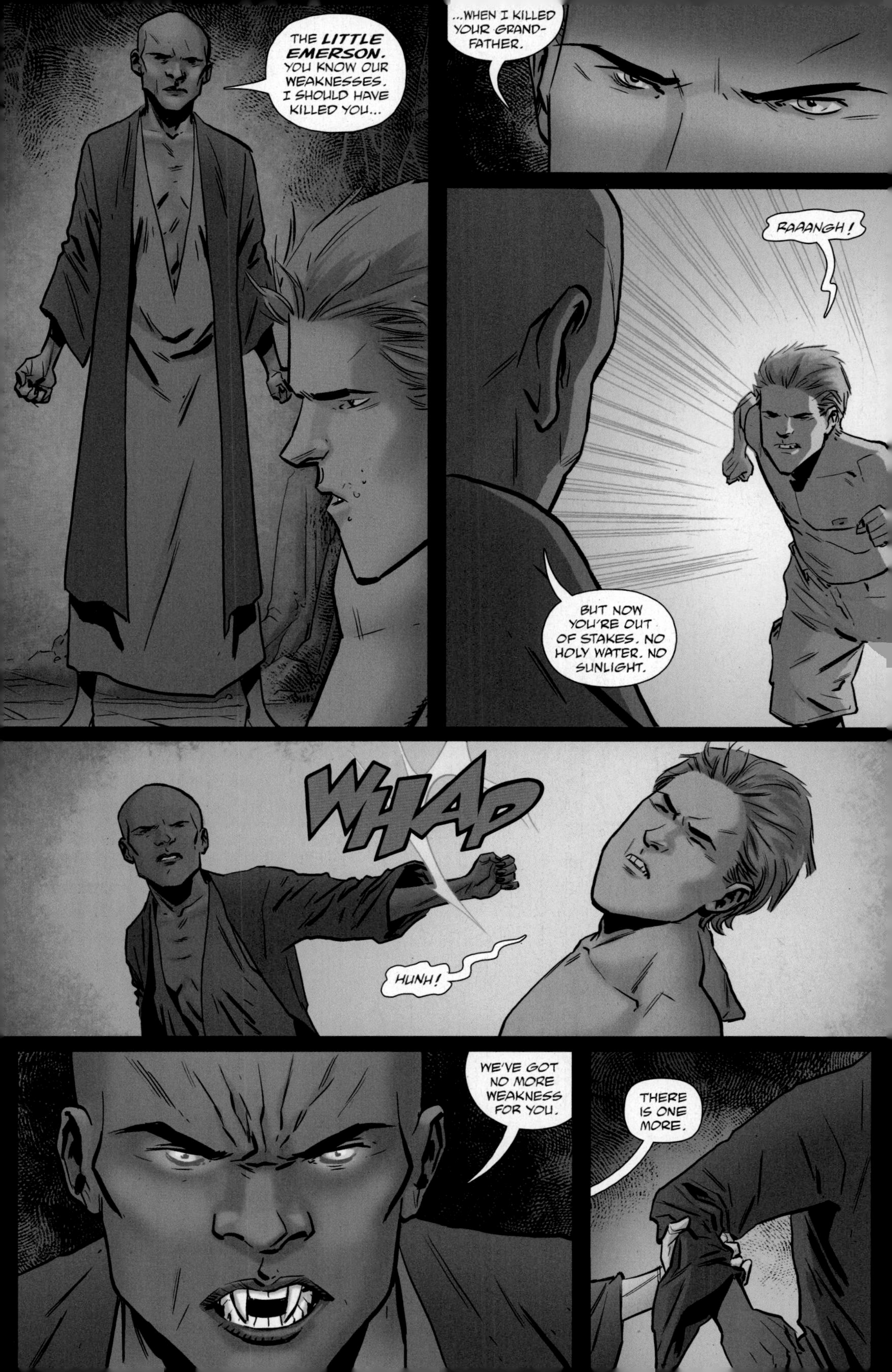
THE **LITTLE EMERSON.** YOU KNOW OUR WEAKNESSES. I SHOULD HAVE KILLED YOU...
...WHEN I KILLED YOUR GRAND-FATHER.
RAAANGH!
BUT NOW YOU'RE OUT OF STAKES. NO HOLY WATER. NO SUNLIGHT.
WHAP
HUNH!
WE'VE GOT NO MORE WEAKNESS FOR YOU.
THERE IS ONE MORE.

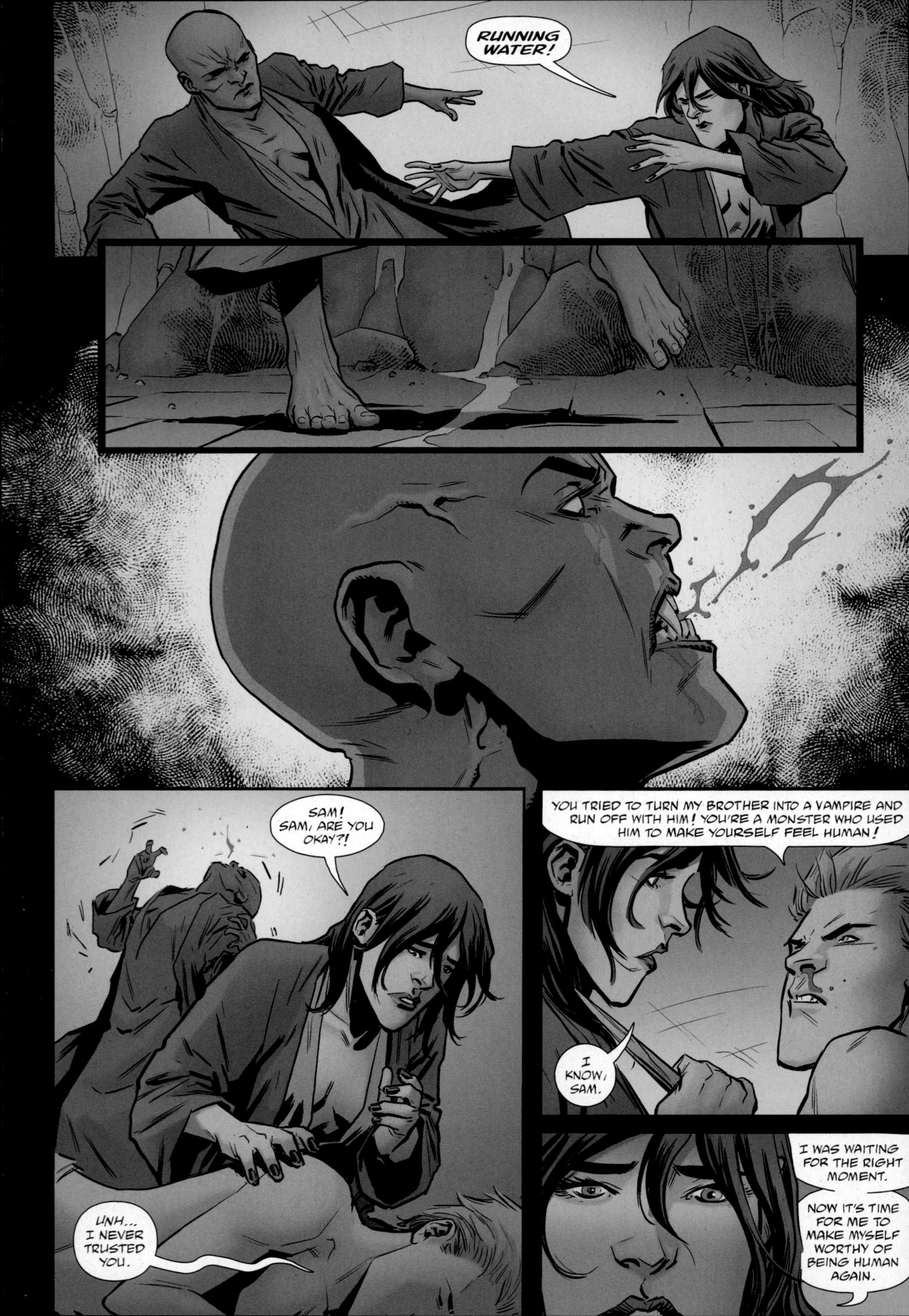
RUNNING WATER!
SAM! SAM, ARE YOU OKAY?!
UNH... I NEVER TRUSTED YOU.
YOU TRIED TO TURN MY BROTHER INTO A VAMPIRE AND RUN OFF WITH HIM! YOU'RE A MONSTER WHO USED HIM TO MAKE YOURSELF FEEL HUMAN!
I KNOW, SAM.
I WAS WAITING FOR THE RIGHT MOMENT.
NOW IT'S TIME FOR ME TO MAKE MYSELF WORTHY OF BEING HUMAN AGAIN.

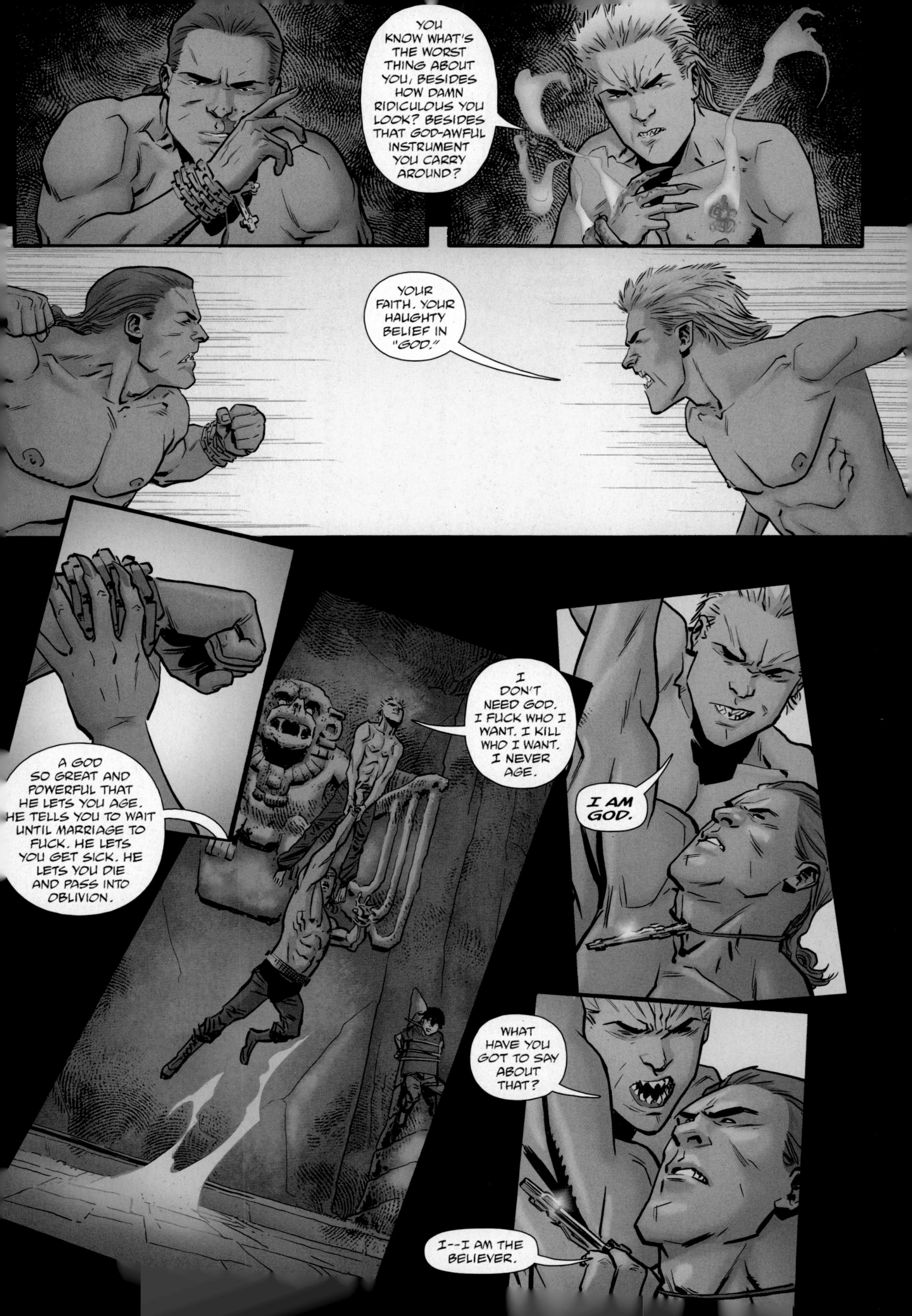
YOU KNOW WHAT'S THE WORST THING ABOUT YOU, BESIDES HOW DAMN RIDICULOUS YOU LOOK? BESIDES THAT GOD-AWFUL INSTRUMENT YOU CARRY AROUND?
YOUR FAITH. YOUR HAUGHTY BELIEF IN "GOD."
A GOD SO GREAT AND POWERFUL THAT HE LETS YOU AGE. HE TELLS YOU TO WAIT UNTIL MARRIAGE TO FUCK. HE LETS YOU GET SICK. HE LETS YOU DIE AND PASS INTO OBLIVION.
I DON'T NEED GOD. I FUCK WHO I WANT. I KILL WHO I WANT. I NEVER AGE.
I AM GOD.
WHAT HAVE YOU GOT TO SAY ABOUT THAT?
I--I AM THE BELIEVER.

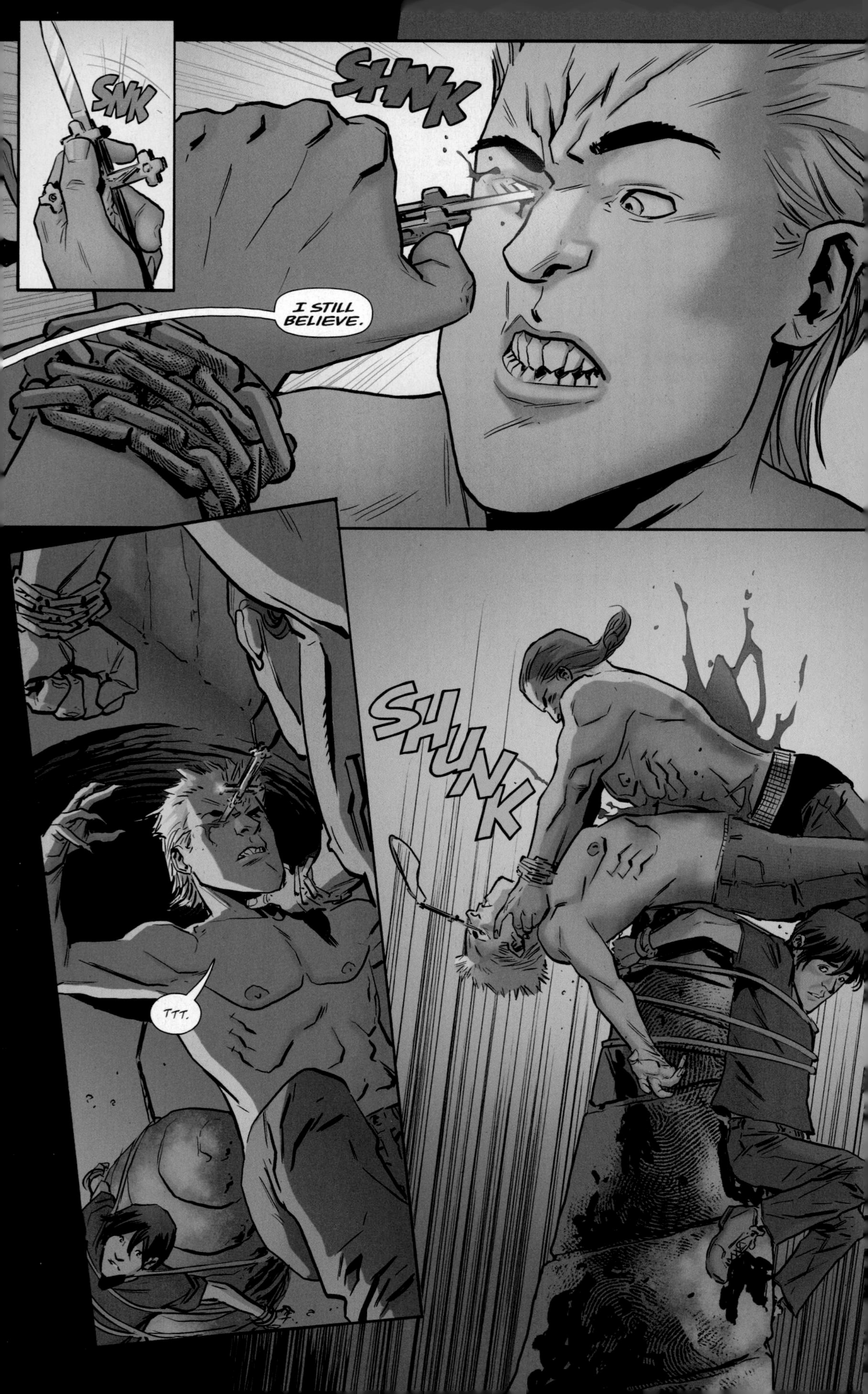
SNK
SHNK
I STILL BELIEVE.
TTT.
SHUNK

GAH! GET ME OFF THIS THING!

JUST CAN'T KEEP FROM GETTING IMPALED, HUH, SUCKHEAD?!

OH. NO. HE-- HE HELPED ME.

HE GAVE HIS LIFE TO EXTINGUISH THE HEART OF HELL. GO WITH GOD, BROTHER HUNTER.

WHAT THE HELL WAS THAT ALL ABOUT?!

WE...ME, EDGAR, AND YOUR BROTHER...WERE PART OF A SACRIFICE.

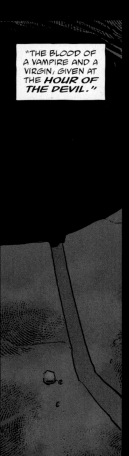

"THE BLOOD OF A VAMPIRE AND A VIRGIN, GIVEN AT THE HOUR OF THE DEVIL."

DAVID... HE IMPLIED MAYBE THAT GUY HAD NEVER DONE A BAD DANCE TO THE SQUEAKY SPRING BEAT.

RMMMBL

DO YOU HEAR THAT? IT'S ANOTHER EARTH-QUAKE!

SAM...

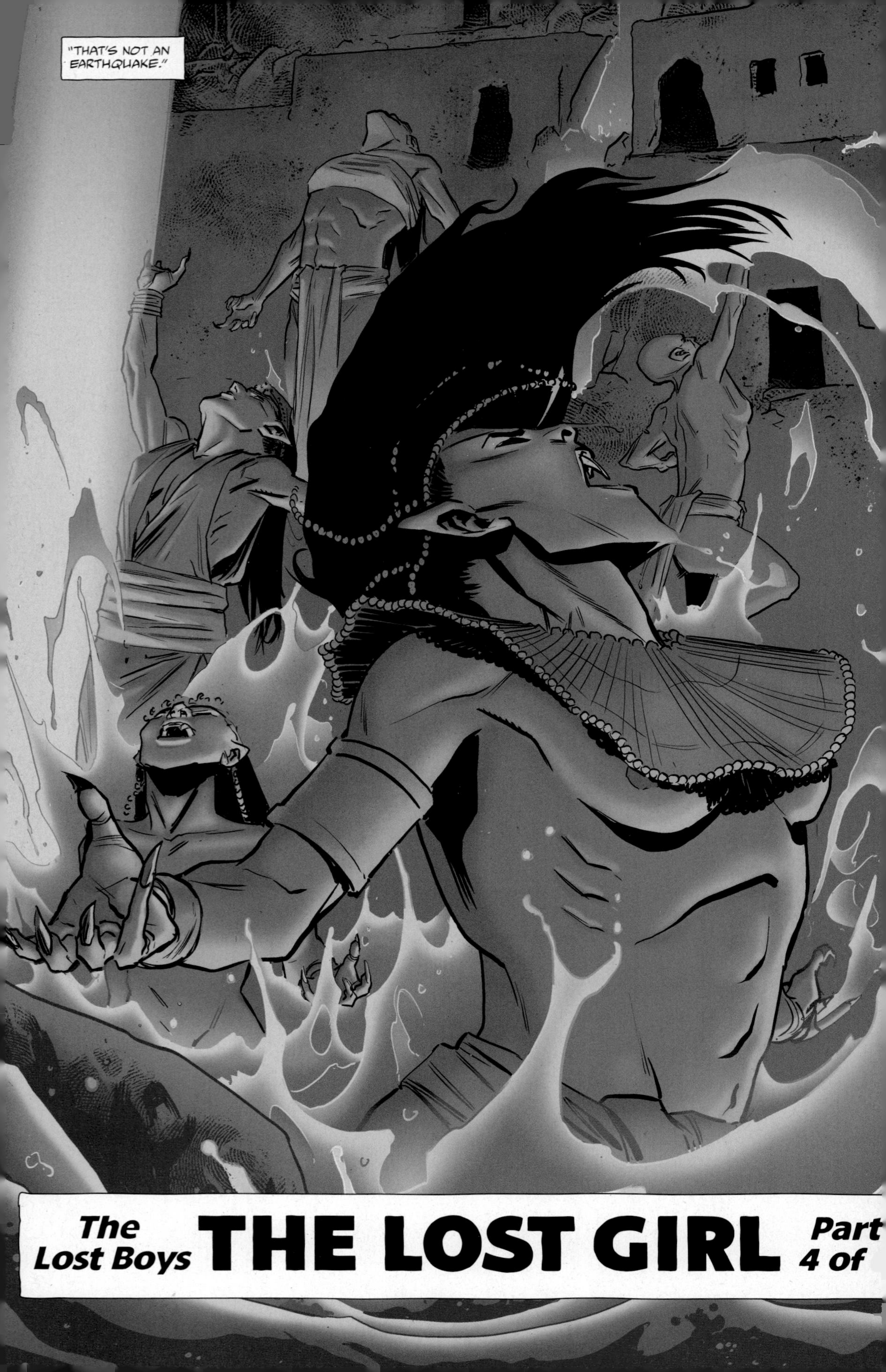
"THAT'S NOT AN EARTHQUAKE."
The Lost Boys
THE LOST GIRL
Part 4 of

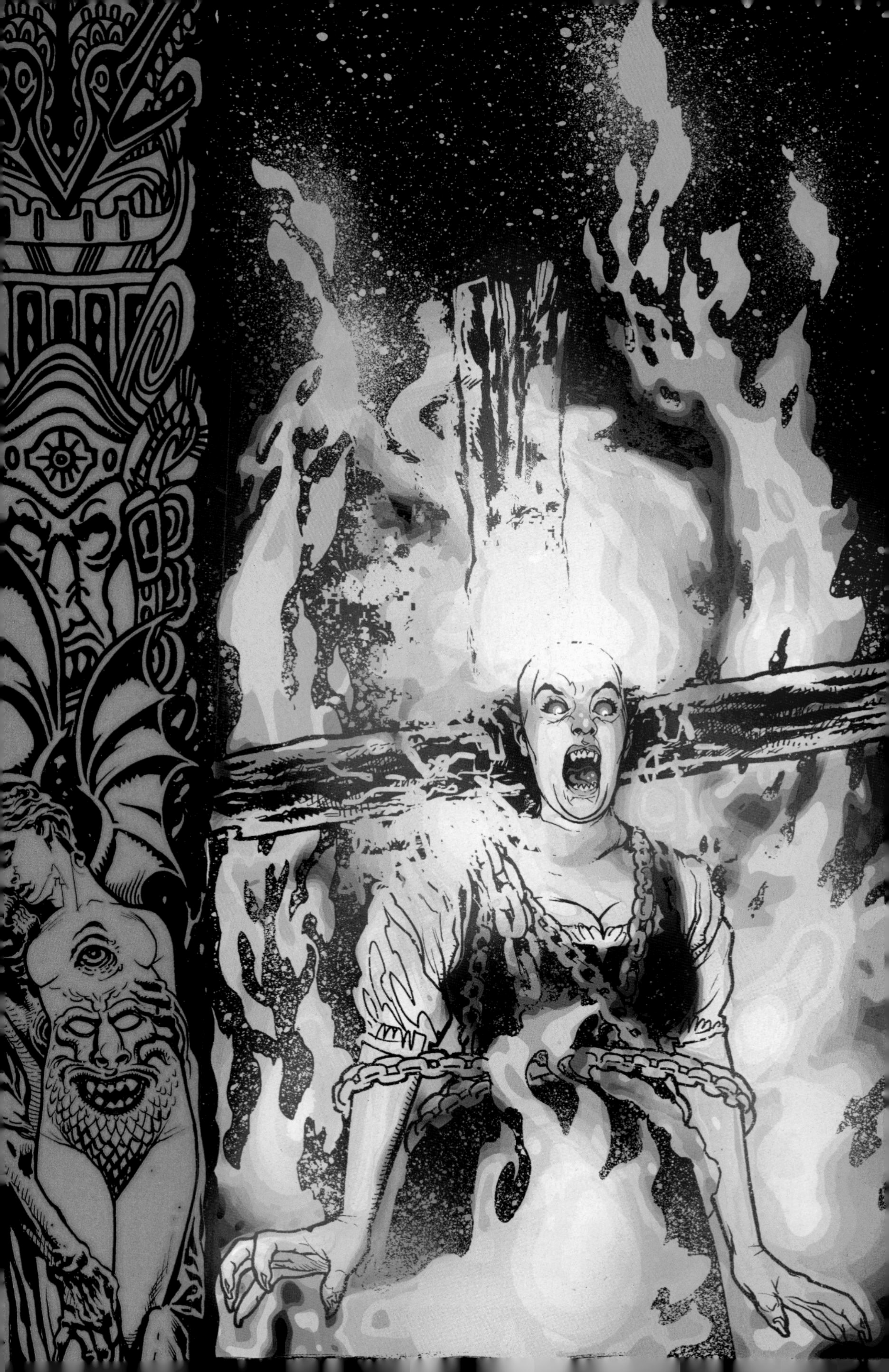

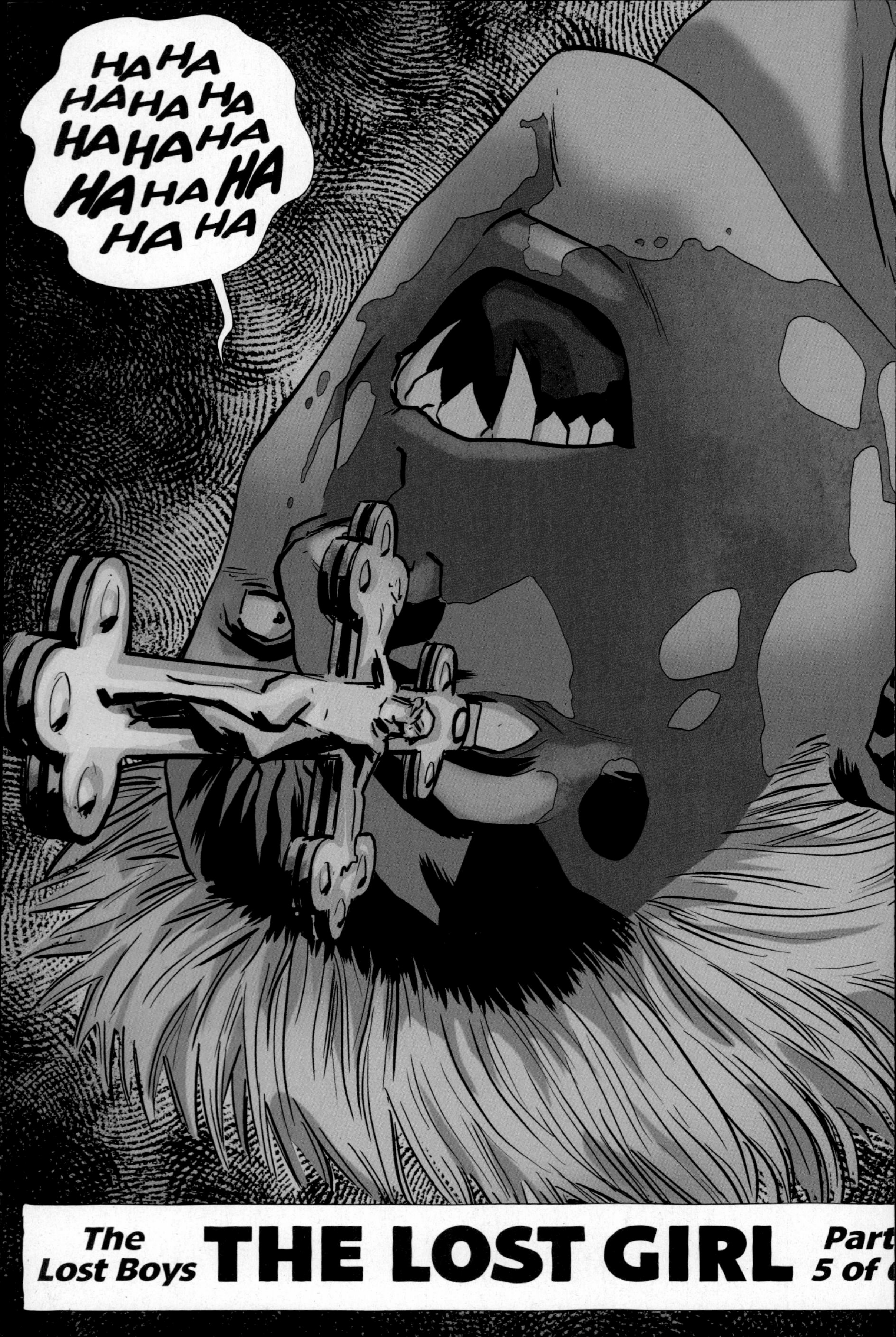
HAHA HAHAHAHA HAHAHAHA HAHAHAHA HAHA
The Lost Boys THE LOST GIRL Part 5 of

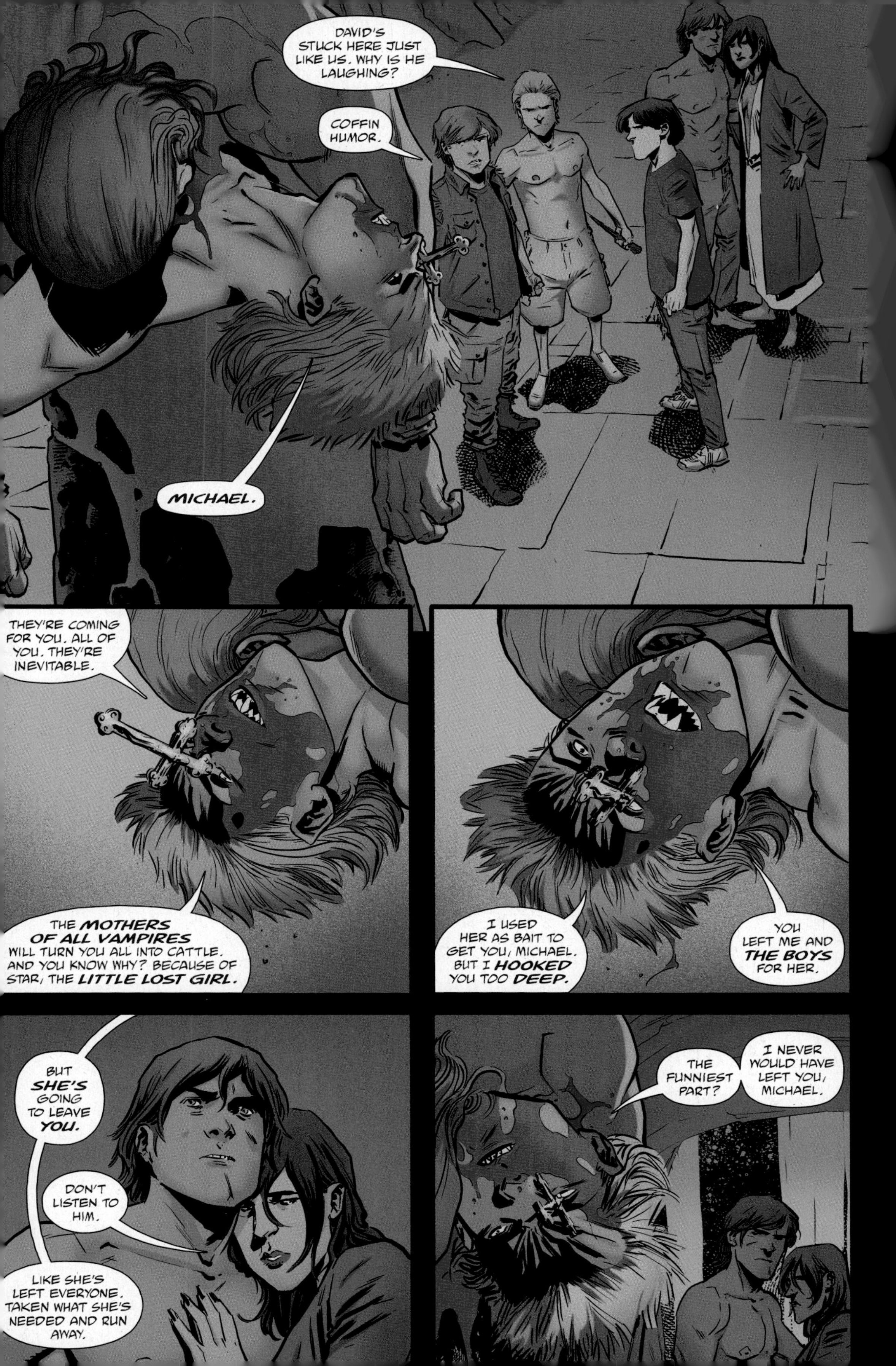
DAVID'S STUCK HERE JUST LIKE US. WHY IS HE LAUGHING?
COFFIN HUMOR.
MICHAEL.
THEY'RE COMING FOR YOU. ALL OF YOU. THEY'RE INEVITABLE.
THE MOTHERS OF ALL VAMPIRES WILL TURN YOU ALL INTO CATTLE. AND YOU KNOW WHY? BECAUSE OF STAR, THE LITTLE LOST GIRL.
I USED HER AS BAIT TO GET YOU, MICHAEL. BUT I HOOKED YOU TOO DEEP.
YOU LEFT ME AND THE BOYS FOR HER.
BUT SHE'S GOING TO LEAVE YOU.
DON'T LISTEN TO HIM.
LIKE SHE'S LEFT EVERYONE. TAKEN WHAT SHE'S NEEDED AND RUN AWAY.
THE FUNNIEST PART?
I NEVER WOULD HAVE LEFT YOU, MICHAEL.

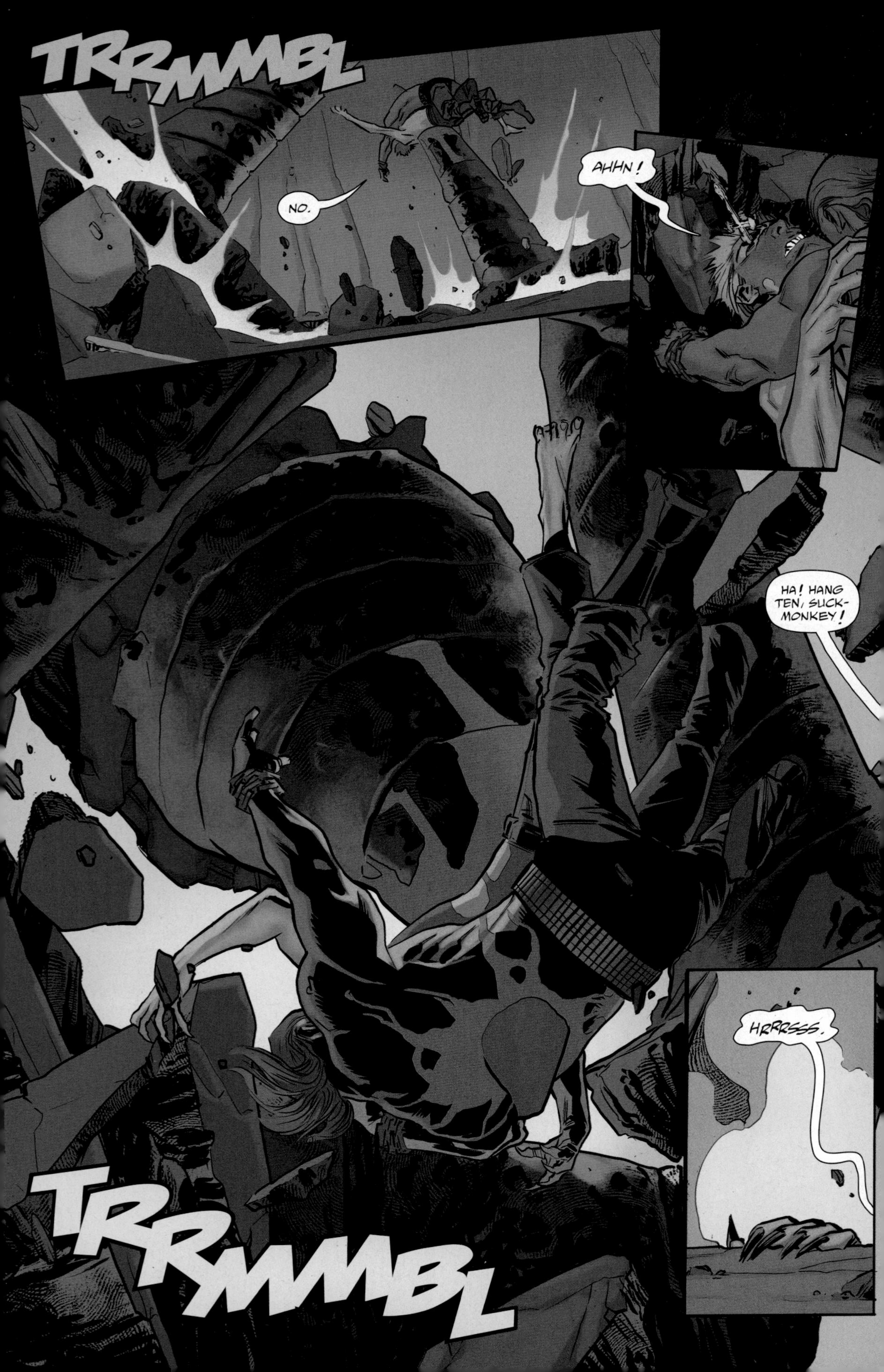
TRRMMBL
NO.
AHHN!
HA! HANG TEN, SUCK-MONKEY!
HRRRSSS.
TRRMMBL

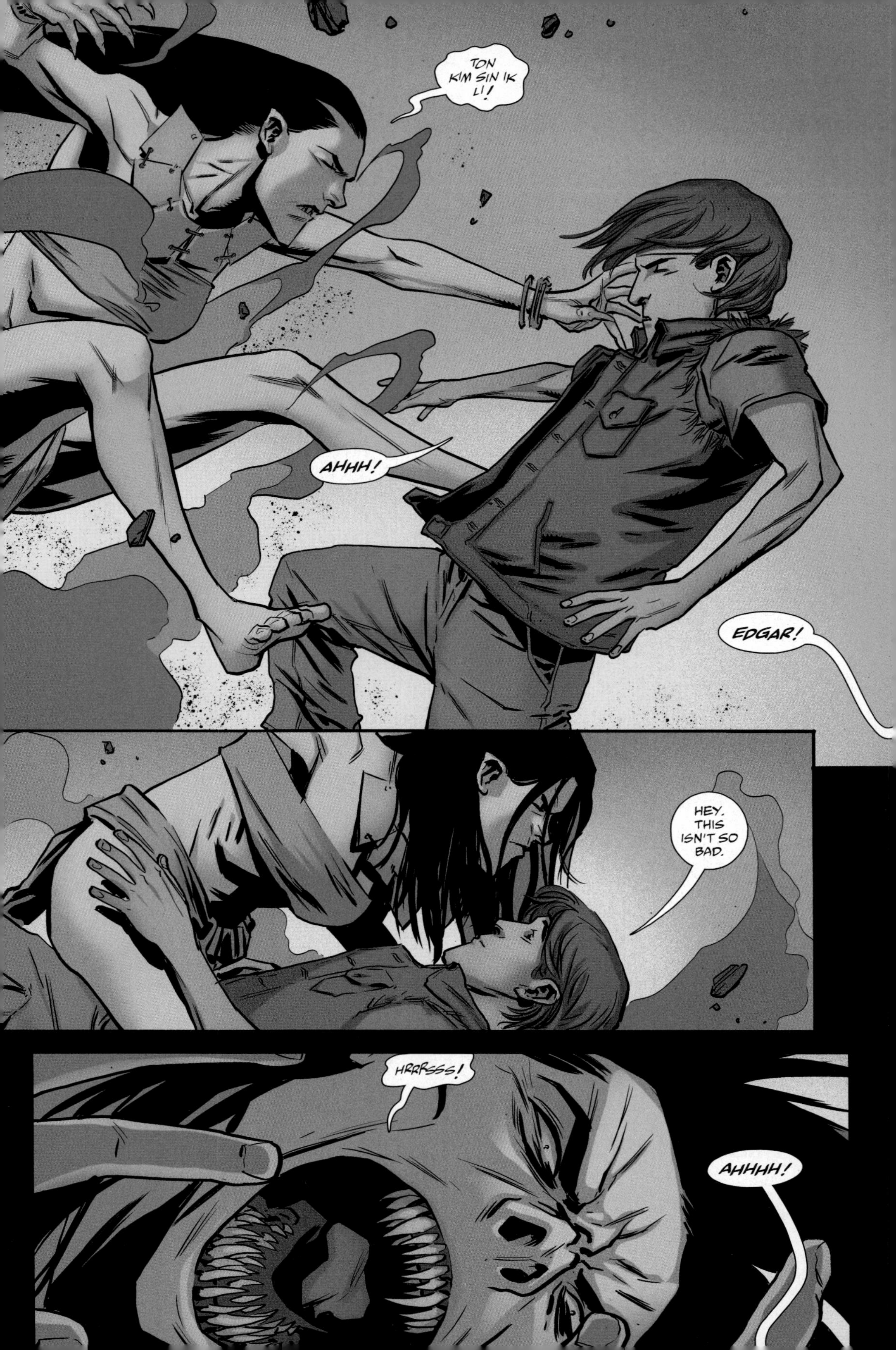
TON KIM SIN IK LI!
AHHH!
EDGAR!
HEY. THIS ISN'T SO BAD.
HRRRSSS!
AHHHH!

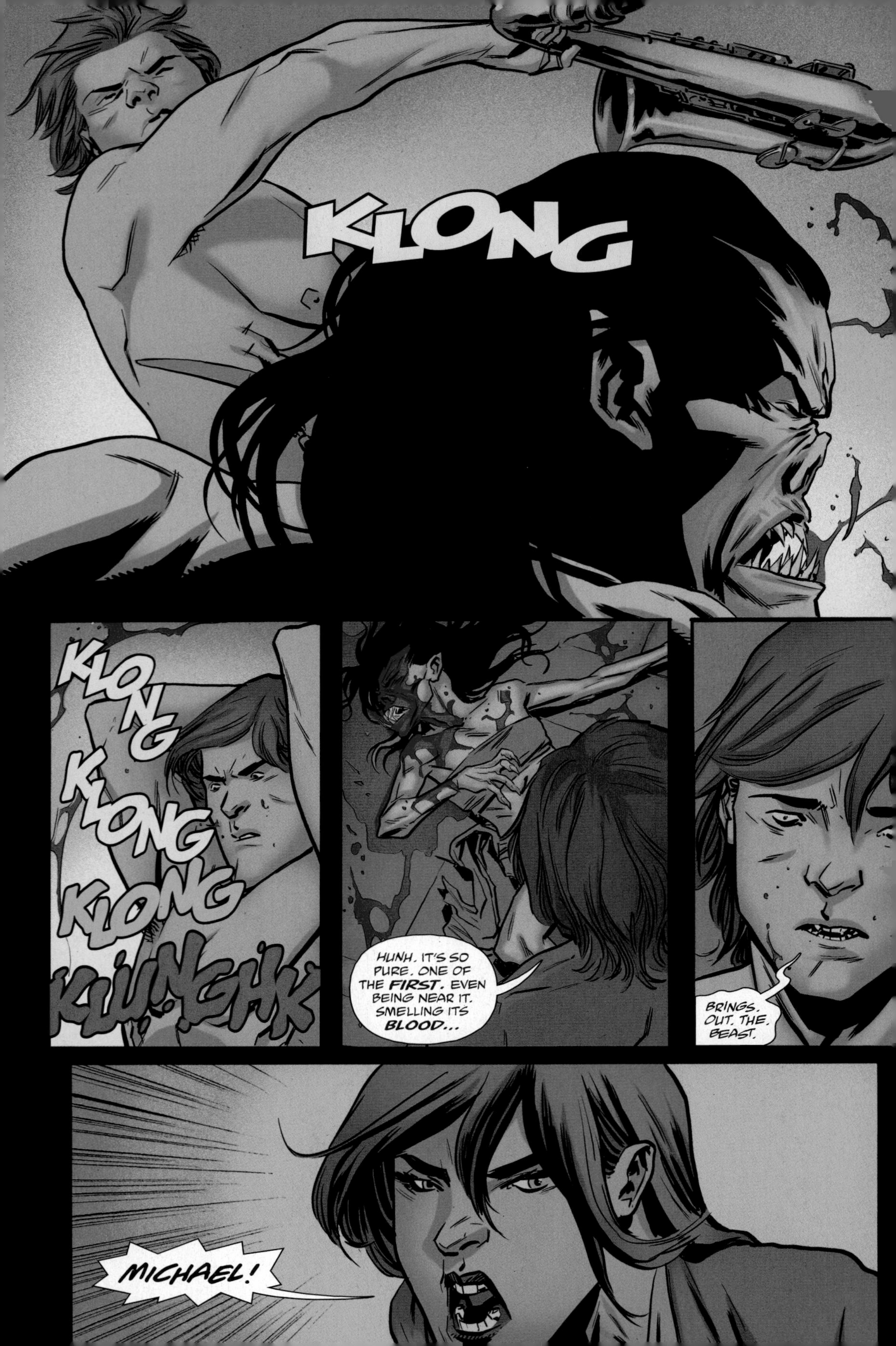
KLONG
KLONG
KLONG
KLONG
KLUNGHK
HUNH. IT'S SO PURE. ONE OF THE FIRST. EVEN BEING NEAR IT. SMELLING ITS BLOOD...
BRINGS. OUT. THE. BEAST.
MICHAEL!

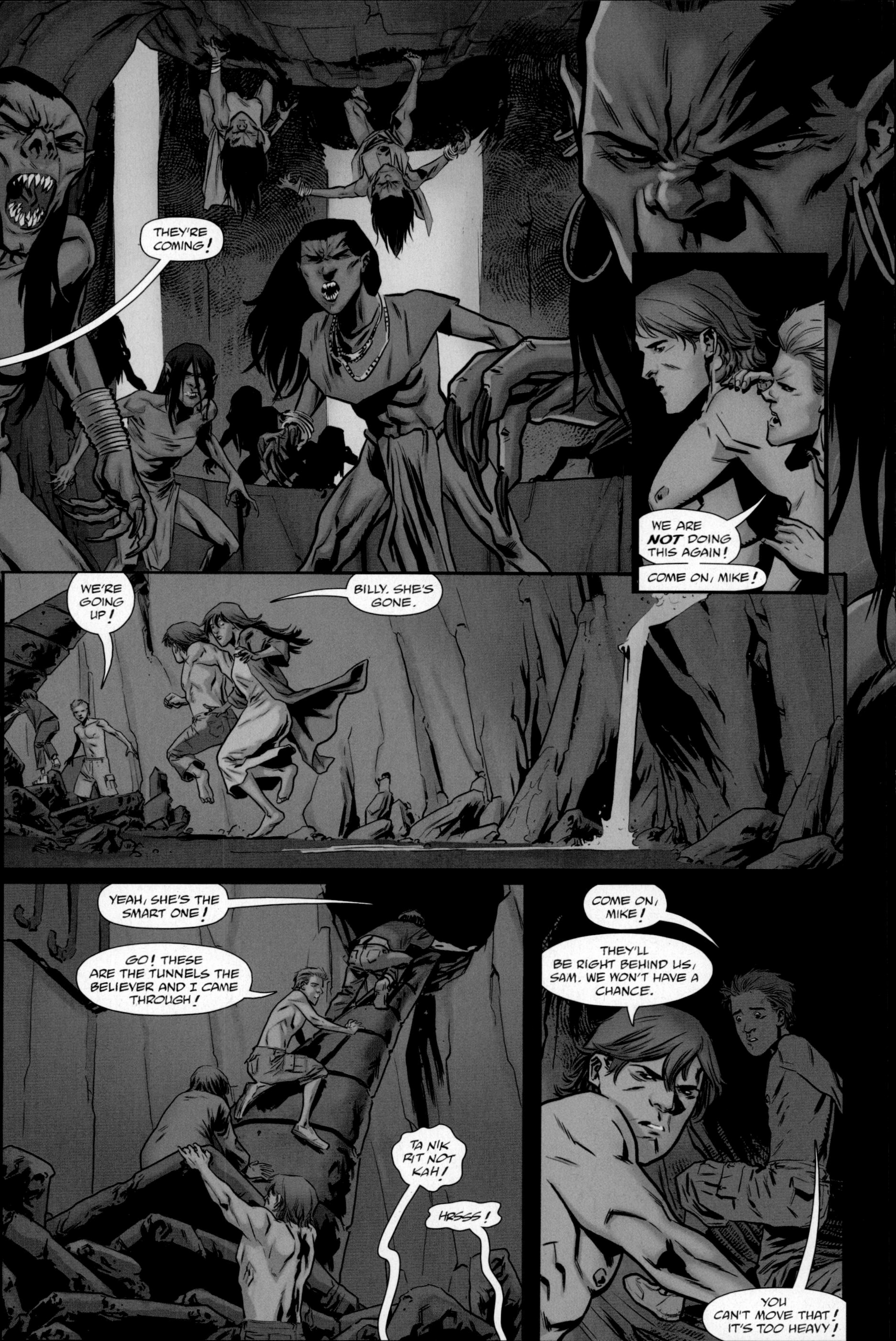
THEY'RE COMING!
WE ARE **NOT** DOING THIS AGAIN!
COME ON, MIKE!
WE'RE GOING UP!
BILLY. SHE'S GONE.
YEAH, SHE'S THE SMART ONE!
GO! THESE ARE THE TUNNELS THE BELIEVER AND I CAME THROUGH!
TA NIK RIT NOT KAH!
HRSSS!
COME ON, MIKE!
THEY'LL BE RIGHT BEHIND US, SAM. WE WON'T HAVE A CHANCE.
YOU CAN'T MOVE THAT! IT'S TOO HEAVY!

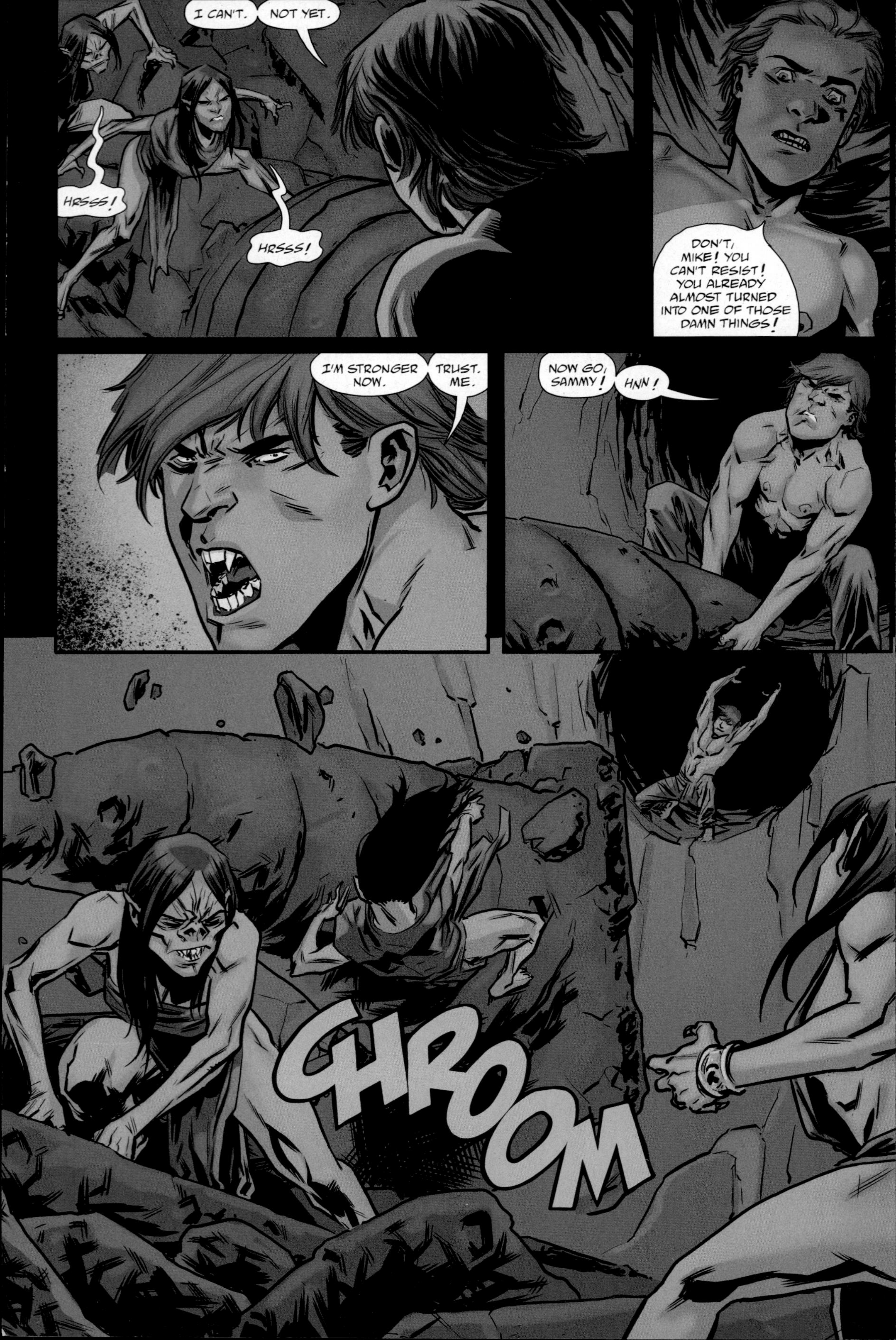

I CAN'T.
NOT YET.
HRSSS!
HRSSS!
DON'T, MIKE! YOU CAN'T RESIST! YOU ALREADY ALMOST TURNED INTO ONE OF THOSE DAMN THINGS!
I'M STRONGER NOW.
TRUST. ME.
NOW GO, SAMMY!
HNN!
CHROOM

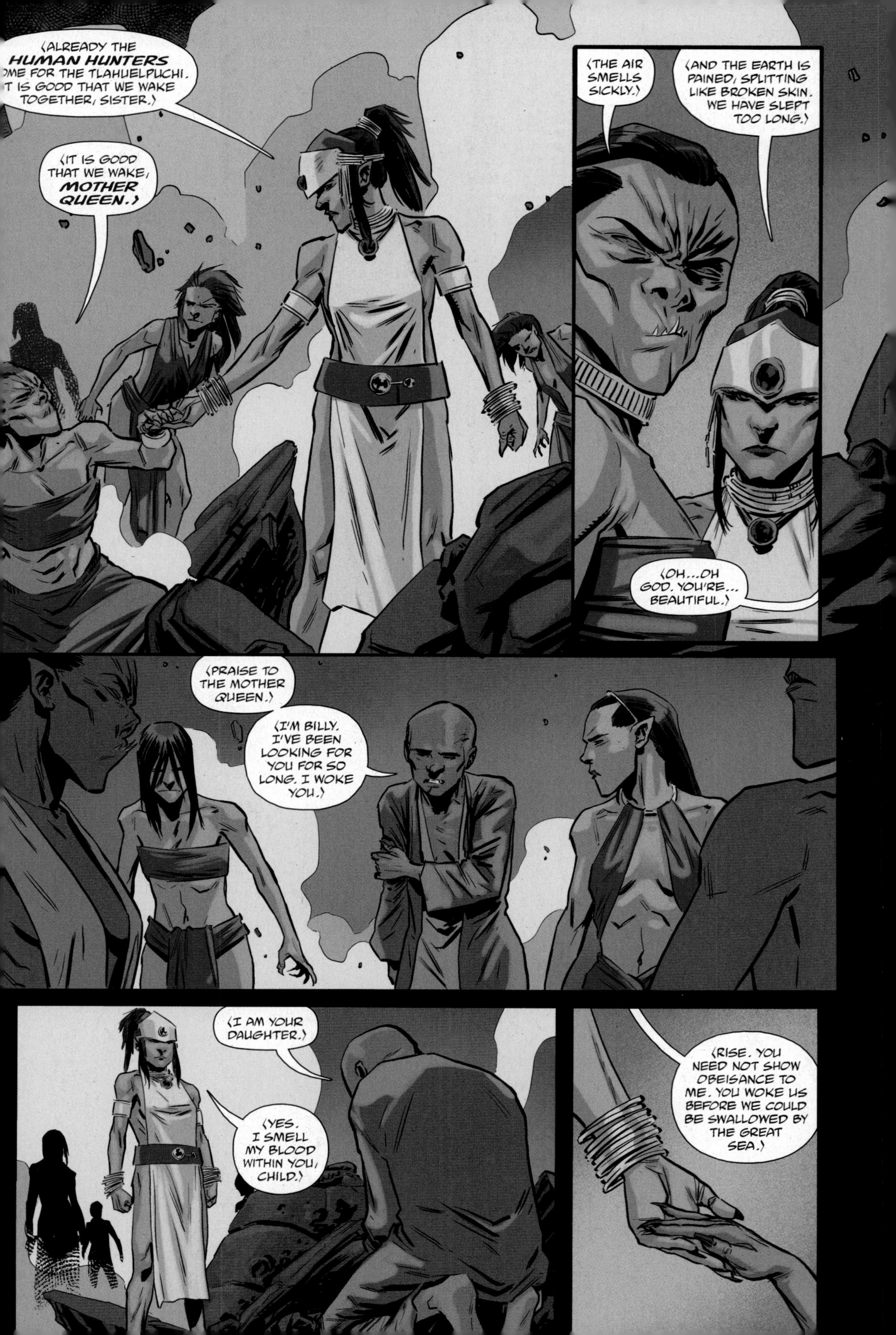

‹ALREADY THE HUMAN HUNTERS OME FOR THE TLAHUELPUCHI. T IS GOOD THAT WE WAKE TOGETHER, SISTER.›
‹IT IS GOOD THAT WE WAKE, MOTHER QUEEN.›
‹THE AIR SMELLS SICKLY.›
‹AND THE EARTH IS PAINED, SPLITTING LIKE BROKEN SKIN. WE HAVE SLEPT TOO LONG.›
‹OH...OH GOD. YOU'RE... BEAUTIFUL.›
‹PRAISE TO THE MOTHER QUEEN.›
‹I'M BILLY. I'VE BEEN LOOKING FOR YOU FOR SO LONG. I WOKE YOU.›
‹I AM YOUR DAUGHTER.›
‹YES. I SMELL MY BLOOD WITHIN YOU, CHILD.›
‹RISE. YOU NEED NOT SHOW OBEISANCE TO ME. YOU WOKE US BEFORE WE COULD BE SWALLOWED BY THE GREAT SEA.›

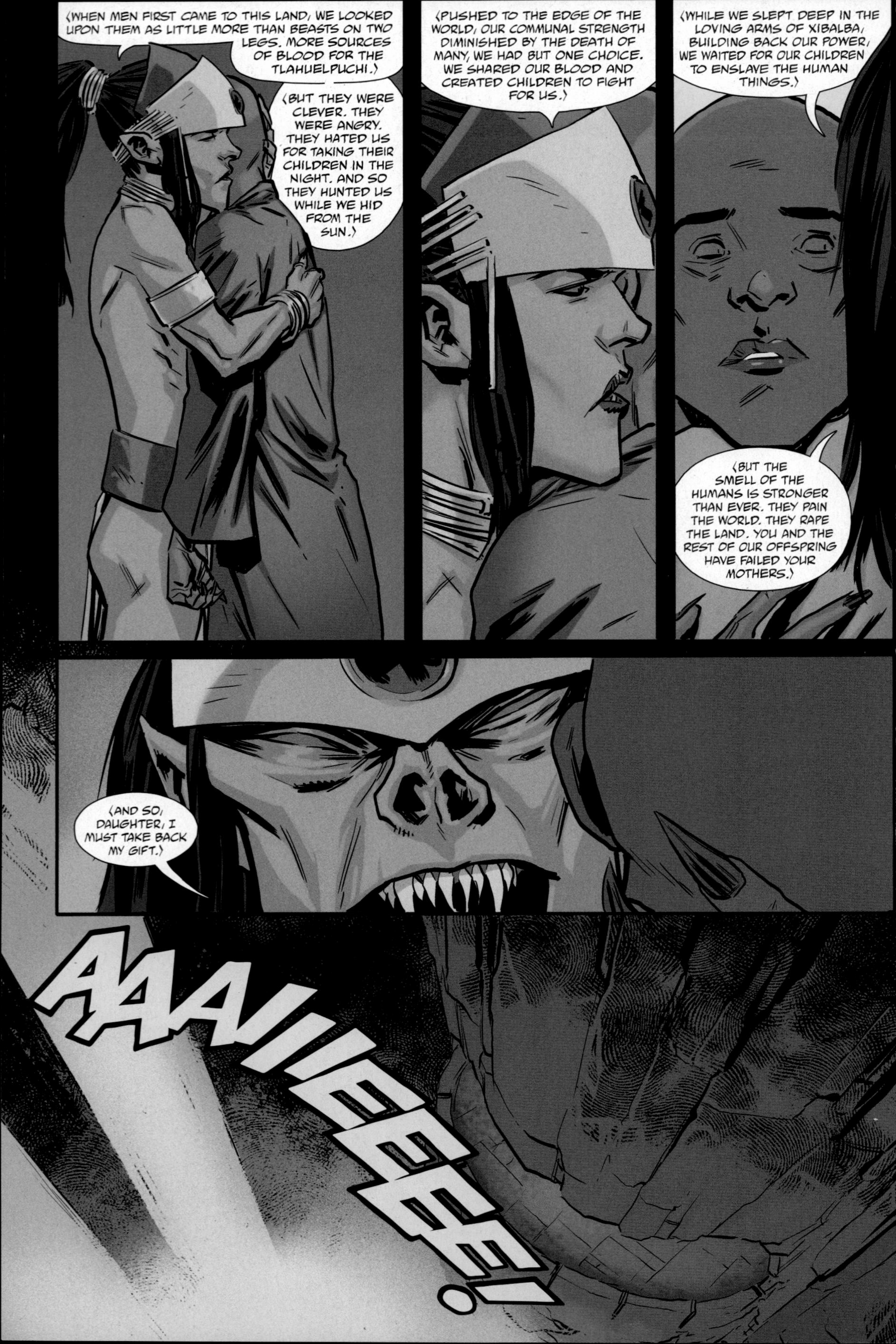
‹WHEN MEN FIRST CAME TO THIS LAND, WE LOOKED UPON THEM AS LITTLE MORE THAN BEASTS ON TWO LEGS. MORE SOURCES OF BLOOD FOR THE TLAHUELPUCHI.›
‹BUT THEY WERE CLEVER. THEY WERE ANGRY. THEY HATED US FOR TAKING THEIR CHILDREN IN THE NIGHT. AND SO THEY HUNTED US WHILE WE HID FROM THE SUN.›
‹PUSHED TO THE EDGE OF THE WORLD, OUR COMMUNAL STRENGTH DIMINISHED BY THE DEATH OF MANY, WE HAD BUT ONE CHOICE. WE SHARED OUR BLOOD AND CREATED CHILDREN TO FIGHT FOR US.›
‹WHILE WE SLEPT DEEP IN THE LOVING ARMS OF XIBALBA, BUILDING BACK OUR POWER, WE WAITED FOR OUR CHILDREN TO ENSLAVE THE HUMAN THINGS.›
‹BUT THE SMELL OF THE HUMANS IS STRONGER THAN EVER. THEY PAIN THE WORLD. THEY RAPE THE LAND. YOU AND THE REST OF OUR OFFSPRING HAVE FAILED YOUR MOTHERS.›
‹AND SO, DAUGHTER, I MUST TAKE BACK MY GIFT.›
AAAIIEEEEE!

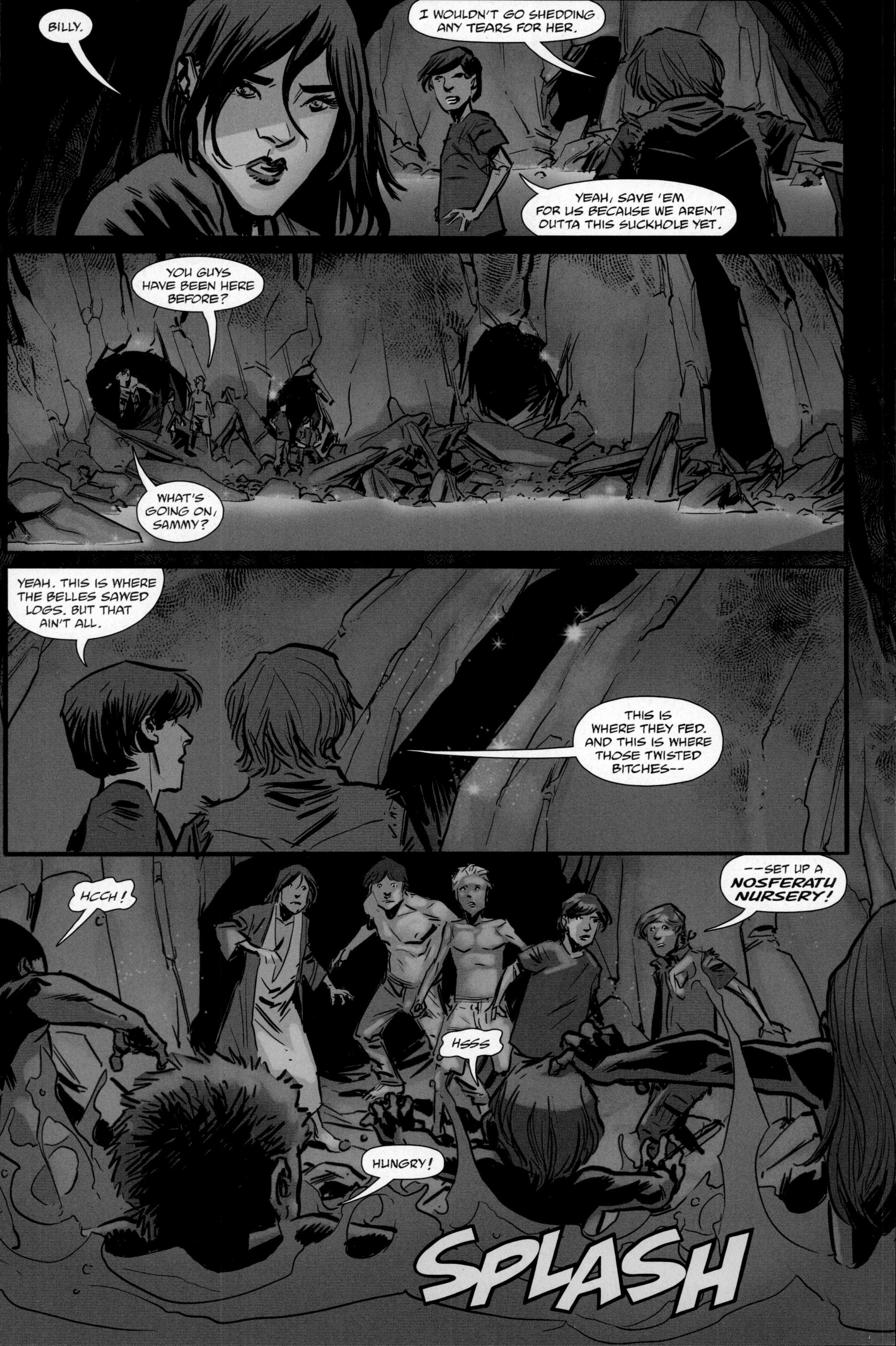
BILLY.
I WOULDN'T GO SHEDDING ANY TEARS FOR HER.
YEAH, SAVE 'EM FOR US BECAUSE WE AREN'T OUTTA THIS SUCKHOLE YET.
YOU GUYS HAVE BEEN HERE BEFORE?
WHAT'S GOING ON, SAMMY?
YEAH. THIS IS WHERE THE BELLES SAWED LOGS. BUT THAT AIN'T ALL.
THIS IS WHERE THEY FED. AND THIS IS WHERE THOSE TWISTED BITCHES--
HCCH!
--SET UP A NOSFERATU NURSERY!
HSSS
HUNGRY!
SPLASH

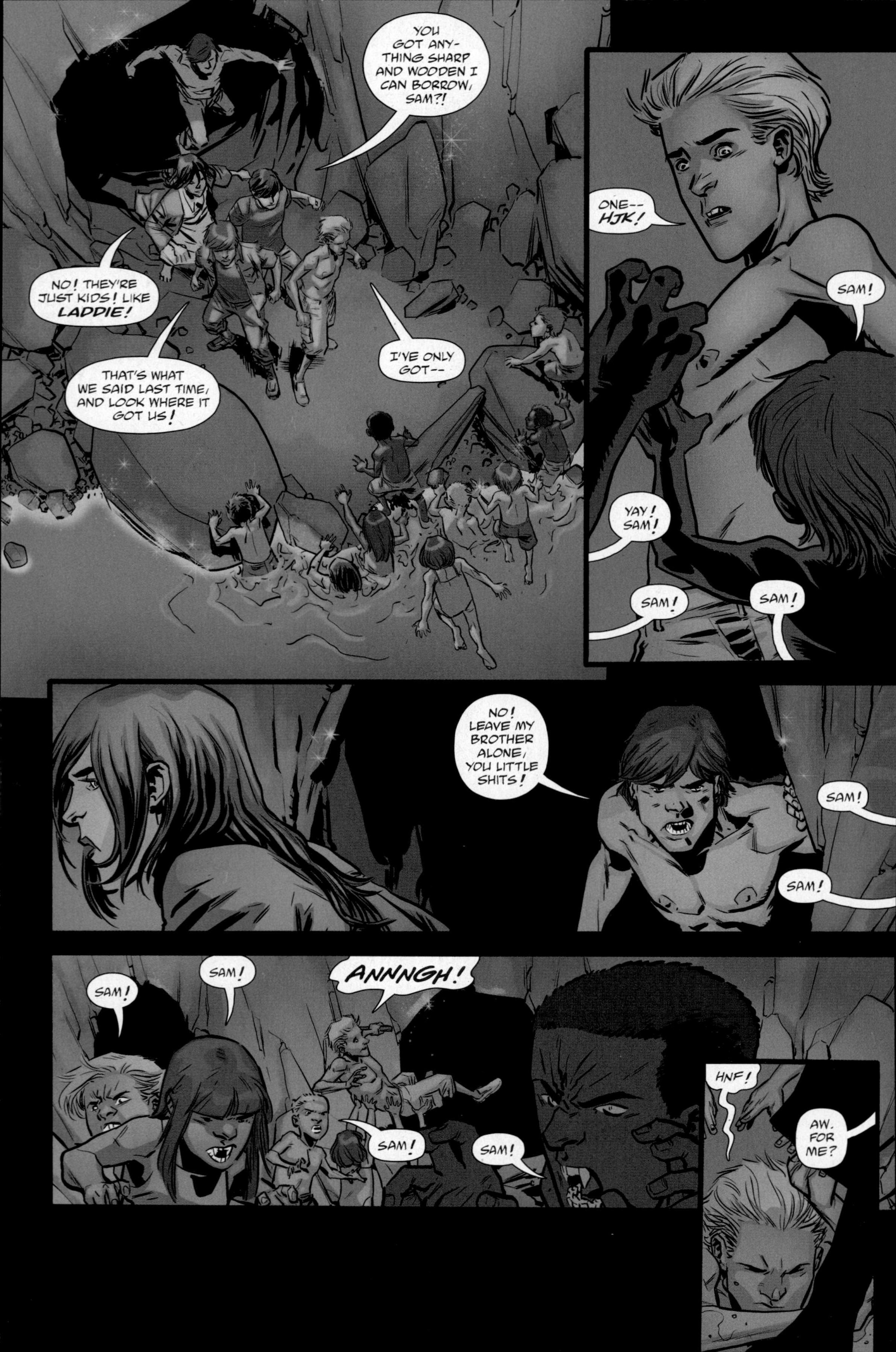
YOU GOT ANY-THING SHARP AND WOODEN I CAN BORROW, SAM?!
NO! THEY'RE JUST KIDS! LIKE LADDIE!
THAT'S WHAT WE SAID LAST TIME, AND LOOK WHERE IT GOT US!
I'VE ONLY GOT--
ONE-- HJK!
SAM!
YAY! SAM!
SAM!
SAM!
NO! LEAVE MY BROTHER ALONE, YOU LITTLE SHITS!
SAM!
SAM!
SAM!
SAM!
ANNNGH!
SAM!
SAM!
HNF!
AW. FOR ME?

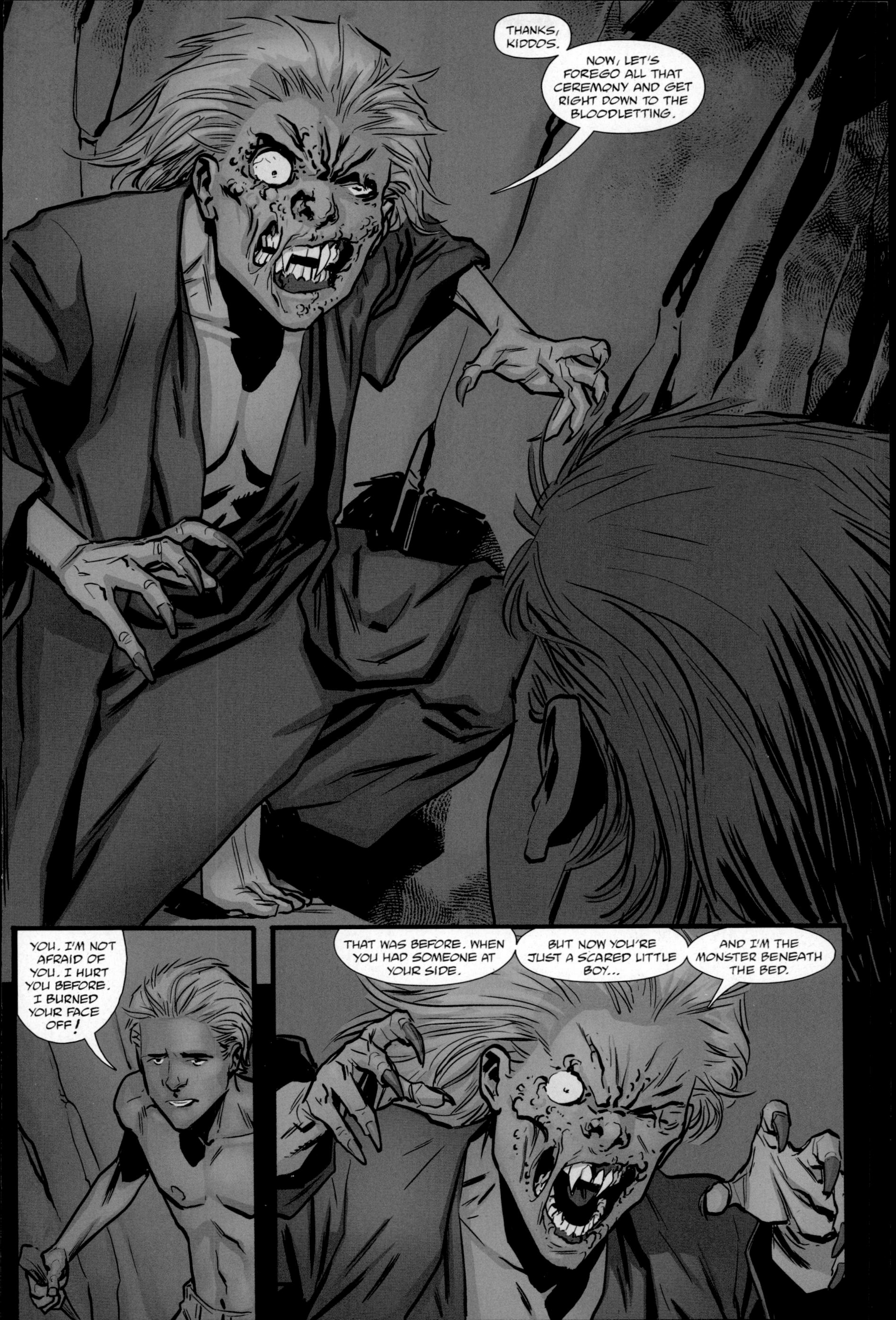
THANKS, KIDDOS.
NOW, LET'S FOREGO ALL THAT CEREMONY AND GET RIGHT DOWN TO THE BLOODLETTING.
YOU. I'M NOT AFRAID OF YOU. I HURT YOU BEFORE. I BURNED YOUR FACE OFF!
THAT WAS BEFORE. WHEN YOU HAD SOMEONE AT YOUR SIDE.
BUT NOW YOU'RE JUST A SCARED LITTLE BOY...
AND I'M THE MONSTER BENEATH THE BED.

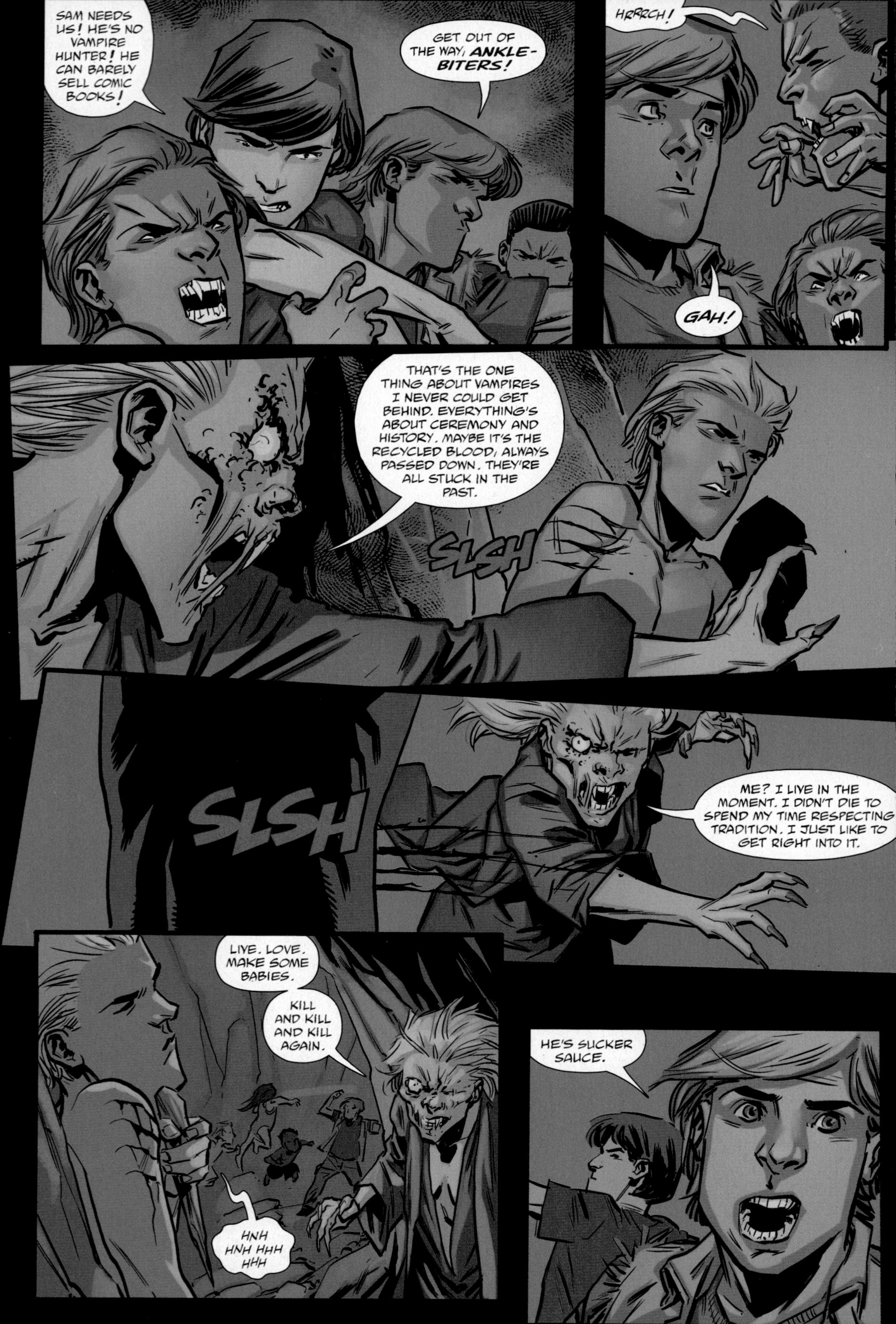
SAM NEEDS US! HE'S NO VAMPIRE HUNTER! HE CAN BARELY SELL COMIC BOOKS!
GET OUT OF THE WAY, ANKLE-BITERS!
HRRRCH!
GAH!
THAT'S THE ONE THING ABOUT VAMPIRES I NEVER COULD GET BEHIND. EVERYTHING'S ABOUT CEREMONY AND HISTORY. MAYBE IT'S THE RECYCLED BLOOD, ALWAYS PASSED DOWN. THEY'RE ALL STUCK IN THE PAST.
SLSH
SLSH
ME? I LIVE IN THE MOMENT. I DIDN'T DIE TO SPEND MY TIME RESPECTING TRADITION. I JUST LIKE TO GET RIGHT INTO IT.
LIVE. LOVE. MAKE SOME BABIES.
KILL AND KILL AND KILL AGAIN.
HNH HNH HHH HHH
HE'S SUCKER SAUCE.

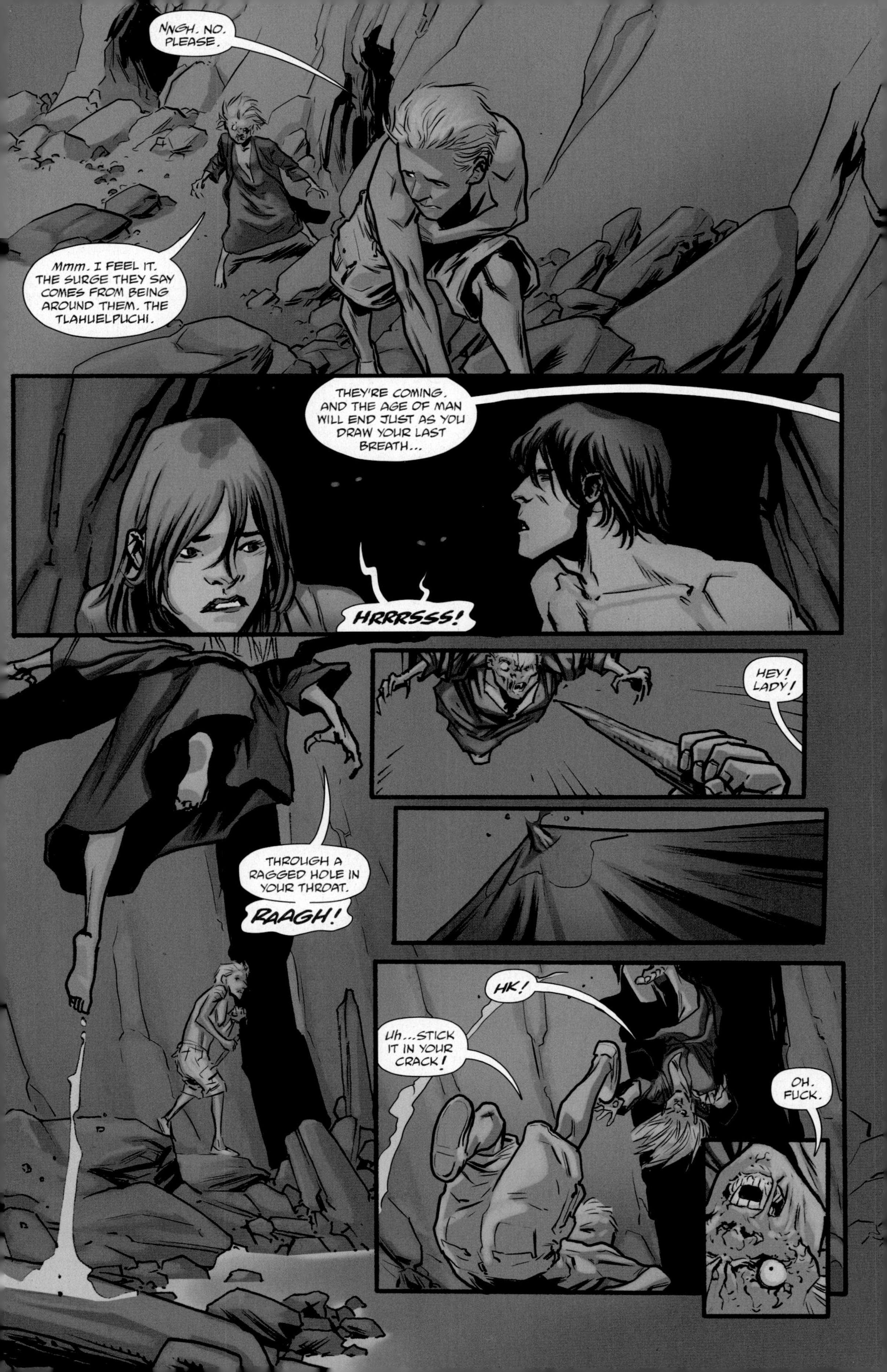
NNGH. NO. PLEASE.
Mmm. I FEEL IT. THE SURGE THEY SAY COMES FROM BEING AROUND THEM. THE TLAHUELPUCHI.
THEY'RE COMING. AND THE AGE OF MAN WILL END JUST AS YOU DRAW YOUR LAST BREATH...
HRRRSSS!
THROUGH A RAGGED HOLE IN YOUR THROAT.
RAAGH!
HEY! LADY!
HK!
Uh...STICK IT IN YOUR CRACK!
OH. FUCK.

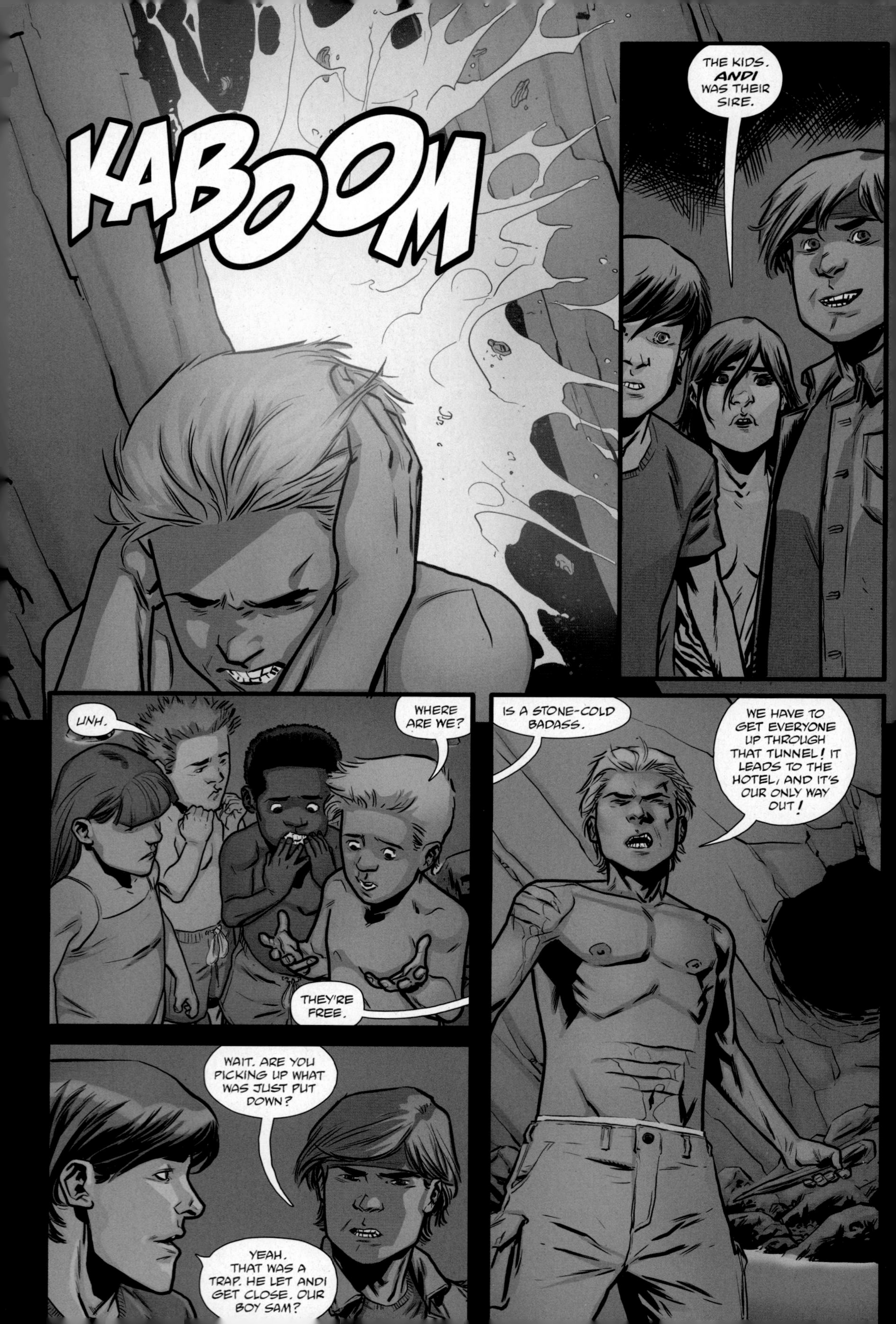
KABOOM
THE KIDS. ANDI WAS THEIR SIRE.
UNH.
WHERE ARE WE?
THEY'RE FREE.
IS A STONE-COLD BADASS.
WE HAVE TO GET EVERYONE UP THROUGH THAT TUNNEL! IT LEADS TO THE HOTEL, AND IT'S OUR ONLY WAY OUT!
WAIT. ARE YOU PICKING UP WHAT WAS JUST PUT DOWN?
YEAH. THAT WAS A TRAP. HE LET ANDI GET CLOSE. OUR BOY SAM?

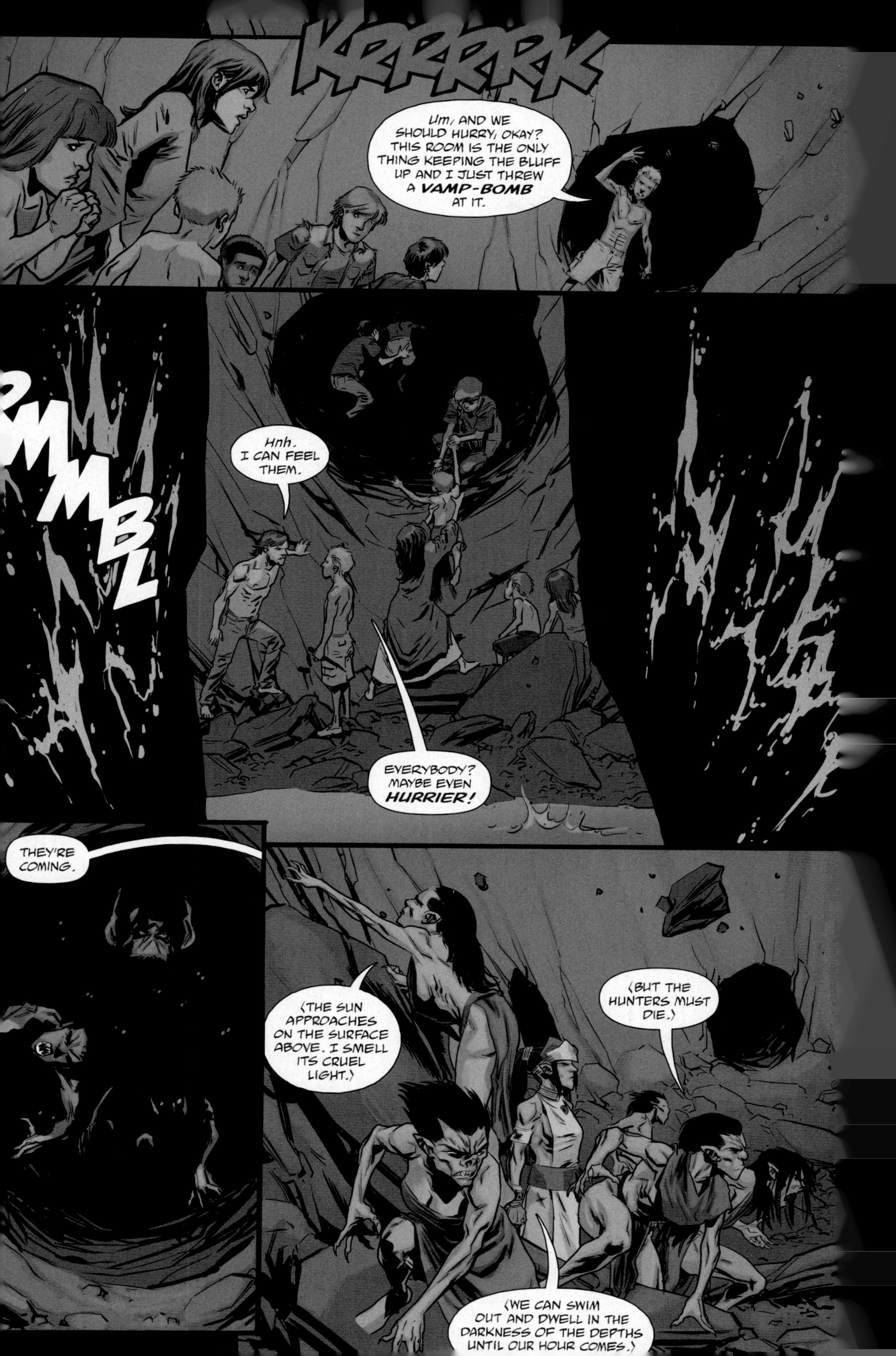
KRRRRK
Um, AND WE SHOULD HURRY, OKAY? THIS ROOM IS THE ONLY THING KEEPING THE BLUFF UP AND I JUST THREW A VAMP-BOMB AT IT.
MMBL
Hnh. I CAN FEEL THEM.
EVERYBODY? MAYBE EVEN HURRIER!
THEY'RE COMING.
‹THE SUN APPROACHES ON THE SURFACE ABOVE. I SMELL ITS CRUEL LIGHT.›
‹BUT THE HUNTERS MUST DIE.›
‹WE CAN SWIM OUT AND DWELL IN THE DARKNESS OF THE DEPTHS UNTIL OUR HOUR COMES.›

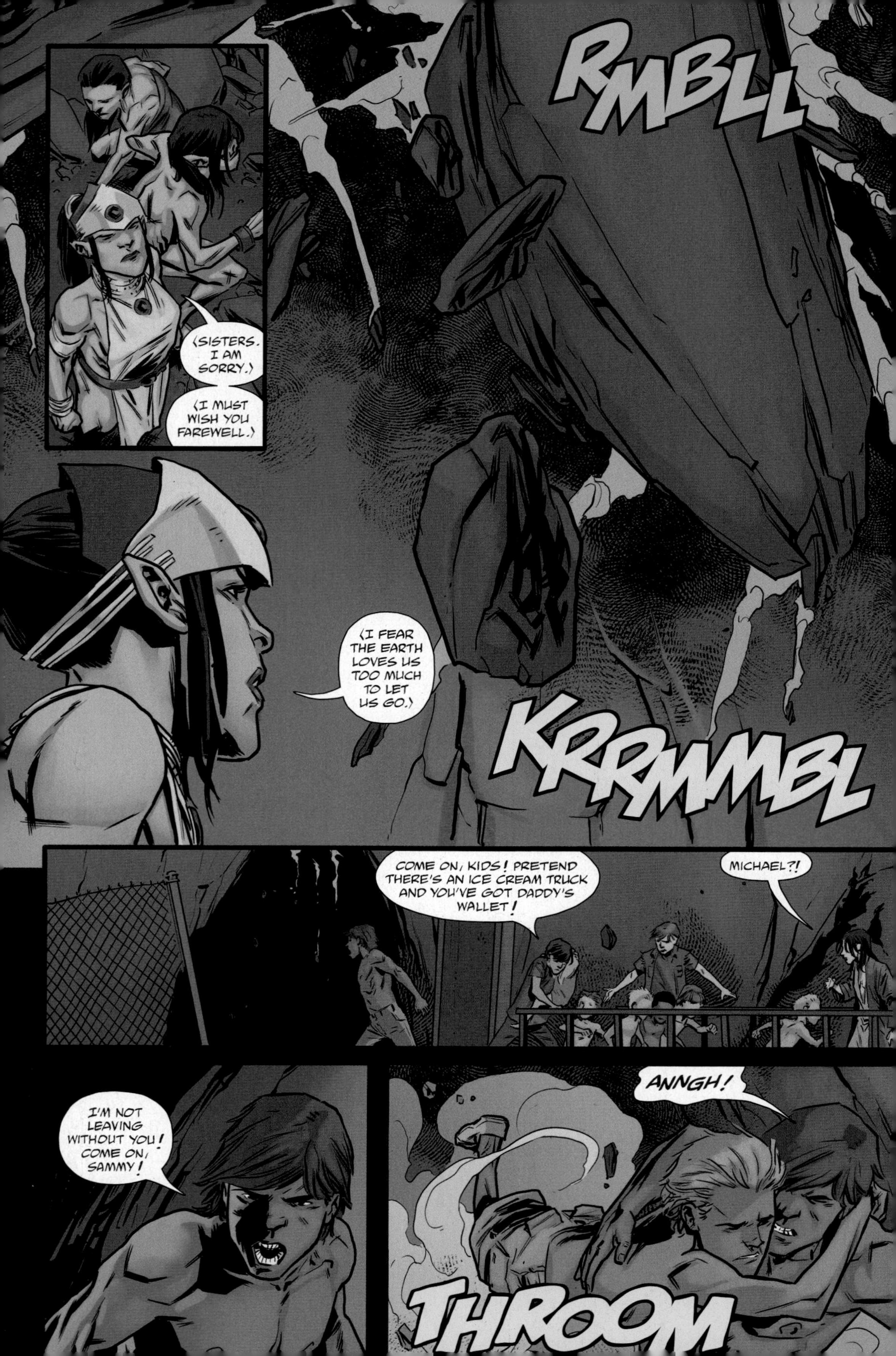
RMBLL
⟨SISTERS. I AM SORRY.⟩
⟨I MUST WISH YOU FAREWELL.⟩
⟨I FEAR THE EARTH LOVES US TOO MUCH TO LET US GO.⟩
KRRMMBL
COME ON, KIDS! PRETEND THERE'S AN ICE CREAM TRUCK AND YOU'VE GOT DADDY'S WALLET!
MICHAEL?!
I'M NOT LEAVING WITHOUT YOU! COME ON, SAMMY!
ANNGH!
THROOM

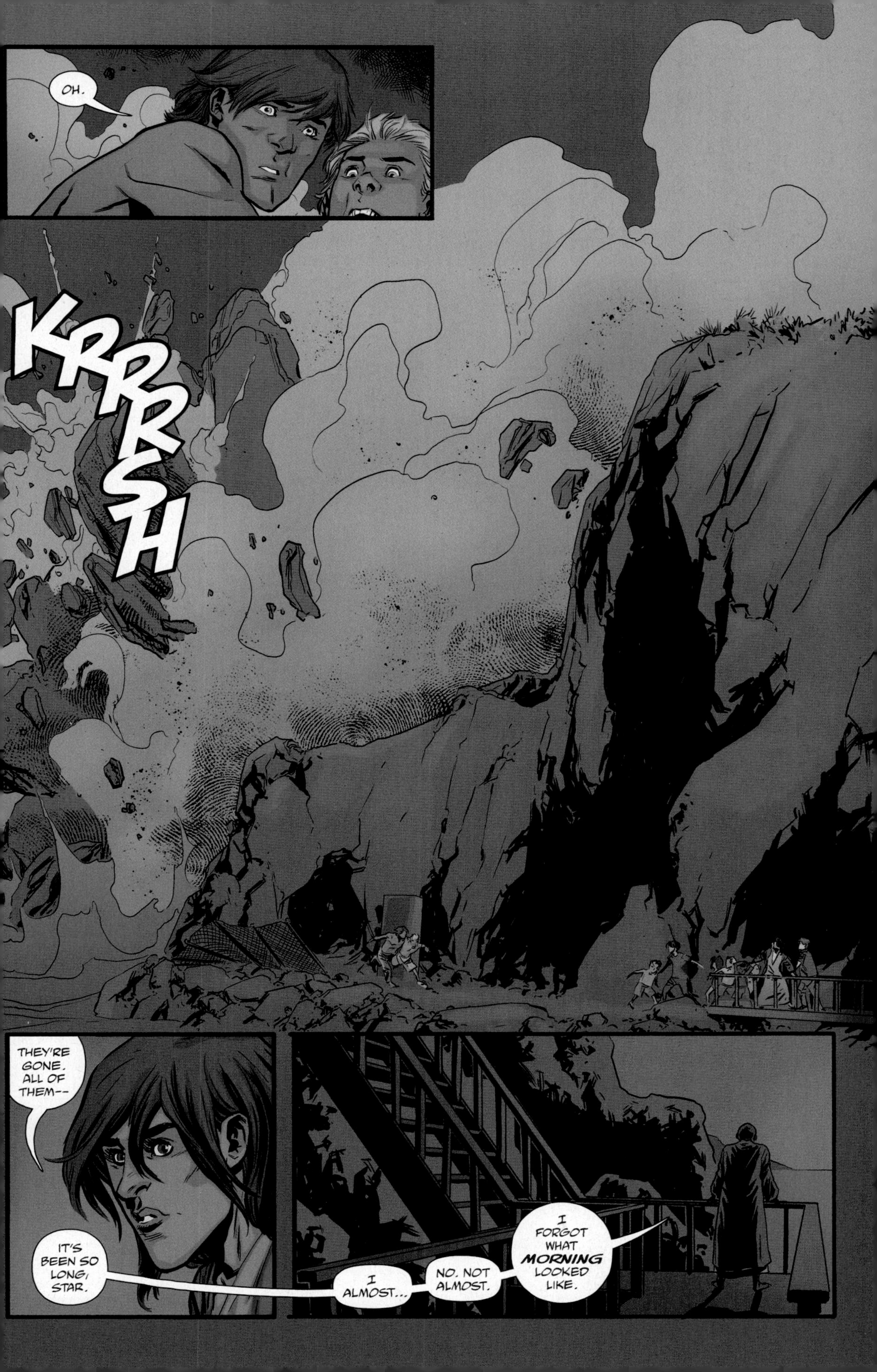
OH.
KRRRSH
THEY'RE GONE. ALL OF THEM--
IT'S BEEN SO LONG, STAR.
I ALMOST...
NO. NOT ALMOST.
I FORGOT WHAT MORNING LOOKED LIKE.

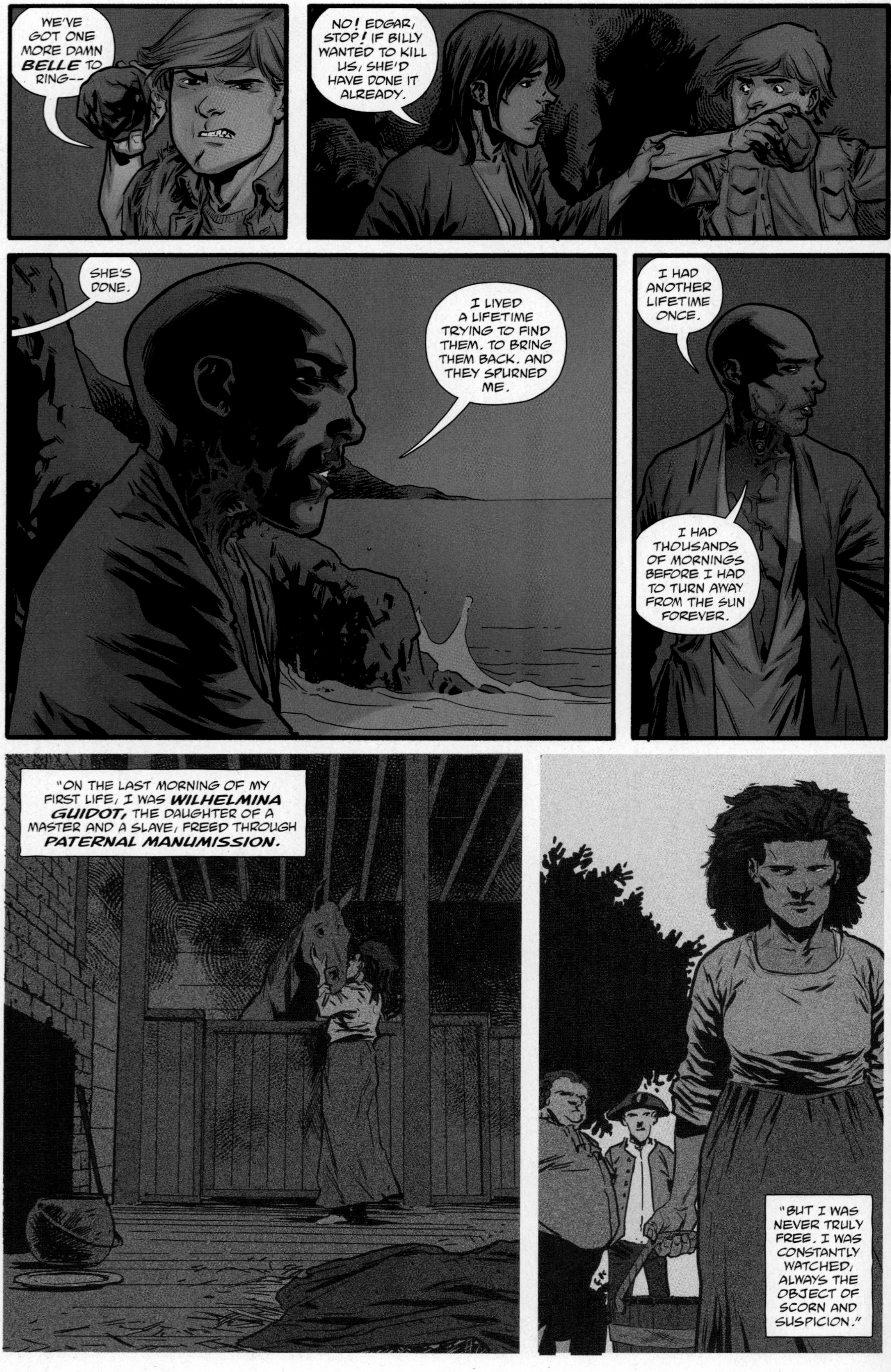
WE'VE GOT ONE MORE DAMN **BELLE** TO RING--
NO! EDGAR, STOP! IF BILLY WANTED TO KILL US, SHE'D HAVE DONE IT ALREADY.
SHE'S DONE.
I LIVED A LIFETIME TRYING TO FIND THEM. TO BRING THEM BACK. AND THEY SPURNED ME.
I HAD ANOTHER LIFETIME ONCE.
I HAD THOUSANDS OF MORNINGS BEFORE I HAD TO TURN AWAY FROM THE SUN FOREVER.
"ON THE LAST MORNING OF MY FIRST LIFE, I WAS **WILHELMINA GUIDOT,** THE DAUGHTER OF A MASTER AND A SLAVE, FREED THROUGH **PATERNAL MANUMISSION.**
"BUT I WAS NEVER TRULY FREE. I WAS CONSTANTLY WATCHED, ALWAYS THE OBJECT OF SCORN AND SUSPICION."

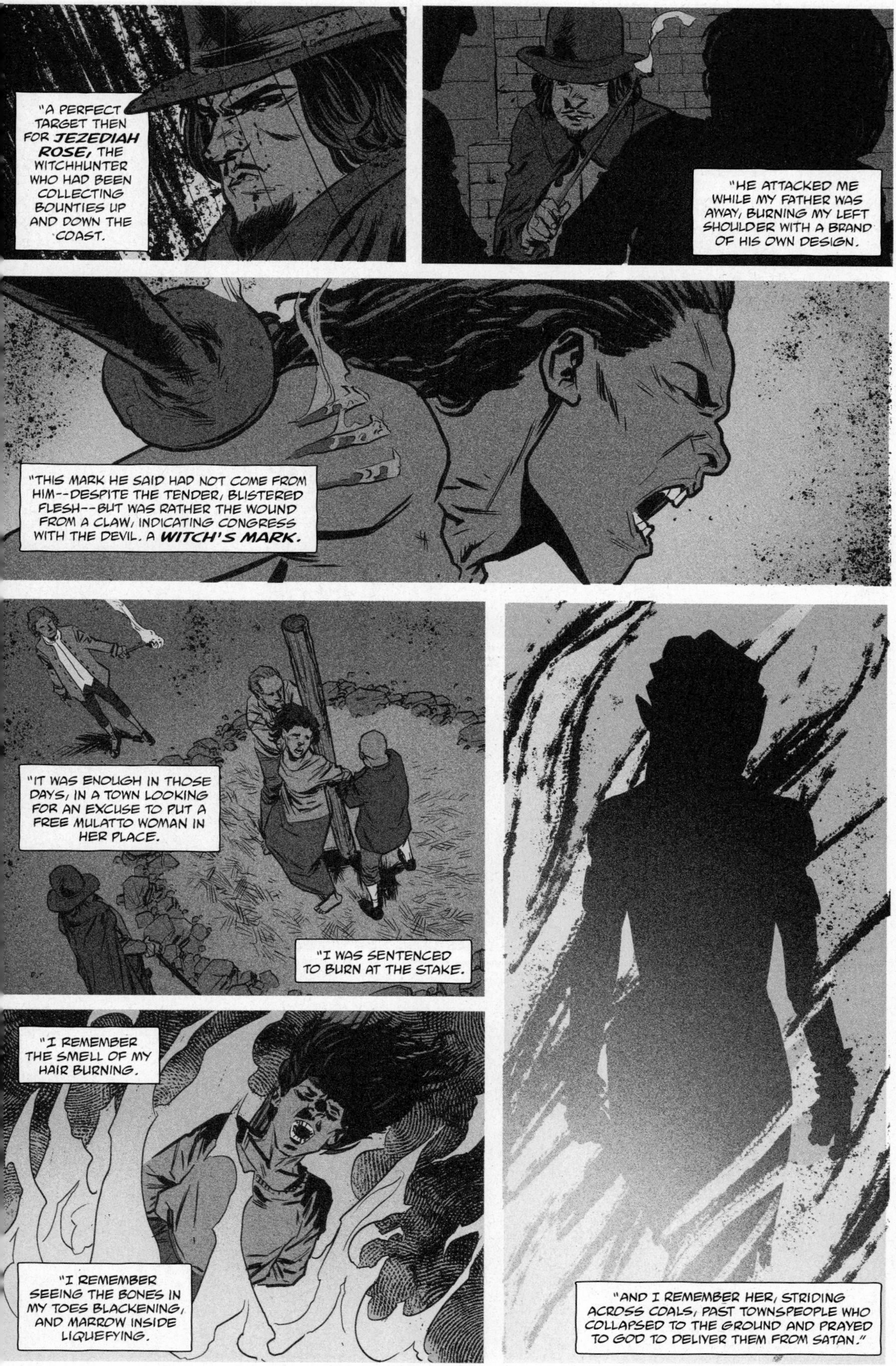
"A PERFECT TARGET THEN FOR JEZEDIAH ROSE, THE WITCHHUNTER WHO HAD BEEN COLLECTING BOUNTIES UP AND DOWN THE COAST.
"HE ATTACKED ME WHILE MY FATHER WAS AWAY, BURNING MY LEFT SHOULDER WITH A BRAND OF HIS OWN DESIGN.
"THIS MARK HE SAID HAD NOT COME FROM HIM--DESPITE THE TENDER, BLISTERED FLESH--BUT WAS RATHER THE WOUND FROM A CLAW, INDICATING CONGRESS WITH THE DEVIL. A WITCH'S MARK.
"IT WAS ENOUGH IN THOSE DAYS, IN A TOWN LOOKING FOR AN EXCUSE TO PUT A FREE MULATTO WOMAN IN HER PLACE.
"I WAS SENTENCED TO BURN AT THE STAKE.
"I REMEMBER THE SMELL OF MY HAIR BURNING.
"I REMEMBER SEEING THE BONES IN MY TOES BLACKENING, AND MARROW INSIDE LIQUEFYING.
"AND I REMEMBER HER, STRIDING ACROSS COALS, PAST TOWNSPEOPLE WHO COLLAPSED TO THE GROUND AND PRAYED TO GOD TO DELIVER THEM FROM SATAN."

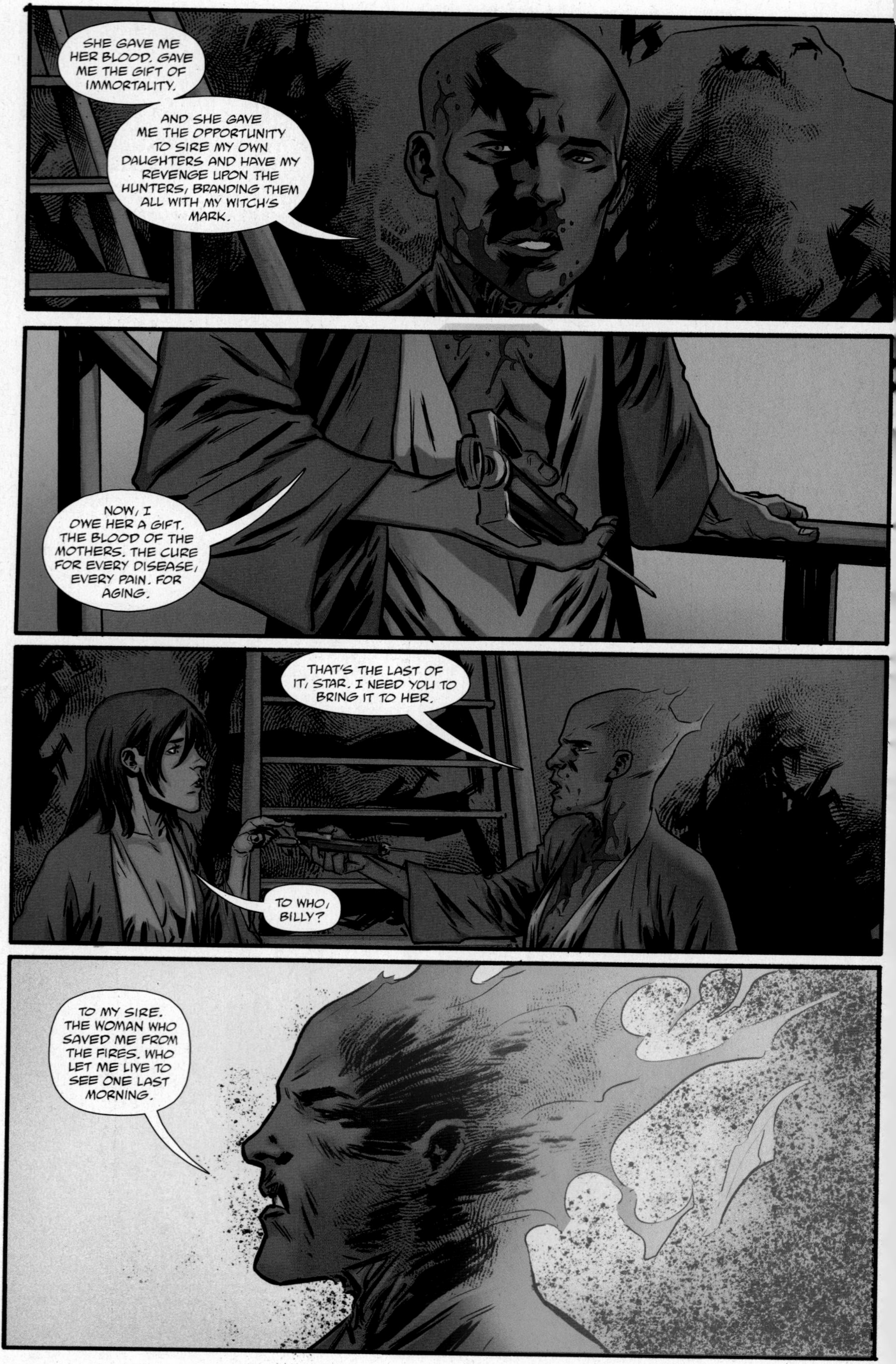
SHE GAVE ME HER BLOOD. GAVE ME THE GIFT OF IMMORTALITY.
AND SHE GAVE ME THE OPPORTUNITY TO SIRE MY OWN DAUGHTERS AND HAVE MY REVENGE UPON THE HUNTERS, BRANDING THEM ALL WITH MY WITCH'S MARK.
NOW, I OWE HER A GIFT. THE BLOOD OF THE MOTHERS. THE CURE FOR EVERY DISEASE, EVERY PAIN. FOR AGING.
THAT'S THE LAST OF IT, STAR. I NEED YOU TO BRING IT TO HER.
TO WHO, BILLY?
TO MY SIRE. THE WOMAN WHO SAVED ME FROM THE FIRES. WHO LET ME LIVE TO SEE ONE LAST MORNING.

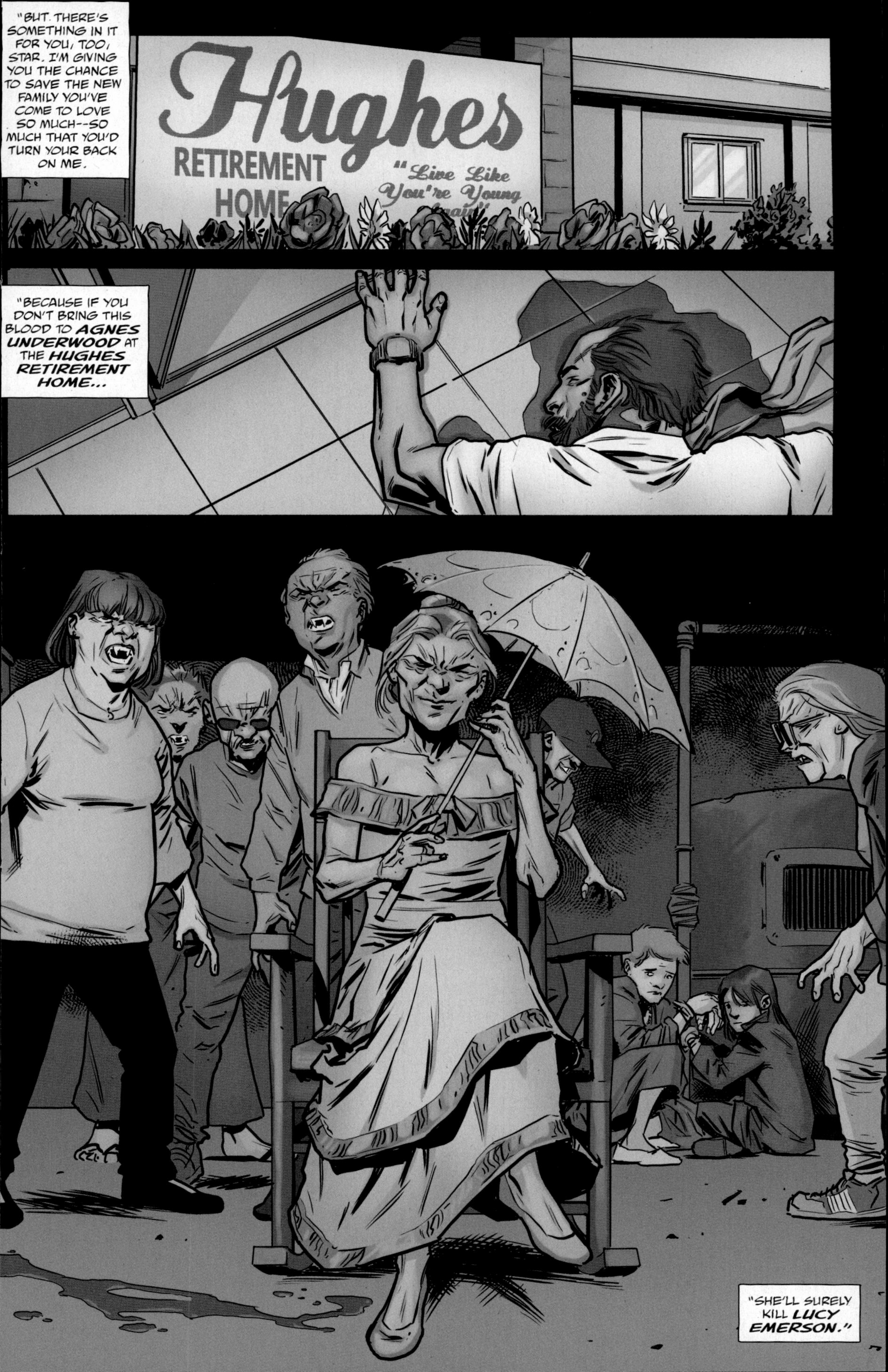
"BUT. THERE'S SOMETHING IN IT FOR YOU, TOO, STAR. I'M GIVING YOU THE CHANCE TO SAVE THE NEW FAMILY YOU'VE COME TO LOVE SO MUCH--SO MUCH THAT YOU'D TURN YOUR BACK ON ME.
Hughes
RETIREMENT
HOME
"Live Like You're Young
"BECAUSE IF YOU DON'T BRING THIS BLOOD TO AGNES UNDERWOOD AT THE HUGHES RETIREMENT HOME...
"SHE'LL SURELY KILL LUCY EMERSON."

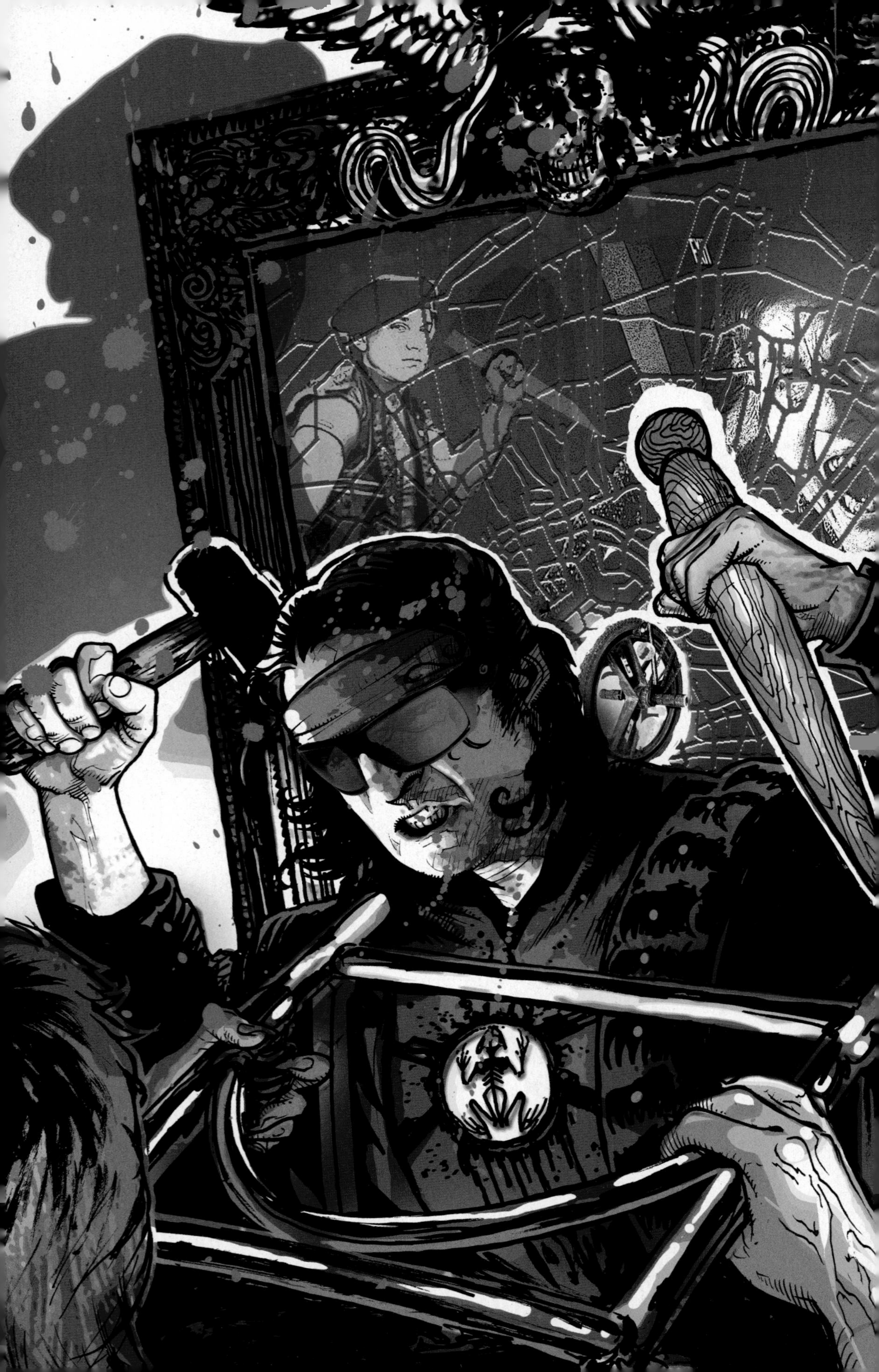

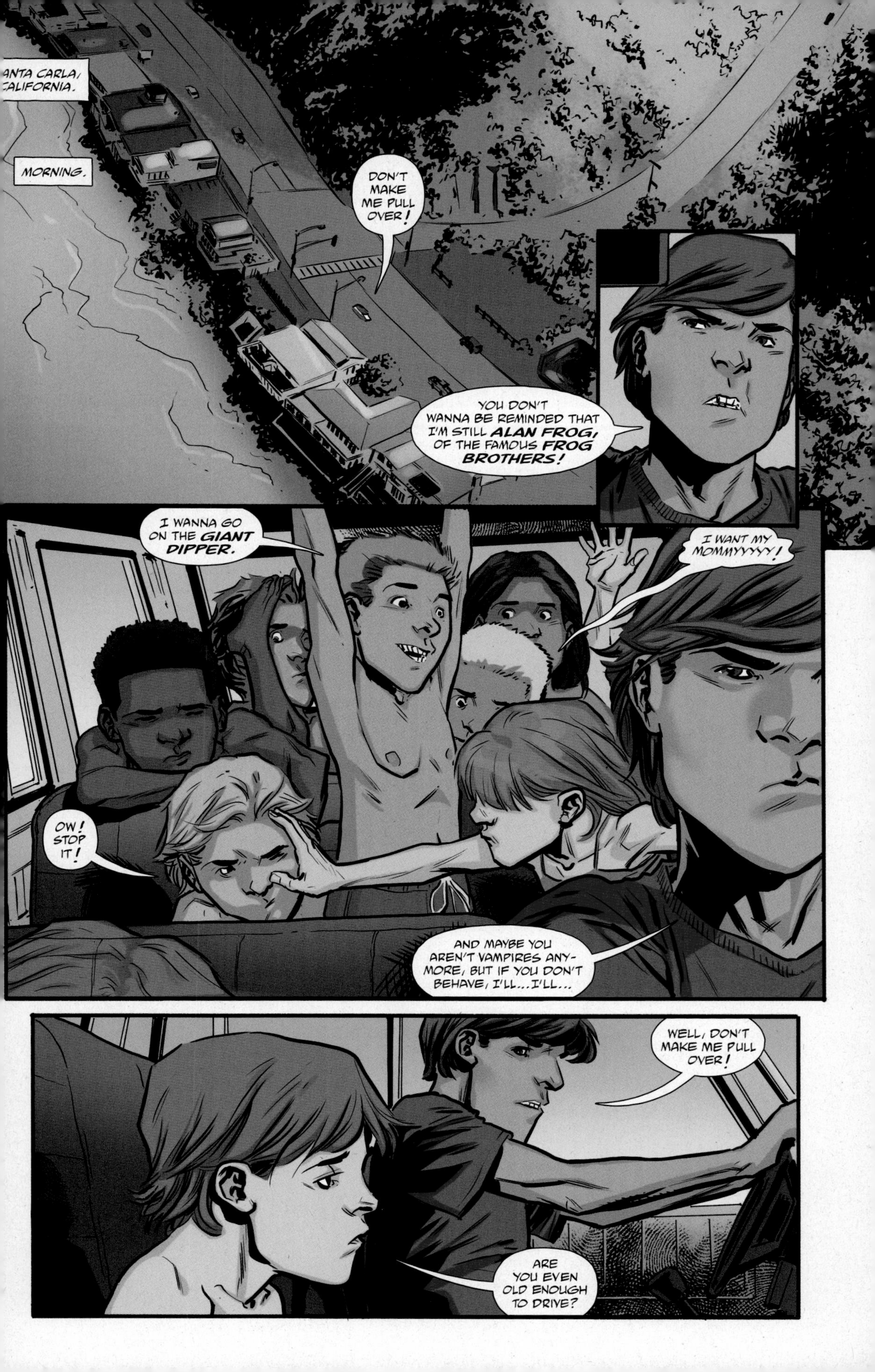
ANTA CARLA, CALIFORNIA.
MORNING.
DON'T MAKE ME PULL OVER!
YOU DON'T WANNA BE REMINDED THAT I'M STILL ALAN FROG, OF THE FAMOUS FROG BROTHERS!
I WANNA GO ON THE GIANT DIPPER.
I WANT MY MOMMYYYYY!
OW! STOP IT!
AND MAYBE YOU AREN'T VAMPIRES ANY-MORE, BUT IF YOU DON'T BEHAVE, I'LL... I'LL...
WELL, DON'T MAKE ME PULL OVER!
ARE YOU EVEN OLD ENOUGH TO DRIVE?

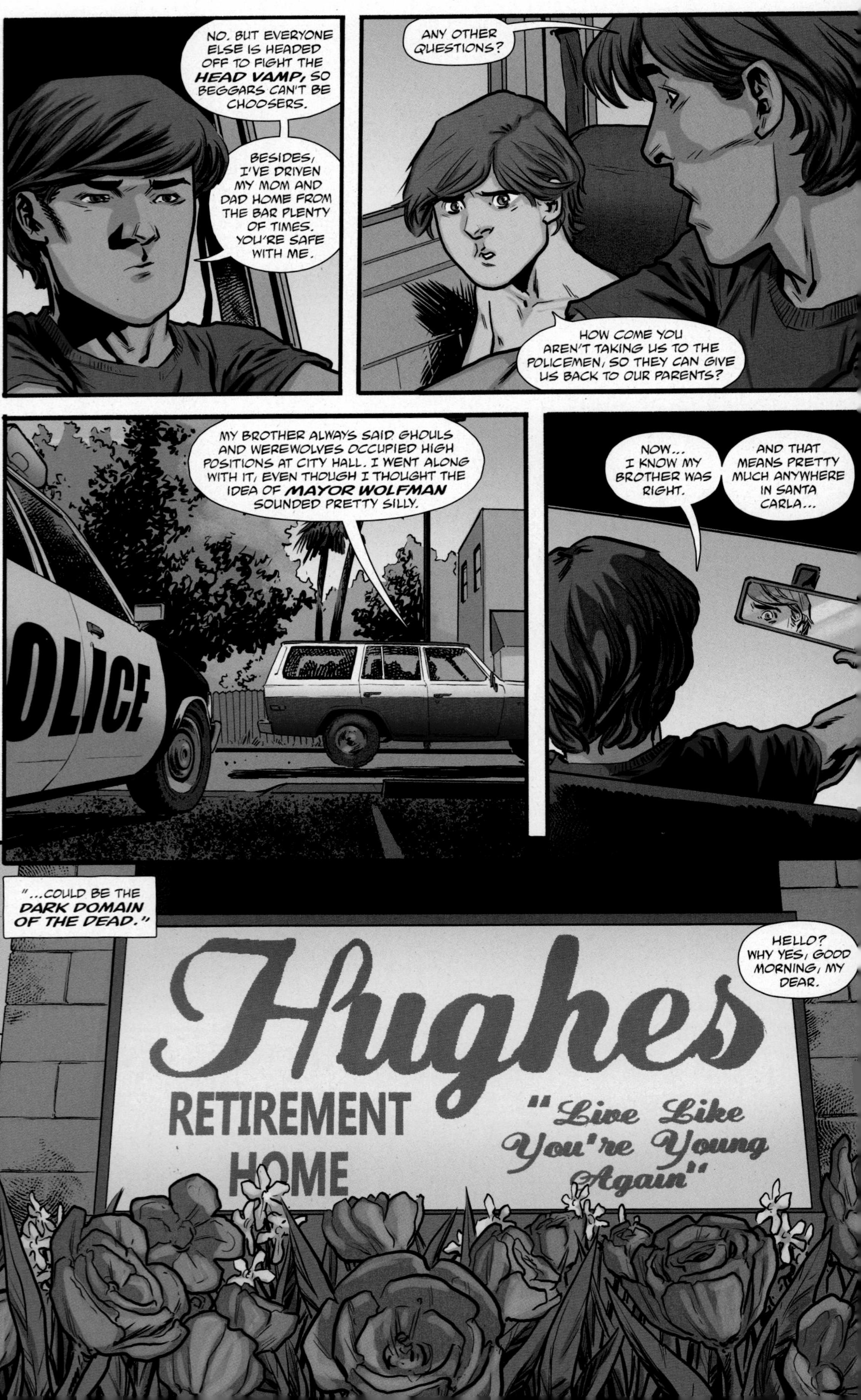
NO. BUT EVERYONE ELSE IS HEADED OFF TO FIGHT THE HEAD VAMP, SO BEGGARS CAN'T BE CHOOSERS.
BESIDES, I'VE DRIVEN MY MOM AND DAD HOME FROM THE BAR PLENTY OF TIMES. YOU'RE SAFE WITH ME.
ANY OTHER QUESTIONS?
HOW COME YOU AREN'T TAKING US TO THE POLICEMEN, SO THEY CAN GIVE US BACK TO OUR PARENTS?
MY BROTHER ALWAYS SAID GHOULS AND WEREWOLVES OCCUPIED HIGH POSITIONS AT CITY HALL. I WENT ALONG WITH IT, EVEN THOUGH I THOUGHT THE IDEA OF MAYOR WOLFMAN SOUNDED PRETTY SILLY.
OLICE
NOW... I KNOW MY BROTHER WAS RIGHT.
AND THAT MEANS PRETTY MUCH ANYWHERE IN SANTA CARLA...
"...COULD BE THE DARK DOMAIN OF THE DEAD."
Hughes
RETIREMENT HOME
"Live Like You're Young Again"
HELLO? WHY YES, GOOD MORNING, MY DEAR.

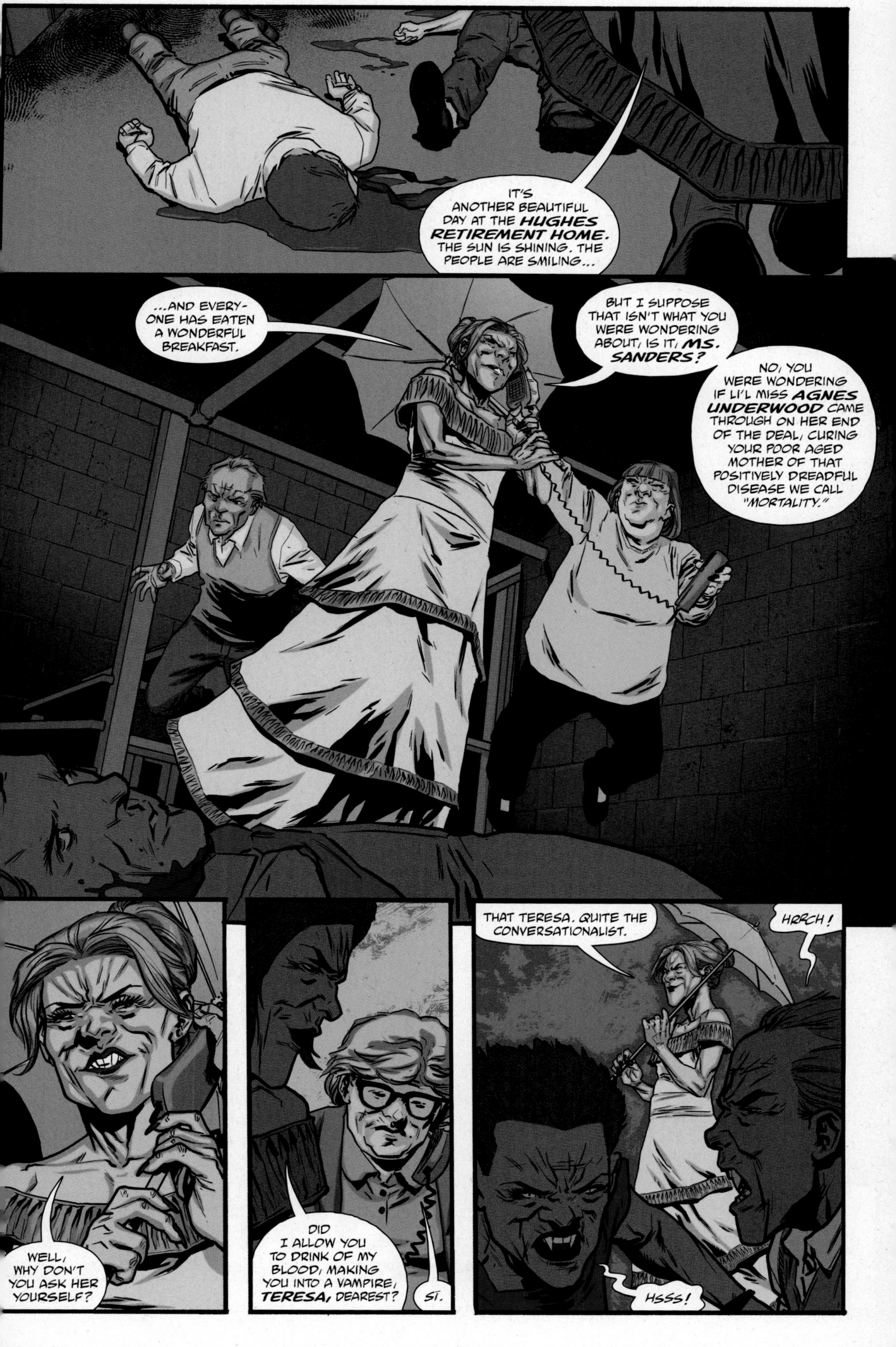

IT'S ANOTHER BEAUTIFUL DAY AT THE HUGHES RETIREMENT HOME. THE SUN IS SHINING. THE PEOPLE ARE SMILING...
...AND EVERY-ONE HAS EATEN A WONDERFUL BREAKFAST.
BUT I SUPPOSE THAT ISN'T WHAT YOU WERE WONDERING ABOUT, IS IT, MS. SANDERS?
NO, YOU WERE WONDERING IF LI'L MISS AGNES UNDERWOOD CAME THROUGH ON HER END OF THE DEAL, CURING YOUR POOR AGED MOTHER OF THAT POSITIVELY DREADFUL DISEASE WE CALL "MORTALITY."
WELL, WHY DON'T YOU ASK HER YOURSELF?
DID I ALLOW YOU TO DRINK OF MY BLOOD, MAKING YOU INTO A VAMPIRE, TERESA, DEAREST?
SÍ.
THAT TERESA. QUITE THE CONVERSATIONALIST.
HRRCH!
HSSS!

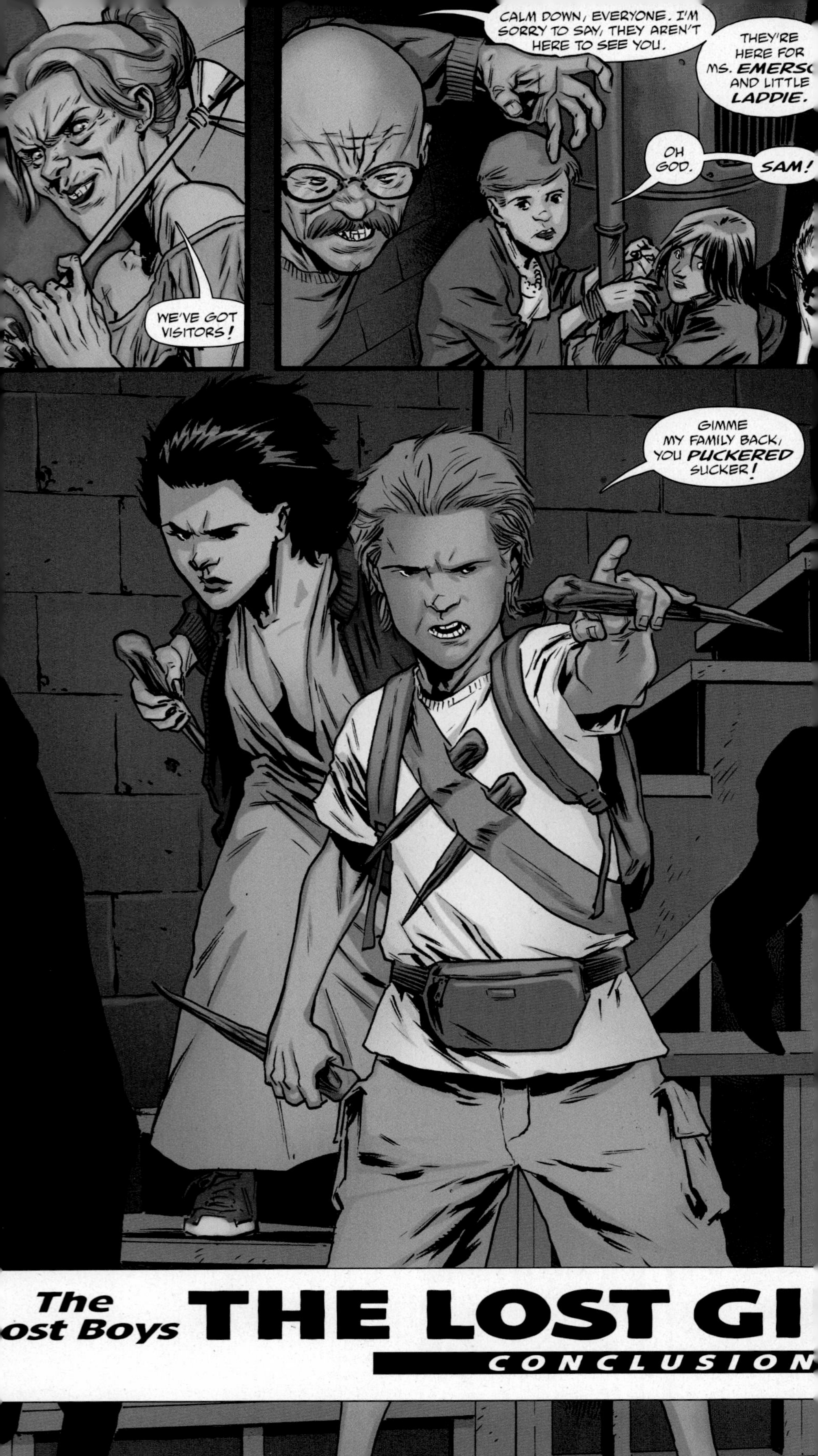
WE'VE GOT VISITORS!
CALM DOWN, EVERYONE. I'M SORRY TO SAY, THEY AREN'T HERE TO SEE YOU.
THEY'RE HERE FOR MS. EMERSO AND LITTLE LADDIE.
OH GOD.
SAM!
GIMME MY FAMILY BACK, YOU PUCKERED SUCKER!
The ost Boys
THE LOST GI
CONCLUSION

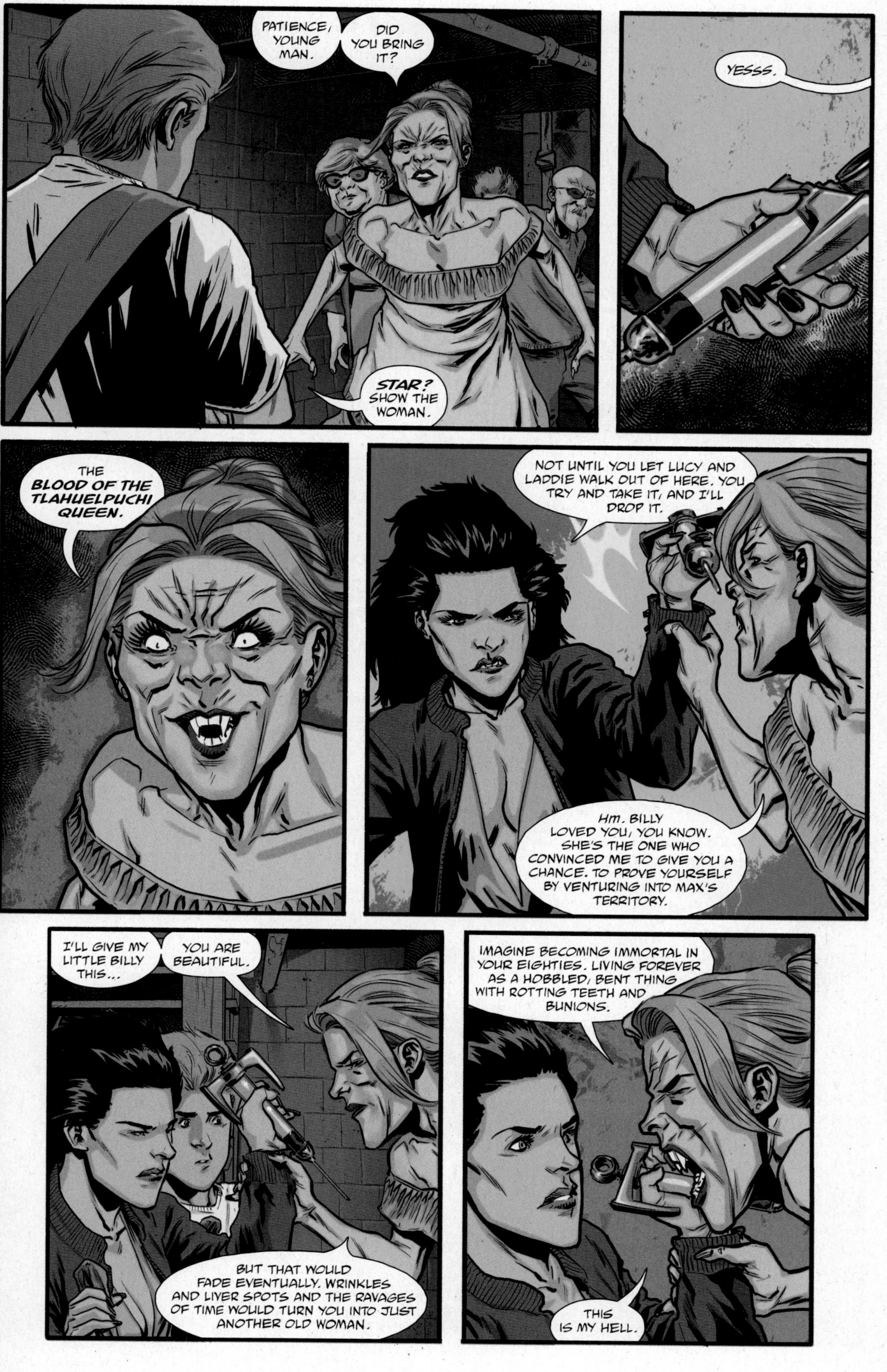
PATIENCE, YOUNG MAN.
DID YOU BRING IT?
STAR? SHOW THE WOMAN.
YESSS.
THE BLOOD OF THE TLAHUELPUCHI QUEEN.
NOT UNTIL YOU LET LUCY AND LADDIE WALK OUT OF HERE. YOU TRY AND TAKE IT, AND I'LL DROP IT.
Hm. BILLY LOVED YOU, YOU KNOW. SHE'S THE ONE WHO CONVINCED ME TO GIVE YOU A CHANCE. TO PROVE YOURSELF BY VENTURING INTO MAX'S TERRITORY.
I'LL GIVE MY LITTLE BILLY THIS...
YOU ARE BEAUTIFUL.
BUT THAT WOULD FADE EVENTUALLY. WRINKLES AND LIVER SPOTS AND THE RAVAGES OF TIME WOULD TURN YOU INTO JUST ANOTHER OLD WOMAN.
IMAGINE BECOMING IMMORTAL IN YOUR EIGHTIES. LIVING FOREVER AS A HOBBLED, BENT THING WITH ROTTING TEETH AND BUNIONS.
THIS IS MY HELL.

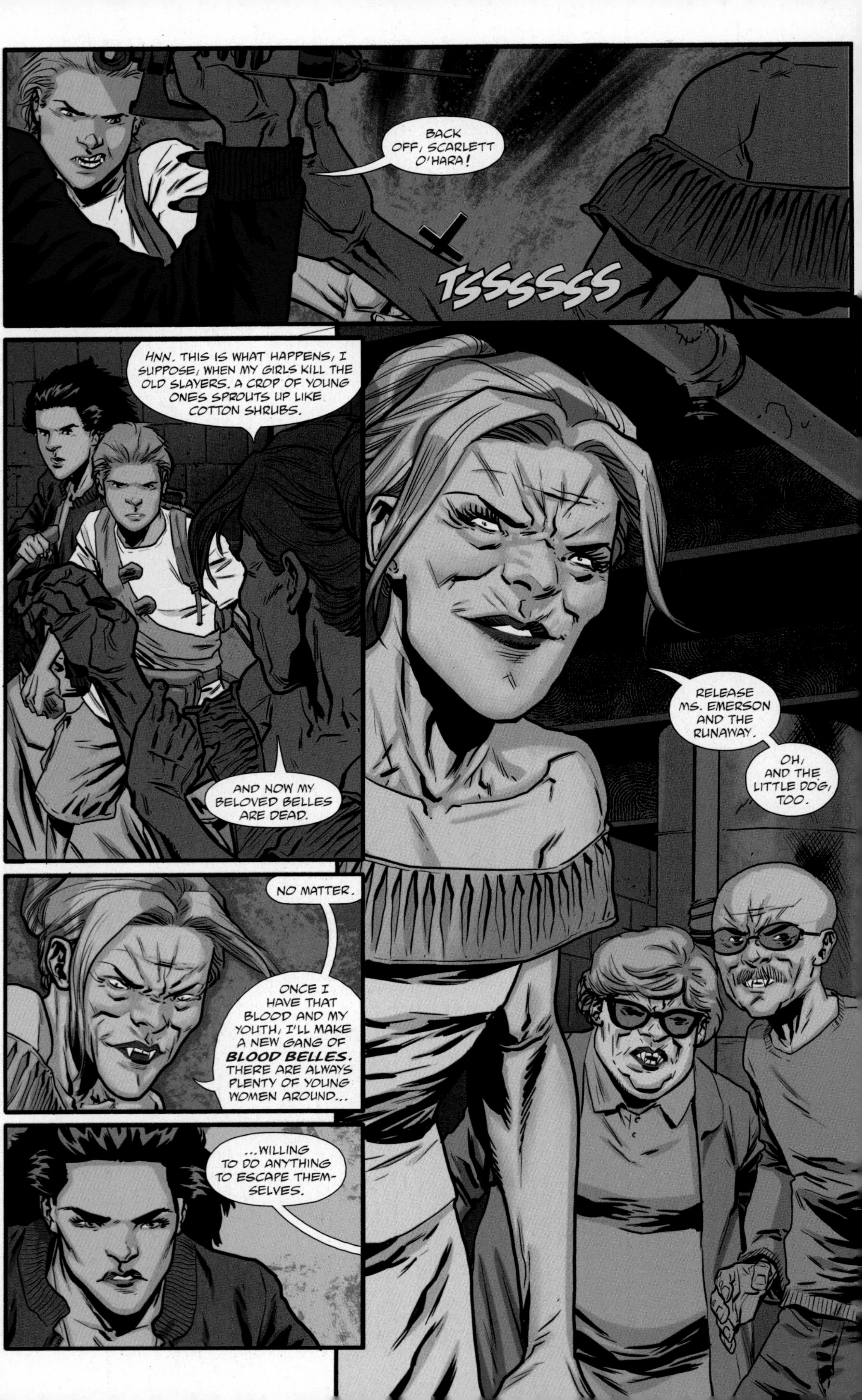
BACK OFF, SCARLETT O'HARA!
TSSSSSS
HNN. THIS IS WHAT HAPPENS, I SUPPOSE, WHEN MY GIRLS KILL THE OLD SLAYERS. A CROP OF YOUNG ONES SPROUTS UP LIKE COTTON SHRUBS.
AND NOW MY BELOVED BELLES ARE DEAD.
RELEASE MS. EMERSON AND THE RUNAWAY.
OH, AND THE LITTLE DOG, TOO.
NO MATTER.
ONCE I HAVE THAT BLOOD AND MY YOUTH, I'LL MAKE A NEW GANG OF **BLOOD BELLES.** THERE ARE ALWAYS PLENTY OF YOUNG WOMEN AROUND...
...WILLING TO DO ANYTHING TO ESCAPE THEMSELVES.

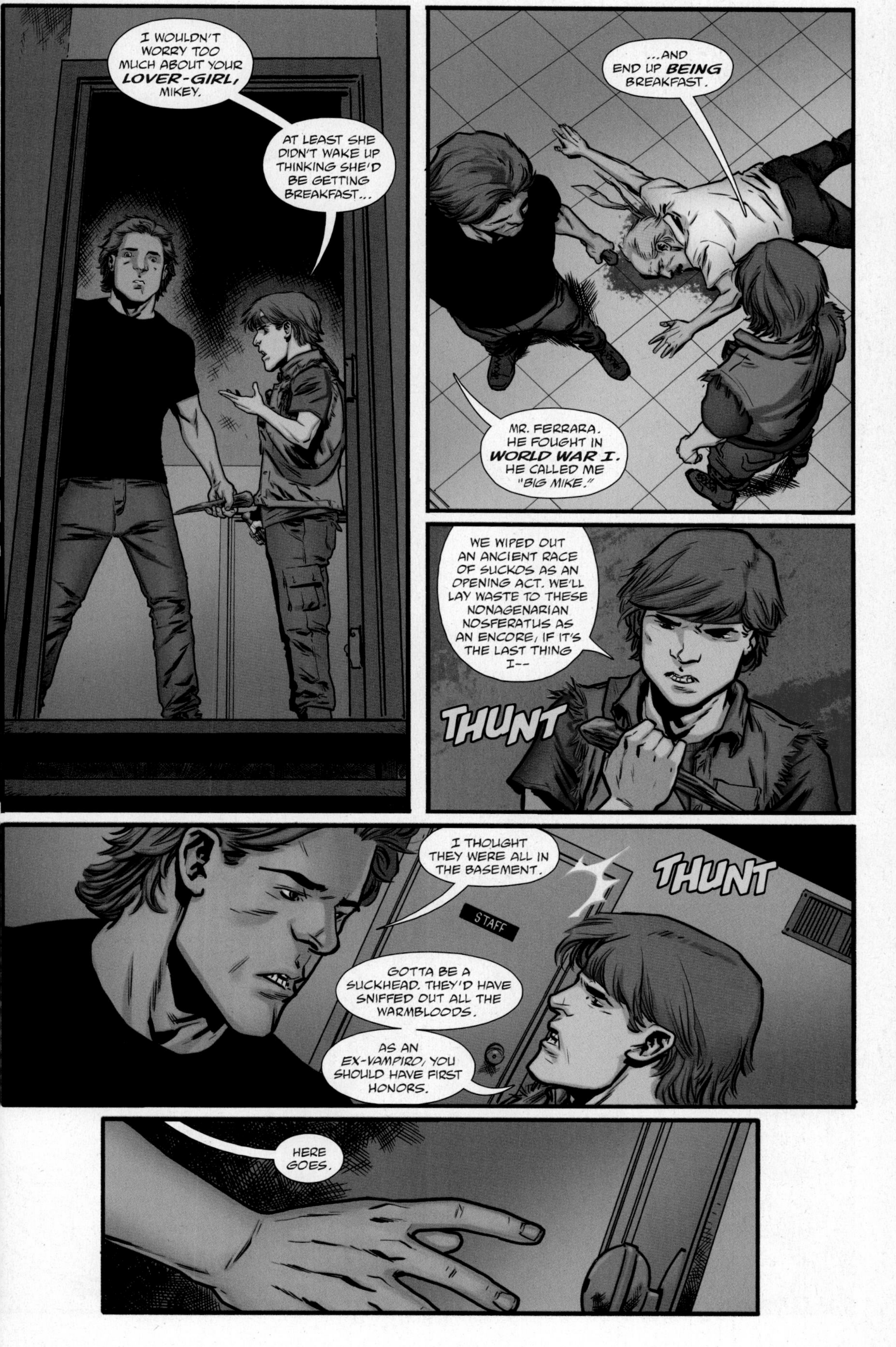
I WOULDN'T WORRY TOO MUCH ABOUT YOUR LOVER-GIRL, MIKEY.
AT LEAST SHE DIDN'T WAKE UP THINKING SHE'D BE GETTING BREAKFAST...
...AND END UP BEING BREAKFAST.
MR. FERRARA. HE FOUGHT IN WORLD WAR I. HE CALLED ME "BIG MIKE."
WE WIPED OUT AN ANCIENT RACE OF SUCKOS AS AN OPENING ACT. WE'LL LAY WASTE TO THESE NONAGENARIAN NOSFERATUS AS AN ENCORE, IF IT'S THE LAST THING I--
THUNT
I THOUGHT THEY WERE ALL IN THE BASEMENT.
THUNT
STAFF
GOTTA BE A SUCKHEAD. THEY'D HAVE SNIFFED OUT ALL THE WARMBLOODS.
AS AN EX-VAMPIRO, YOU SHOULD HAVE FIRST HONORS.
HERE GOES.

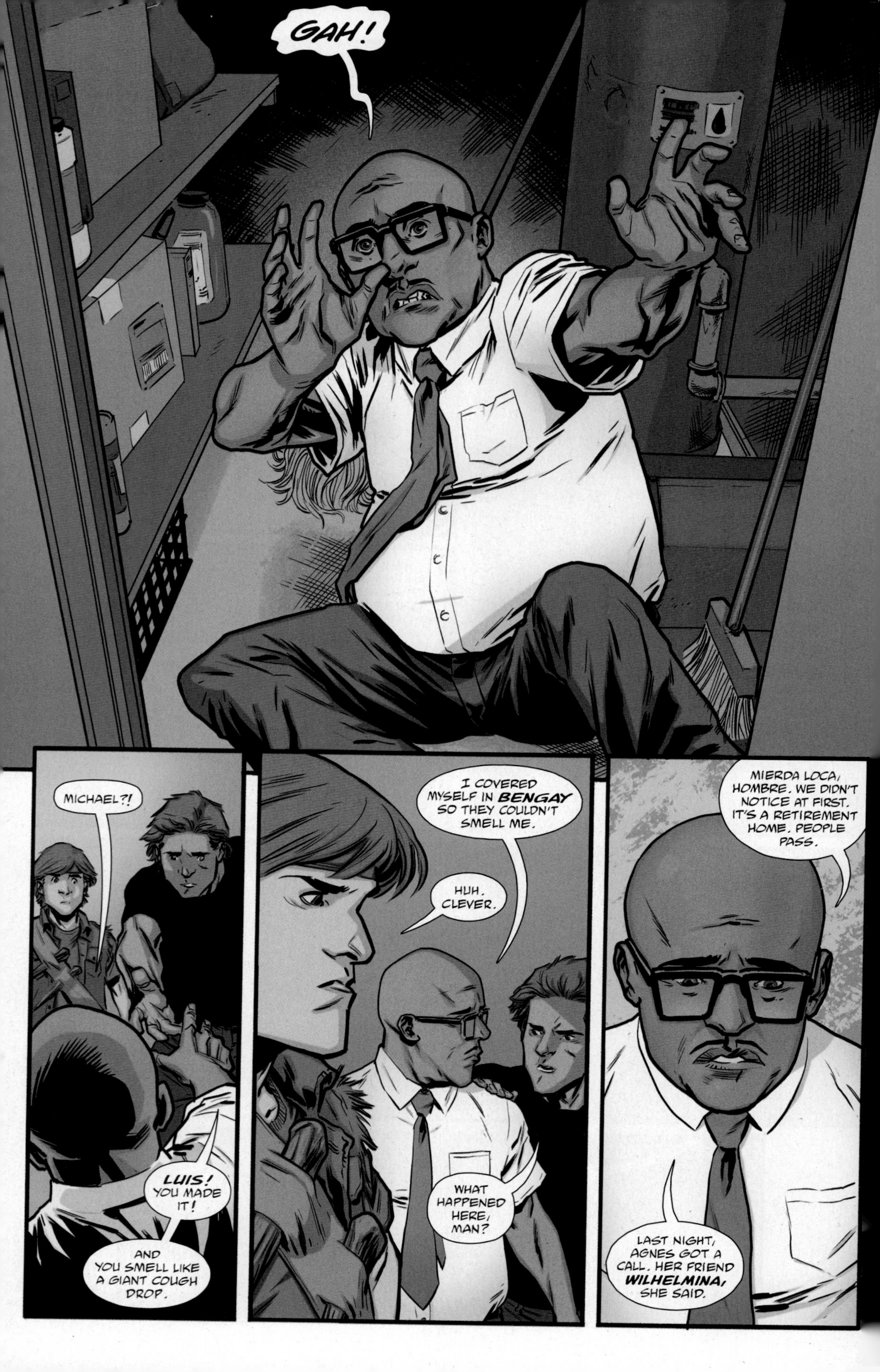
GAH!
MICHAEL?!
LUIS! YOU MADE IT!
AND YOU SMELL LIKE A GIANT COUGH DROP.
I COVERED MYSELF IN BENGAY SO THEY COULDN'T SMELL ME.
HUH. CLEVER.
WHAT HAPPENED HERE, MAN?
MIERDA LOCA, HOMBRE. WE DIDN'T NOTICE AT FIRST. IT'S A RETIREMENT HOME. PEOPLE PASS.
LAST NIGHT, AGNES GOT A CALL. HER FRIEND WILHELMINA, SHE SAID.

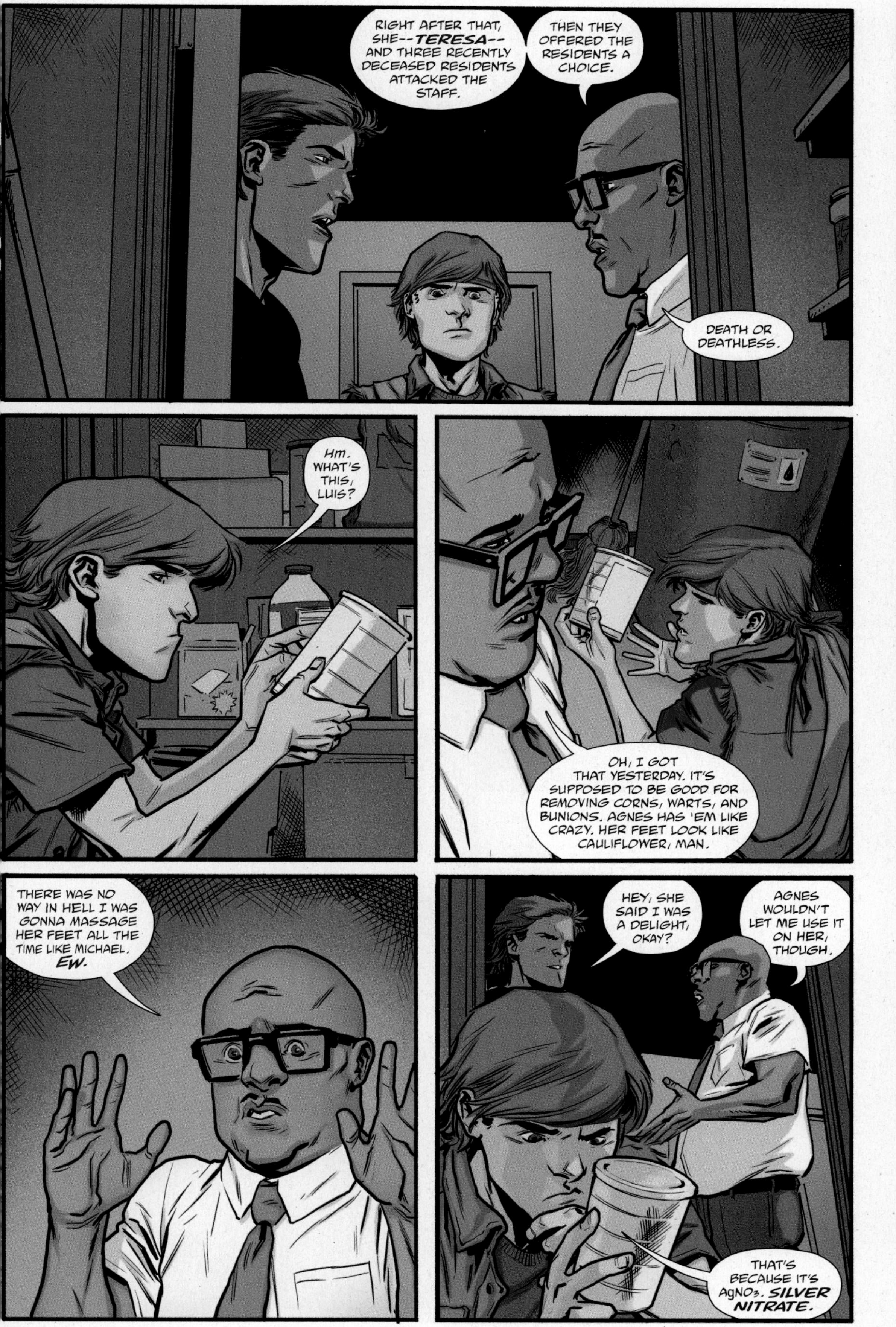
RIGHT AFTER THAT, SHE--TERESA--AND THREE RECENTLY DECEASED RESIDENTS ATTACKED THE STAFF.
THEN THEY OFFERED THE RESIDENTS A CHOICE.
DEATH OR DEATHLESS.
Hm. WHAT'S THIS, LUIS?
OH, I GOT THAT YESTERDAY. IT'S SUPPOSED TO BE GOOD FOR REMOVING CORNS, WARTS, AND BUNIONS. AGNES HAS 'EM LIKE CRAZY. HER FEET LOOK LIKE CAULIFLOWER, MAN.
THERE WAS NO WAY IN HELL I WAS GONNA MASSAGE HER FEET ALL THE TIME LIKE MICHAEL. EW.
HEY, SHE SAID I WAS A DELIGHT, OKAY?
AGNES WOULDN'T LET ME USE IT ON HER, THOUGH.
THAT'S BECAUSE IT'S AgNO3. SILVER NITRATE.

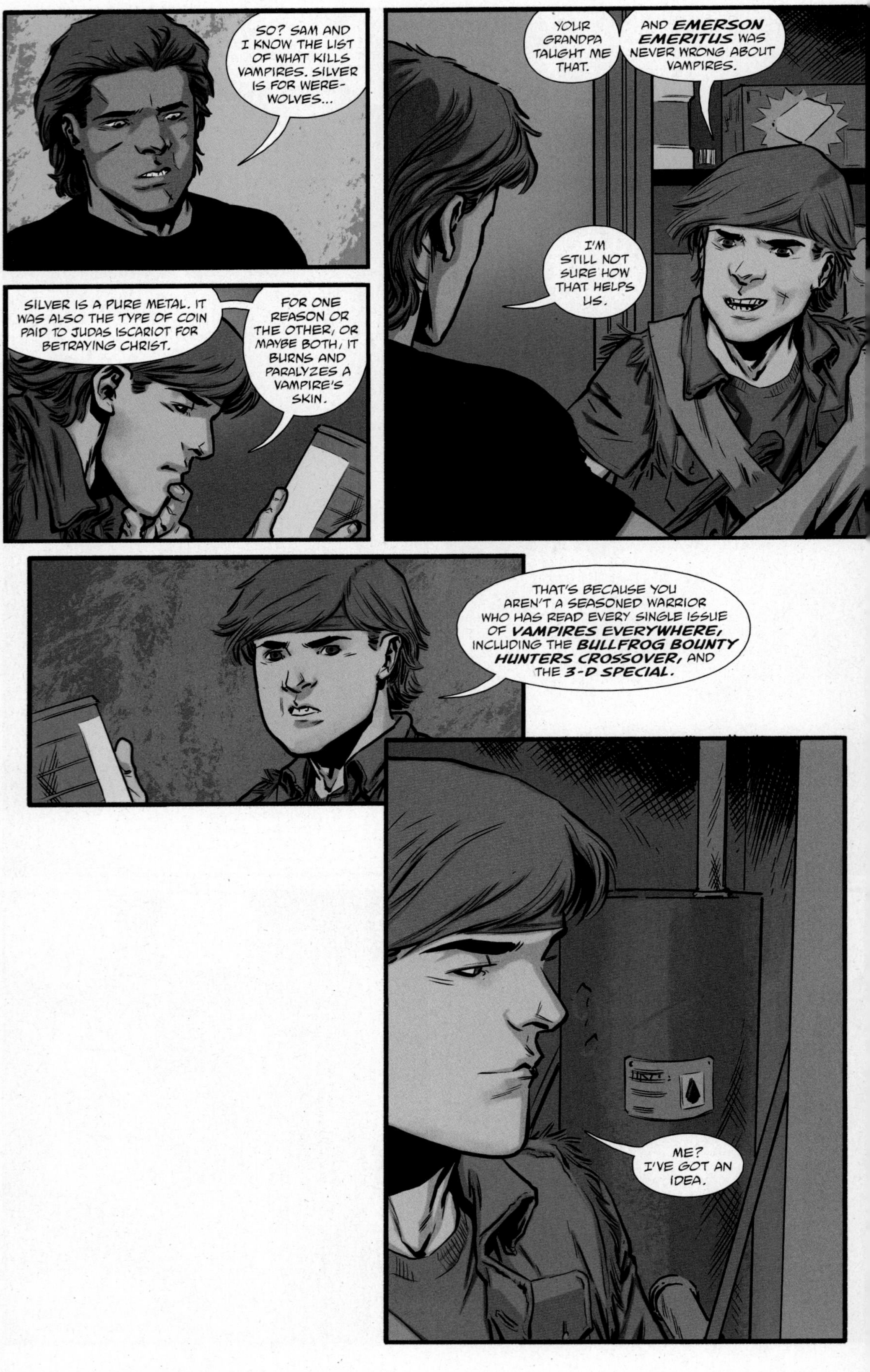
SO? SAM AND I KNOW THE LIST OF WHAT KILLS VAMPIRES. SILVER IS FOR WERE-WOLVES...
YOUR GRANDPA TAUGHT ME THAT.
AND EMERSON EMERITUS WAS NEVER WRONG ABOUT VAMPIRES.
I'M STILL NOT SURE HOW THAT HELPS US.
SILVER IS A PURE METAL. IT WAS ALSO THE TYPE OF COIN PAID TO JUDAS ISCARIOT FOR BETRAYING CHRIST.
FOR ONE REASON OR THE OTHER, OR MAYBE BOTH, IT BURNS AND PARALYZES A VAMPIRE'S SKIN.
THAT'S BECAUSE YOU AREN'T A SEASONED WARRIOR WHO HAS READ EVERY SINGLE ISSUE OF VAMPIRES EVERYWHERE, INCLUDING THE BULLFROG BOUNTY HUNTERS CROSSOVER, AND THE 3-D SPECIAL.
ME? I'VE GOT AN IDEA.

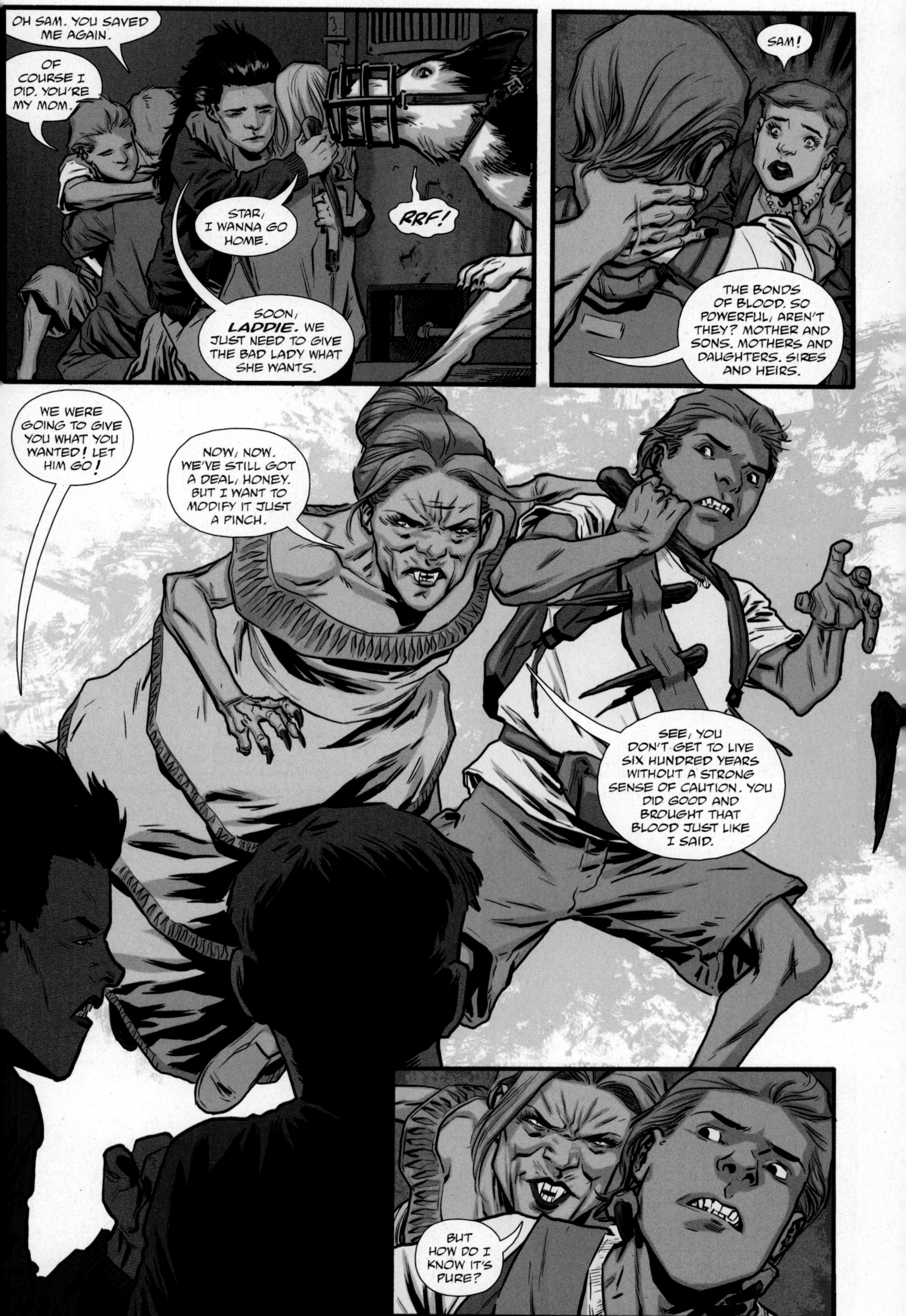
OH SAM. YOU SAVED ME AGAIN.
OF COURSE I DID. YOU'RE MY MOM.
STAR, I WANNA GO HOME.
SOON, LADDIE. WE JUST NEED TO GIVE THE BAD LADY WHAT SHE WANTS.
RRF!
SAM!
THE BONDS OF BLOOD. SO POWERFUL, AREN'T THEY? MOTHER AND SONS. MOTHERS AND DAUGHTERS. SIRES AND HEIRS.
WE WERE GOING TO GIVE YOU WHAT YOU WANTED! LET HIM GO!
NOW, NOW. WE'VE STILL GOT A DEAL, HONEY. BUT I WANT TO MODIFY IT JUST A PINCH.
SEE, YOU DON'T GET TO LIVE SIX HUNDRED YEARS WITHOUT A STRONG SENSE OF CAUTION. YOU DID GOOD AND BROUGHT THAT BLOOD JUST LIKE I SAID.
BUT HOW DO I KNOW IT'S PURE?

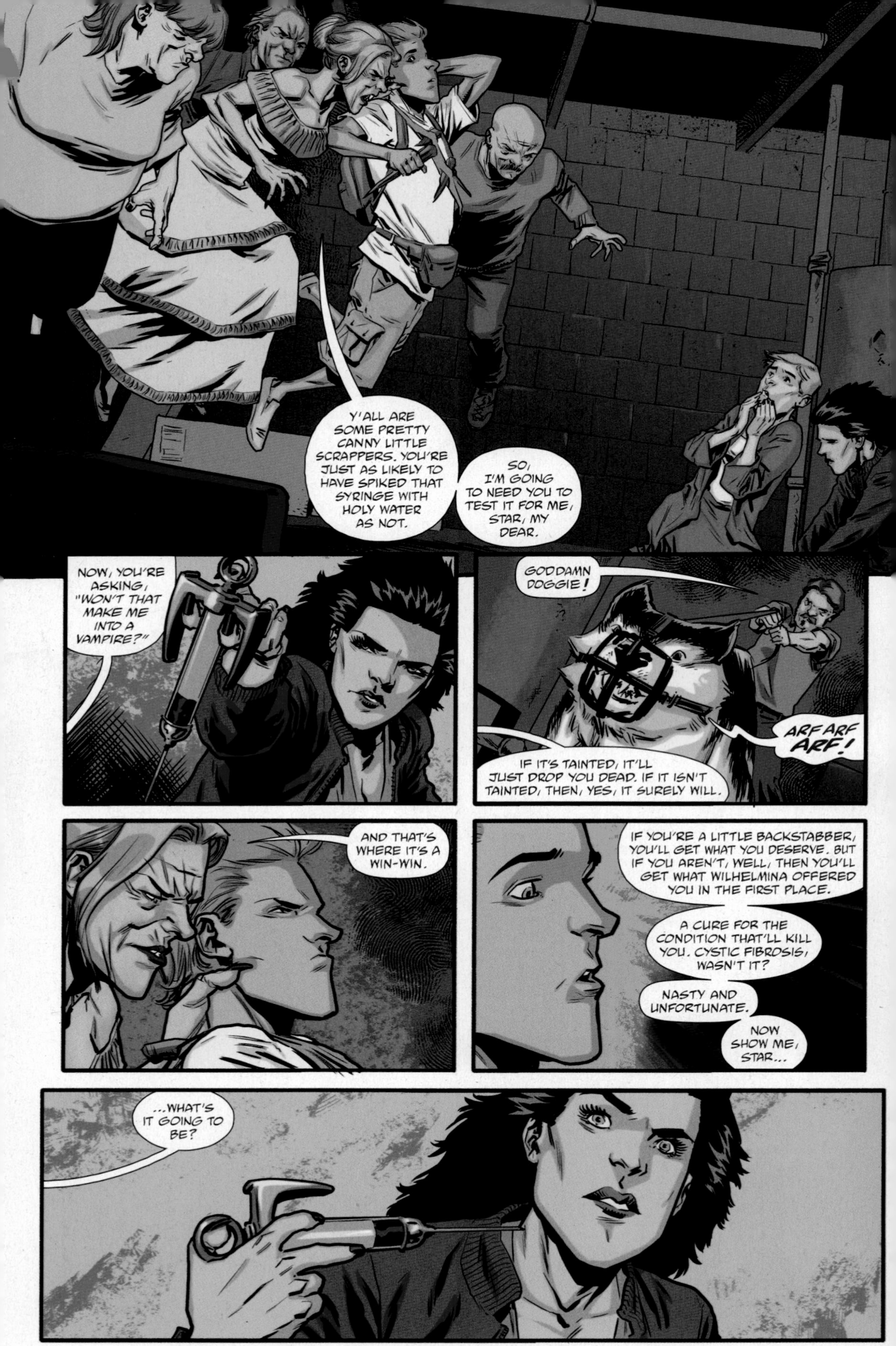
Y'ALL ARE SOME PRETTY CANNY LITTLE SCRAPPERS. YOU'RE JUST AS LIKELY TO HAVE SPIKED THAT SYRINGE WITH HOLY WATER AS NOT.
SO, I'M GOING TO NEED YOU TO TEST IT FOR ME, STAR, MY DEAR.
NOW, YOU'RE ASKING, "WON'T THAT MAKE ME INTO A VAMPIRE?"
GODDAMN DOGGIE!
ARF ARF ARF!
IF IT'S TAINTED, IT'LL JUST DROP YOU DEAD. IF IT ISN'T TAINTED, THEN, YES, IT SURELY WILL.
AND THAT'S WHERE IT'S A WIN-WIN.
IF YOU'RE A LITTLE BACKSTABBER, YOU'LL GET WHAT YOU DESERVE. BUT IF YOU AREN'T, WELL, THEN YOU'LL GET WHAT WILHELMINA OFFERED YOU IN THE FIRST PLACE.
A CURE FOR THE CONDITION THAT'LL KILL YOU. CYSTIC FIBROSIS, WASN'T IT?
NASTY AND UNFORTUNATE.
NOW SHOW ME, STAR...
...WHAT'S IT GOING TO BE?

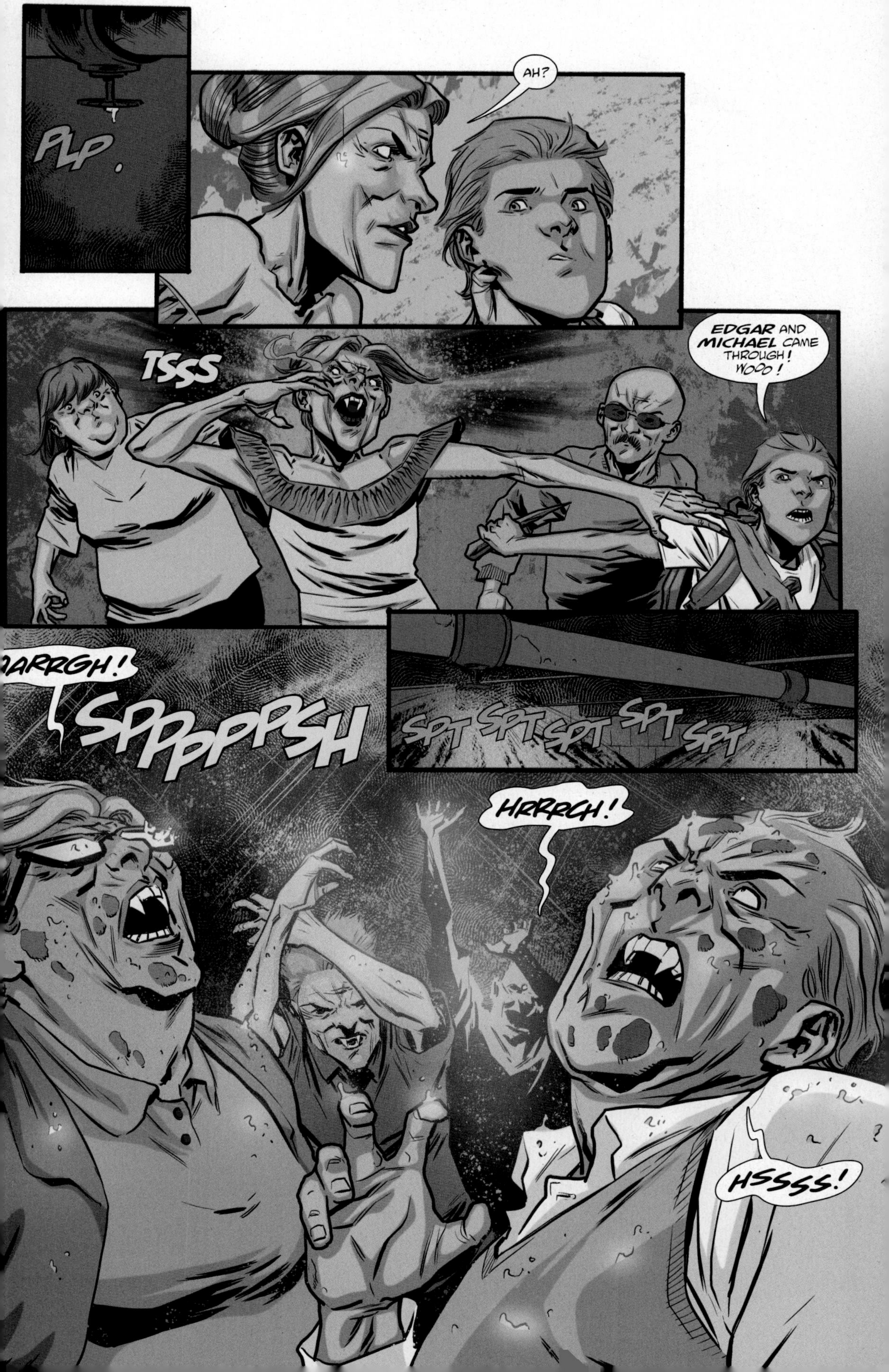
PLP
AH?
TSSS
EDGAR AND MICHAEL CAME THROUGH! WOOO!
AARRGH!
SPPPPPPSH
SPT SPT SPT SPT SPT
HRRRGH!
HSSSS!

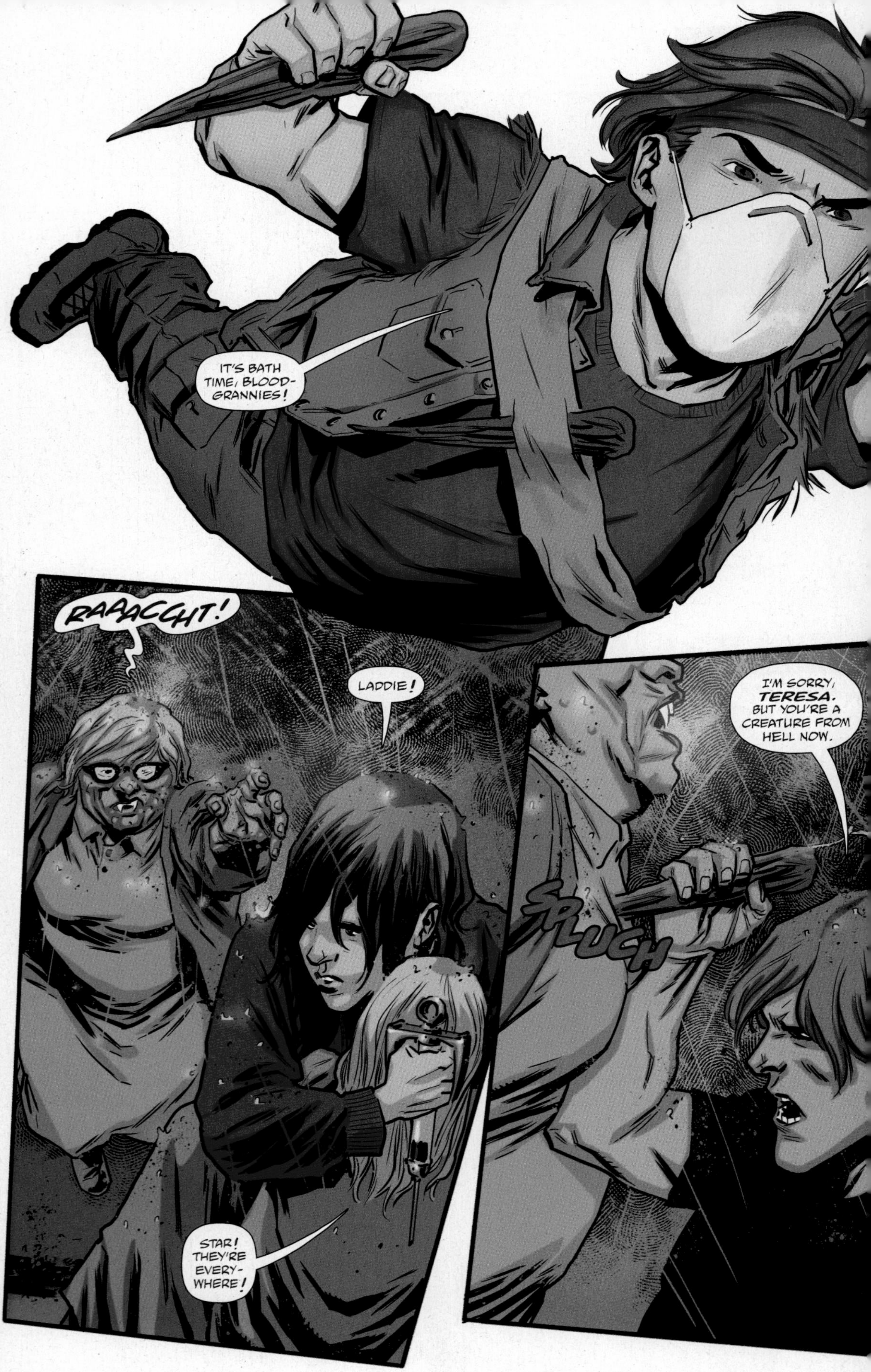
IT'S BATH TIME, BLOOD-GRANNIES!
RAAACCHT!
LADDIE!
STAR! THEY'RE EVERY-WHERE!
I'M SORRY, TERESA. BUT YOU'RE A CREATURE FROM HELL NOW.
SPLUCH

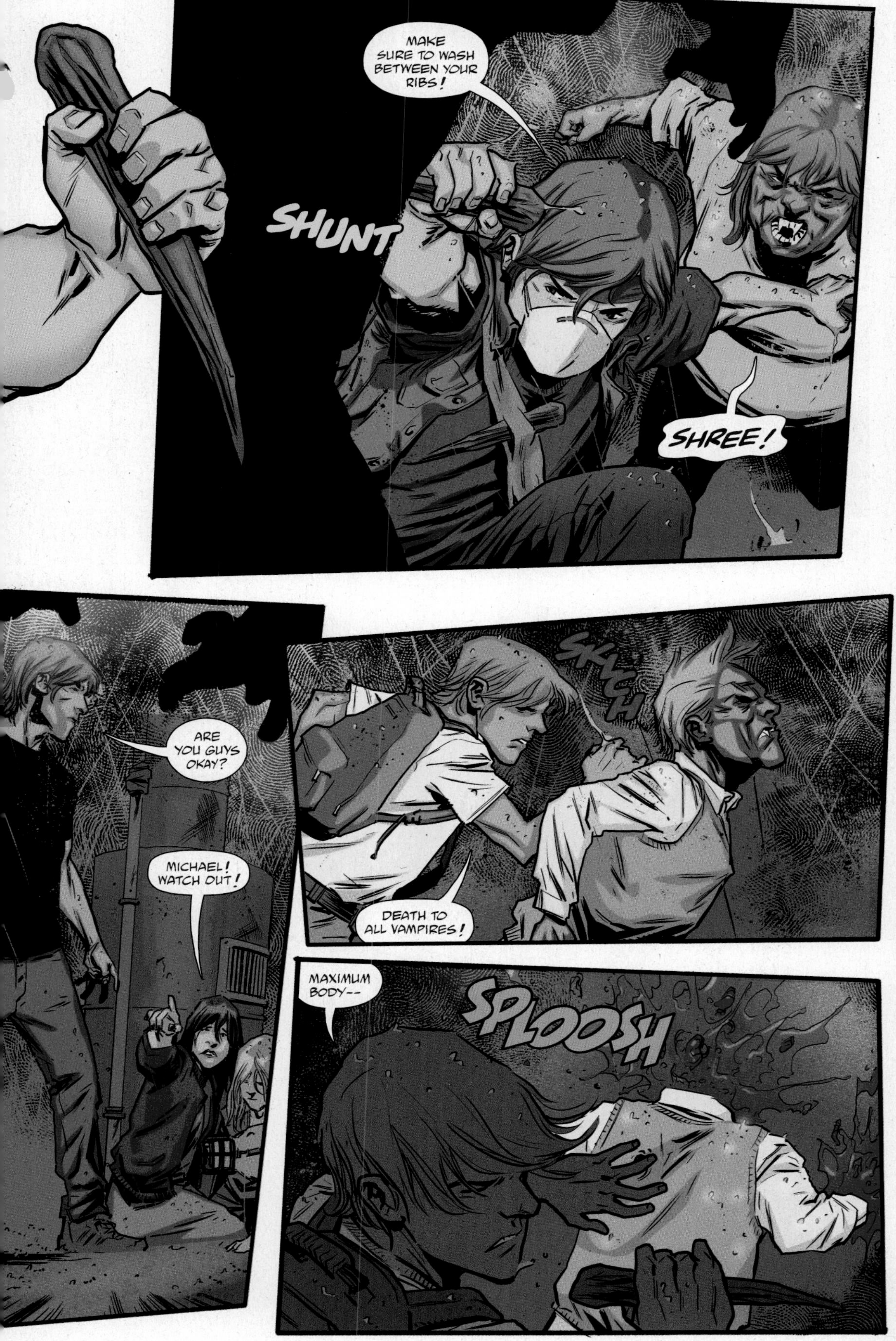
MAKE SURE TO WASH BETWEEN YOUR RIBS!
SHUNT
SHREE!
ARE YOU GUYS OKAY?
MICHAEL! WATCH OUT!
SKWCH
DEATH TO ALL VAMPIRES!
MAXIMUM BODY--
SPLOOSH

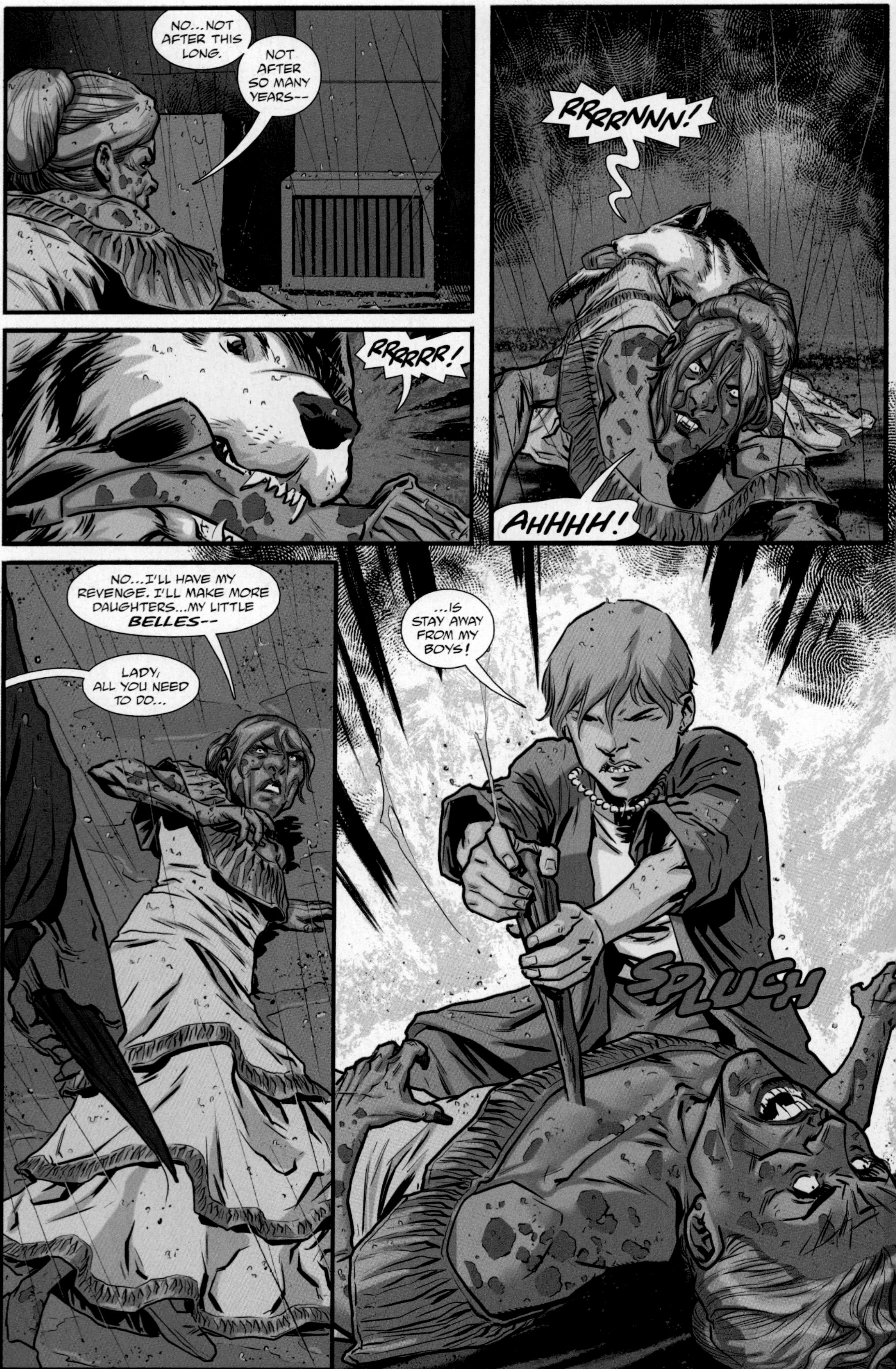
NO...NOT AFTER THIS LONG.
NOT AFTER SO MANY YEARS--
RRRRNNN!
RRRRRR!
AHHHH!
NO...I'LL HAVE MY REVENGE. I'LL MAKE MORE DAUGHTERS...MY LITTLE BELLES--
LADY, ALL YOU NEED TO DO...
...IS STAY AWAY FROM MY BOYS!
SPLUCH

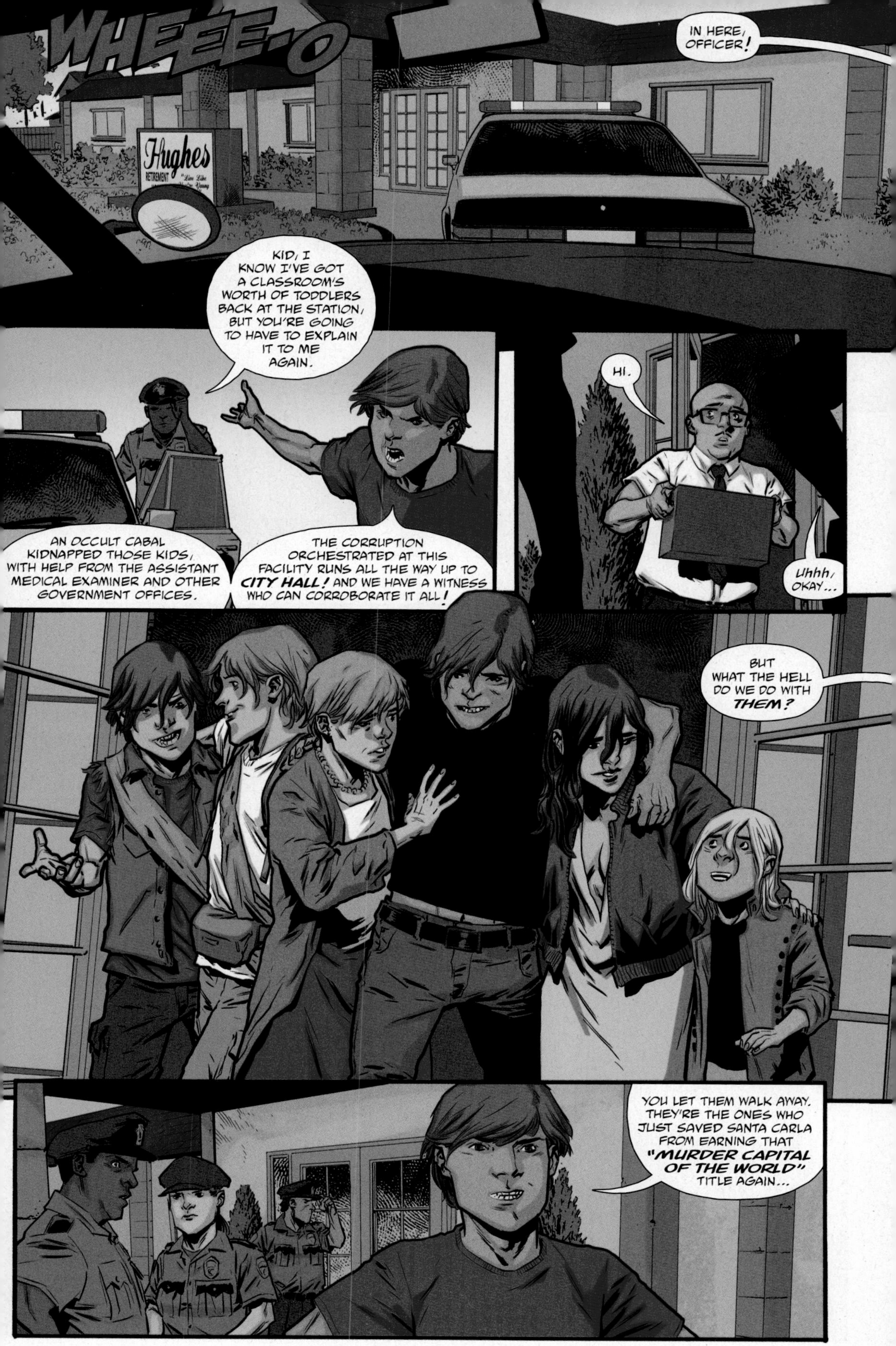
WHEEE-O
IN HERE, OFFICER!
Hughes RETIREMENT
KID, I KNOW I'VE GOT A CLASSROOM'S WORTH OF TODDLERS BACK AT THE STATION, BUT YOU'RE GOING TO HAVE TO EXPLAIN IT TO ME AGAIN.
AN OCCULT CABAL KIDNAPPED THOSE KIDS, WITH HELP FROM THE ASSISTANT MEDICAL EXAMINER AND OTHER GOVERNMENT OFFICES.
THE CORRUPTION ORCHESTRATED AT THIS FACILITY RUNS ALL THE WAY UP TO CITY HALL! AND WE HAVE A WITNESS WHO CAN CORROBORATE IT ALL!
HI.
Uhhh, OKAY...
BUT WHAT THE HELL DO WE DO WITH THEM?
YOU LET THEM WALK AWAY. THEY'RE THE ONES WHO JUST SAVED SANTA CARLA FROM EARNING THAT "MURDER CAPITAL OF THE WORLD" TITLE AGAIN...

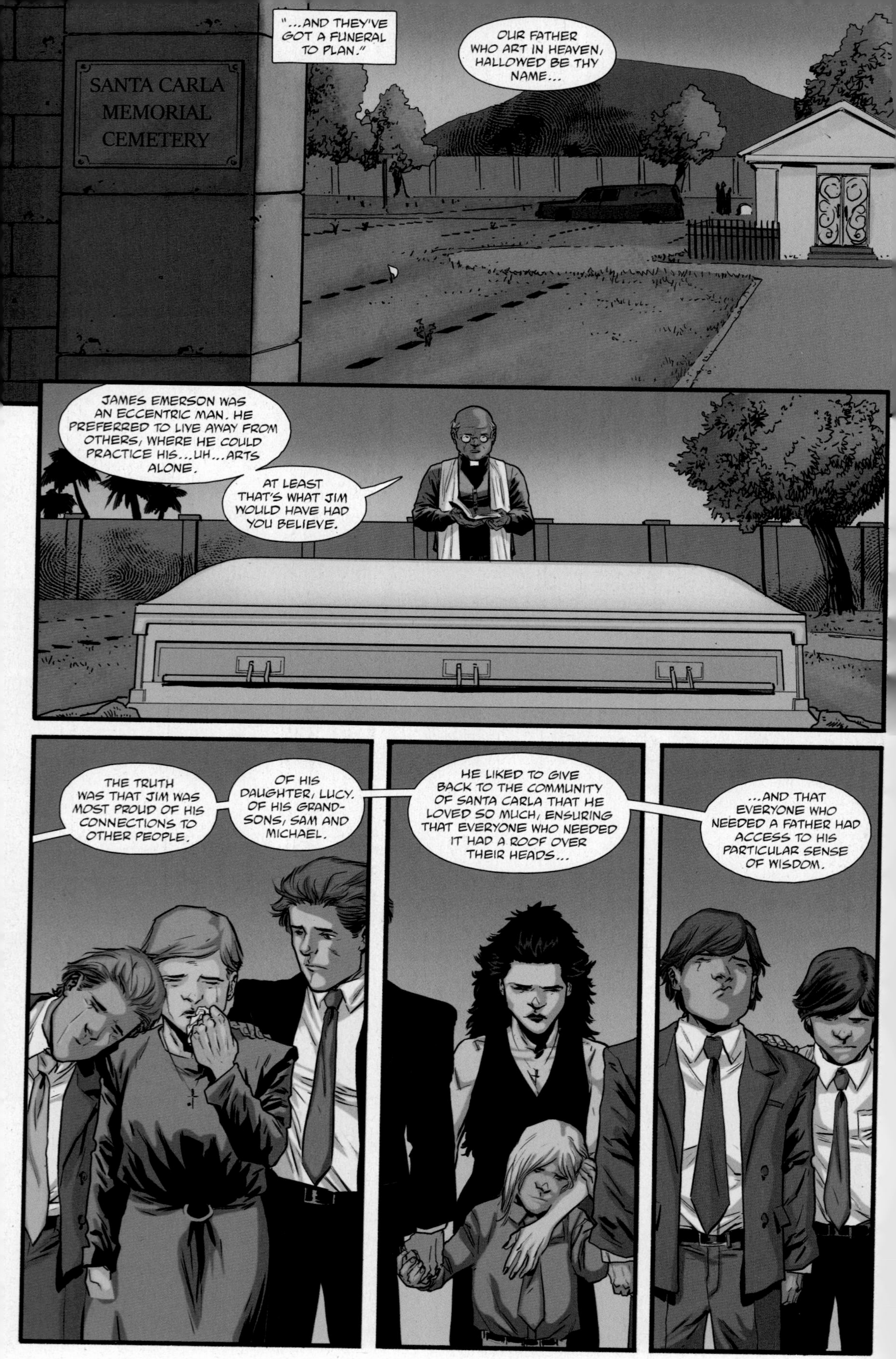
SANTA CARLA MEMORIAL CEMETERY
"...AND THEY'VE GOT A FUNERAL TO PLAN."
OUR FATHER WHO ART IN HEAVEN, HALLOWED BE THY NAME...
JAMES EMERSON WAS AN ECCENTRIC MAN. HE PREFERRED TO LIVE AWAY FROM OTHERS, WHERE HE COULD PRACTICE HIS...UH...ARTS ALONE.
AT LEAST THAT'S WHAT JIM WOULD HAVE HAD YOU BELIEVE.
THE TRUTH WAS THAT JIM WAS MOST PROUD OF HIS CONNECTIONS TO OTHER PEOPLE.
OF HIS DAUGHTER, LUCY. OF HIS GRANDSONS, SAM AND MICHAEL.
HE LIKED TO GIVE BACK TO THE COMMUNITY OF SANTA CARLA THAT HE LOVED SO MUCH, ENSURING THAT EVERYONE WHO NEEDED IT HAD A ROOF OVER THEIR HEADS...
...AND THAT EVERYONE WHO NEEDED A FATHER HAD ACCESS TO HIS PARTICULAR SENSE OF WISDOM.

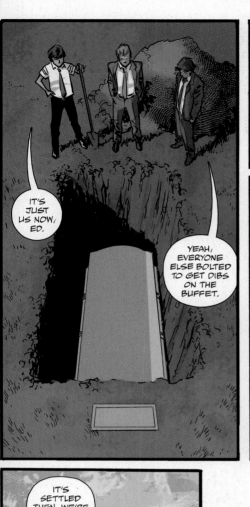

IT'S JUST US NOW, ED.

YEAH, EVERYONE ELSE BOLTED TO GET DIBS ON THE BUFFET.

NO, I MEAN *IT'S JUST US.* WE'RE THE LAST VAMPIRE HUNTERS IN SANTA CARLA. MAYBE IN THE WORLD.

THAT MEANS IT'S UP TO US TO RECRUIT AND TRAIN THE NEXT GENERATION.

FIRST NEW RECRUIT! I NOMINATE SAM "THE BADASS" EMERSON!

OW!

IT'S SETTLED THEN, WE'RE S.C.H.U. 2.

POP POP POP

ROOT BEER

ROOT BEER

TO GRANDPA!

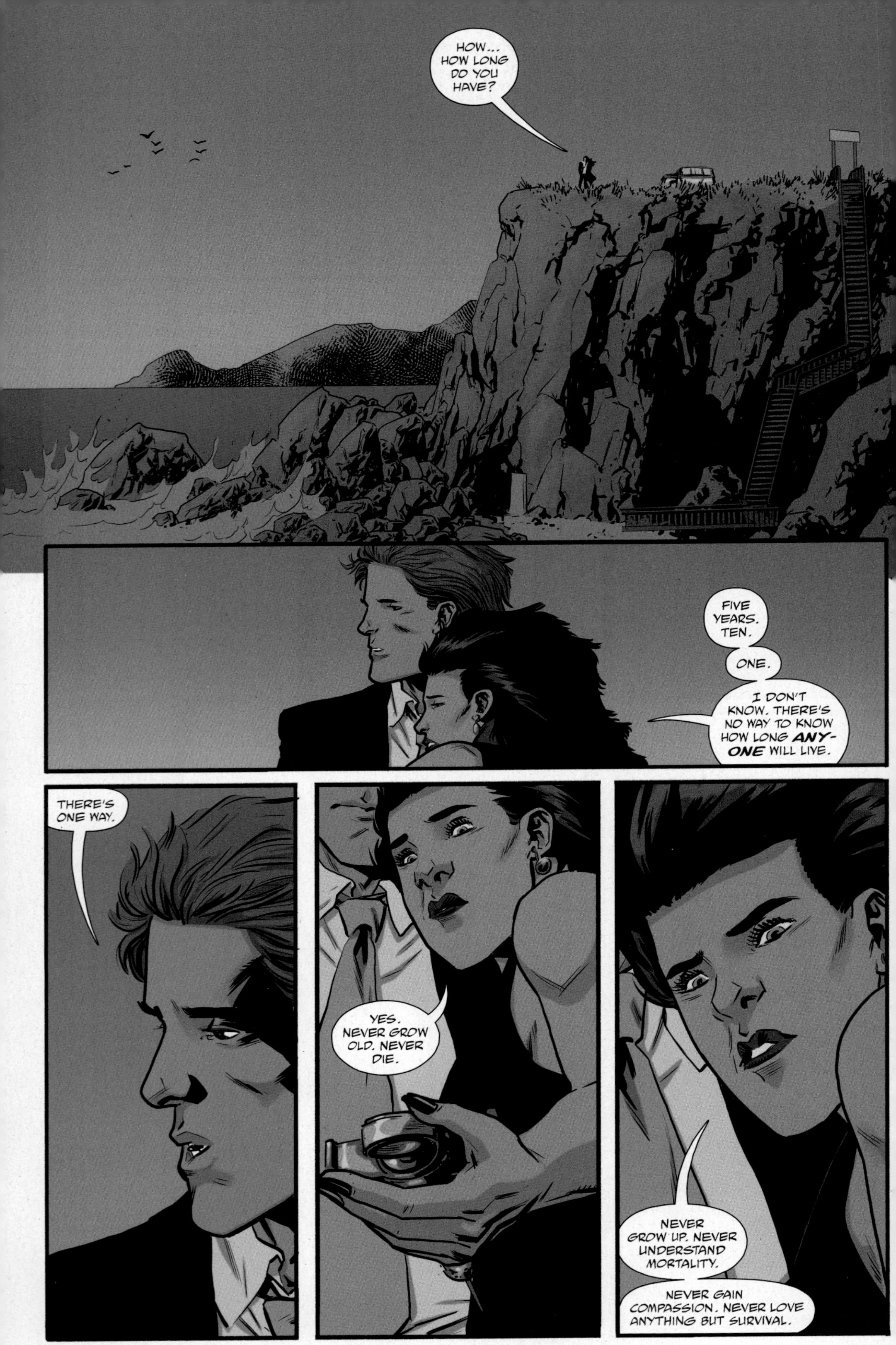
HOW... HOW LONG DO YOU HAVE?
FIVE YEARS. TEN.
ONE.
I DON'T KNOW. THERE'S NO WAY TO KNOW HOW LONG **ANY-ONE** WILL LIVE.
THERE'S ONE WAY.
YES. NEVER GROW OLD. NEVER DIE.
NEVER GROW UP. NEVER UNDERSTAND MORTALITY.
NEVER GAIN COMPASSION. NEVER LOVE ANYTHING BUT SURVIVAL.

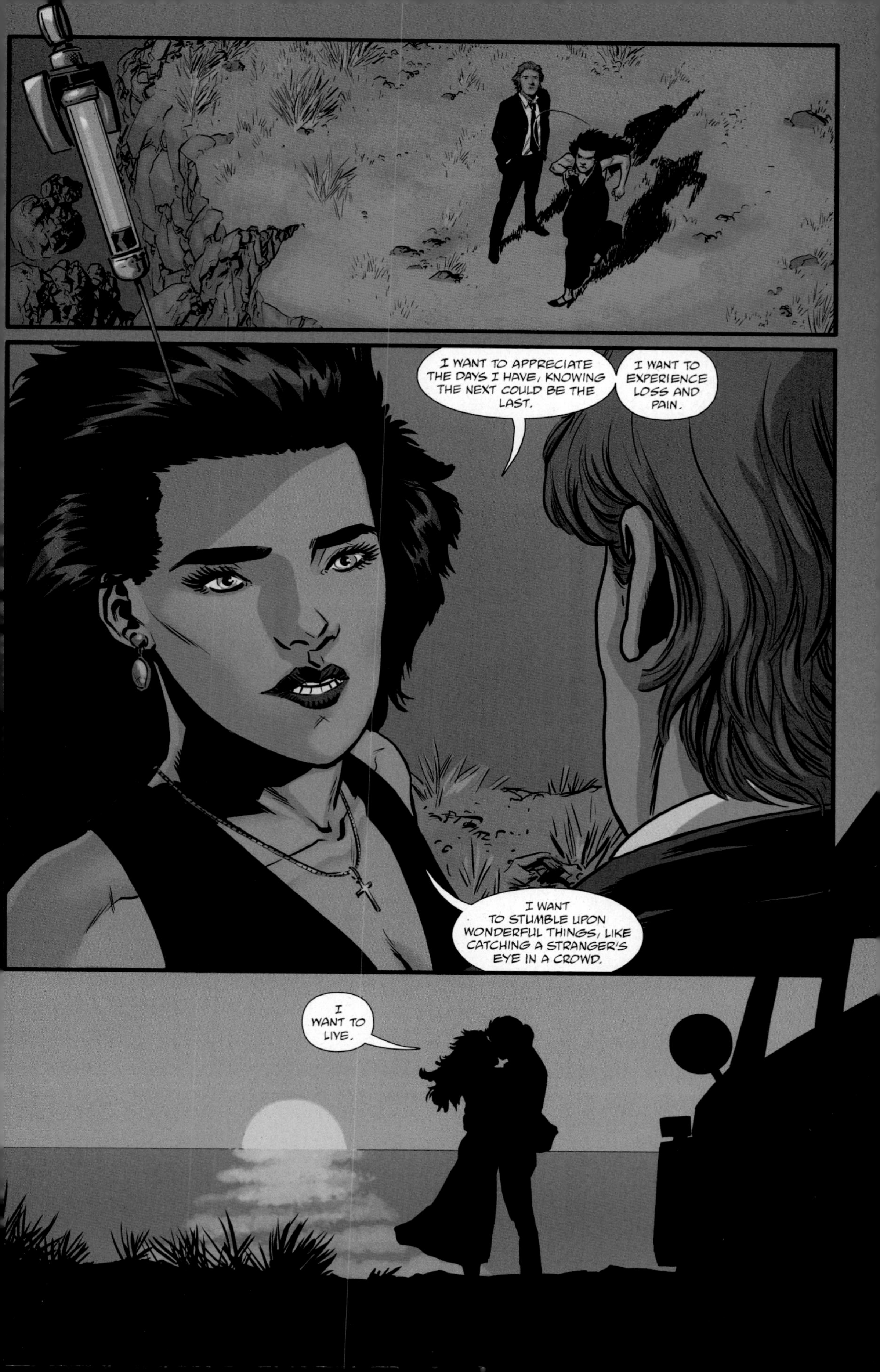
I WANT TO APPRECIATE THE DAYS I HAVE, KNOWING THE NEXT COULD BE THE LAST.
I WANT TO EXPERIENCE LOSS AND PAIN.
I WANT TO STUMBLE UPON WONDERFUL THINGS, LIKE CATCHING A STRANGER'S EYE IN A CROWD.
I WANT TO LIVE.

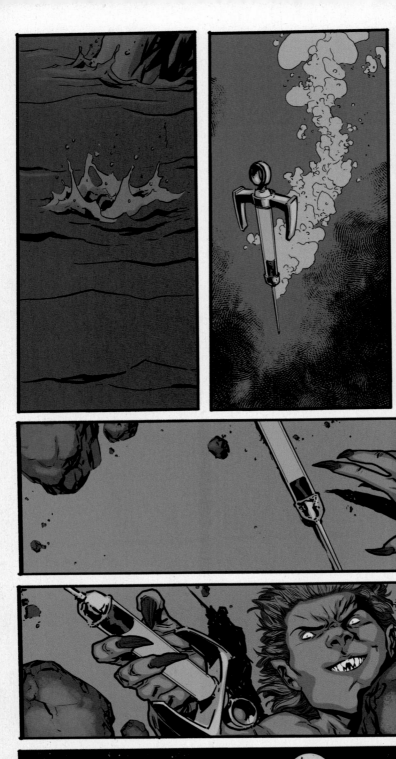

HUH. HUH HUNH.

HAHAHAHAHAHAHAHA

Variant cover art for issue #1 by Joelle Jones and Trish Mu

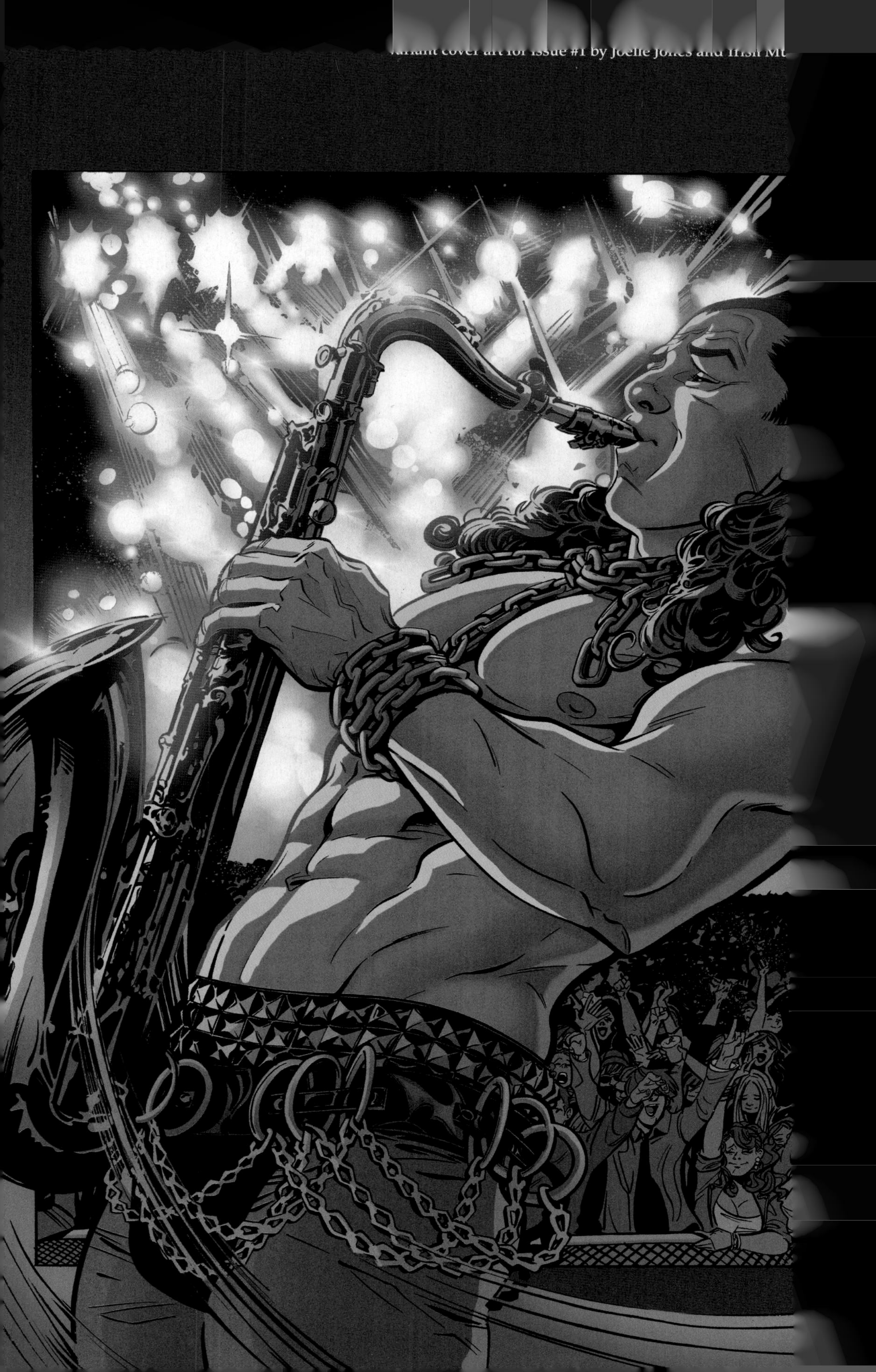

"Looking for a vampire story with some real bite? Then, boys and girls, Scott Snyder has a comic book for you."
—USA WEEKEND

FROM THE *NEW YORK TIMES* #1 BESTSELLING AUTHOR OF *BATMAN VOL. 1: THE COURT OF OWL*

SCOTT SNYDER

with RAFAEL ALBUQUERQUE and STEPHEN KING

AMERICAN VAMPIRE VOL. 2

with RAFAEL ALBUQUERQUE and MATEUS SANTOLOUCO

AMERICAN VAMPIRE VOL. 3

with RAFAEL ALBUQUERQUE and SEAN MURPHY

AMERICAN VAMPIRE VOL. 4

with RAFAEL ALBUQUERQUE and JORDI BERNET

"At a time when vampire stories engulf pop culture, this one's actually fresh and original."
— ENTERTAINMENT WEEKLY

AMERICAN VAMPIRE

SCOTT SNYDER   RAFAEL ALBUQUERQUE
and
STEPHEN KING

VERTIGO